All About
Attention Deficit Disorder

Symptoms, Diagnosis and Treatment:
Children and Adults

Second Edition

All About
Attention
Deficit Disorder

Second Edition

Thomas W. Phelan, Ph.D.

CHILD MANAGEMENT INC ™

Glen Ellyn, Illinois

Cover design and illustrations by Margaret Mayer
Cover photography by Steve Orlick
Child Management Logo by Steve Roe

Printed in the United States of America
10 9 8 7 6 5 4 3 2 1

For more information, contact:
Child Management, Inc.
800 Roosevelt Road
Glen Ellyn, Illinois 60137

Publisher's Cataloging-in-Publication
(*Provided by Quality Books, Inc.*)

Phelan, Thomas W., 1943-
    All about attention deficit disorder / Thomas
W. Phelan. -- 2nd ed.
    p. cm.
    ISBN: 1-889140-11-2

    1. Attention-deficit hyperactivity disorder--
Popular works. I. Title.

RJ506.H9P54 2000   618.92'8589
                    QBI00-432

Contents

PART III: TREATMENT

PART IV: ADULTS WITH ADD

Introduction

In ten short years Attention Deficit Disorder (ADD or ADHD) has jumped from obscurity to center stage. In the early 1980s those of us who were both parents of ADD children and mental health professionals had ADD "coming out of our ears," both at home and at work. But no one else, it seemed, had ever heard of the problem, even though—then as well as now—ADD was the number one psychological condition in children.

Today all that is different. With the phenomenal growth of our ADD support groups throughout the country and with voluminous media exposure, ADD has become a household word. Today everybody has heard of ADD. And everyone has an opinion—or two—about it.

Certainly this sudden expansion of knowledge has been largely for the good. More ADD children are being properly diagnosed and treated. More classroom teachers are being trained to understand and manage Attention Deficit Disorders, producing corresponding benefits to ADD children, to their classmates and to the teachers themselves. Fewer parents these days have to feel guilty that they somehow caused ADD in their children due to their bad parenting, and fewer Moms and Dads argue about "which one of us messed up this kid." Further benefits have come from the recognition that most ADD kids do not outgrow their symptoms, which has led to diagnosis and effective treatment for many ADD adults as well as to useful accommodations for college students with the disorder and ADD employees in the workplace.

Yet the increase in public awareness about ADD has had its negative side. Many people worry about the extent to which the condition is being overdiagnosed, although recent data suggests this is not a problem. Others cannot seem to fathom the apparent paradox involved in giving stimulant medications to "hyperactive" children. And still others argue that ADD is being used as an excuse for all kinds of harmful and negligent behavior, from classroom disruption to criminal activities.

In the past few years there have been exciting and promising new developments in the field. We are recognizing that many—or perhaps most—children and adults with Attention Deficit are not of the "squeaky clean" variety; that is, they often have another psychological condition (or two), such as anxiety, mood disorder, learning disability or substance abuse. Imaging studies are suggesting possible differences in the structure of parts of the brains of people with ADD. Genetic researchers are busy examining chromosomes and genes in the hopes of finding identifiable links to the problem. More is understood about the effects of stimulant medications on dopamine transmission, and—surprise—new medications are being developed that, according to some writers, may someday make our current ones look like "jalopies"!

This second edition of *All About Attention Deficit Disorder* will explain the current state of the ADD art in plain English. This book will bring you up-to-date on the important changes that have occurred in the past few years. The popularity of the first edition (70,000 copies sold) indicated that there is great interest in a book written from the point of view of someone who is *both* the parent of an ADD child and a clinical psychologist working with ADD children.

ADD will always have a personal, family side as well as a clinical, scientific side. To really grasp the problem and deal effectively with it, you need to understand both.

Part I

What Is ADD?

1

Impact

Attention Deficit Disorder dramatically alters family life. Families with one or more ADD children experience fundamental differences in their daily living that other families do not have to endure. There is more tension and more arguing. Sibling rivalry is awful and unending. Noise is constant. Dinnertime may not be fun, and eating out is nearly impossible. Instead of being carefree and fun, vacations become unhappy experiences where it seems all you do is switch from one prison (the car) to another (the motel room). Marital conflict is seriously aggravated; divorce and separation are more common. Parents get discouraged and sometimes depressed; siblings feel embarrassed, neglected and angry.

This is no way for any child to grow up. It's also no way for a family to live, but there are millions of families with ADD children who do live this way—day in and day out. *All* family members are affected.

People often forget that the first person to get badly hurt by the entry of an ADD child into a family is not the ADD child. He's too little to know what's going on. It's not usually the father, either. Dad is out working with people who are—at least hopefully—sane. The first person to get seriously burned is the mother.

Mom

"Doctor Eriksen, you've got to help me with my son. He's only four, but he's been kicked out of two preschools—and that's not the half of it. They say he's too aggressive with the other children. He pushes and sometimes hits. They say Jeff is loud and always has to have his way. He won't follow the rules.

"I hate to say it, but they're right. He's the same way at home. He tortures his little sister all the time. He's really mean sometimes! Getting him to bed is World War III.

"Everything—and I mean everything—is a big deal. He won't take no for an answer. When he wants something, it's NOW! Is this normal? It can't be normal. What am I doing wrong?

"Jeffery was always cute as a button, but he was a difficult baby. Slept and ate in fits. Never seemed content or happy. He's still cute as a button. I mean, it's deceptive to look at him, because he's a terrible toddler. He never stops moving. He never stops making noise.

"What did I do wrong? I think maybe I didn't hold him right or something. I think I was too nervous after he came home from the hospital. I have no doubt that's what my mother—and probably my husband— think. I mean, he was my first one and all, but I really don't think I was that bad. I'm not stupid. I'm not a mean person, but I've got to be doing something wrong. This just isn't right. My husband doesn't have as much trouble with him. None of his cousins are like this—that I know of. I had a good pregnancy and I honestly looked forward to having him. But I never dreamed it would be like this.

"We can't go on this way. That's why I came to see you. We're going nuts."

Dad

The road stretches out endlessly through the rolling farm country. Des Moines is still 85 miles away and Jim doesn't think his sanity will last that long. The kids are warming up for another fight in the back seat. Four-year-old Mark, who's always been a difficult child, is about to provoke his sister, Mary, for the millionth time during the trip. Ten minutes ago Jim almost lost control of the car while reaching around trying to hit his son.

The all-too-predictable fight starts. Mary is screaming and crying; it looks like there's a spot of blood on her cheek. That's it! Jim jerks the car off to the side. His startled wife yells at him for his carelessness. He doesn't care: right now he wants to kill this kid. Jim jumps out and jerks open the back door. Mark is now quiet—terrified by the insane look in his father's eyes. Mom is yelling, "Jim, for Pete's sake, please, don't!"

The boy is yanked from the car. He hits his head on the door on the way out and starts crying. Cars and trucks speed by. Jim drags the little monster down the grassy hill, spanking him as hard as he can, screaming at the top of his lungs how sick and tired he is of this and how it's going to stop once and for all.

There is a sudden screech behind them as a car pulls up. An angry man jumps out, yelling, "What the h—l do you think you're doing to that kid!" The Good Samaritan has arrived. Jim tells the newcomer where to put his good intentions. Back in the car Mom and Mary are sobbing.

Siblings

"My younger brother, Jeffrey, makes me so mad I could scream. He never shuts up, and if he's not talking or yelling about something, he's making noise some other way. He drives my parents crazy half the time, but they don't know what to do with him. Jeffrey usually gets his way because he badgers them into whatever he wants. I don't do that, because I feel bad—for my Mom especially—but it's not fair.

"Jeffrey gets into my stuff all the time. I'll tell my parents, but they don't do anything. I want a lock on my door. Why can't I have a stupid lock and me just keep the key? Mom and Dad can have an extra key if they want. That's not fair either.

"Sometimes Jeffrey's fun, but not very often. He has more energy than all the rest of us put together. But if you have a friend over, he won't leave you alone. My mother told us once, "Why don't you let him play with you?" I was ready to kill her for saying that. Are you kidding!? So I just don't invite friends over very much anymore. He acts so stupid I'm embarrassed he's my brother.

"I wish I could go on a real long vacation with just my Mom and Dad and no Jeffrey. It would be so fun! Actually, I wish I could just spend some time with my parents in the evening. But that's homework time—three straight hours of civil war. I put in earplugs and I shut up and do my homework. Why can't he? Mom tried to tell me he's got some problem called Attention Deficit something or other. Why does she make excuses for him? I can tell you his problem—he's lazy and he's a brat! Sometimes I feel bad I don't even like my own brother."

The Happy Couple

Bob and Sally nervously enter the restaurant with four-year-old Janie. Janie is cute, curious, talkative and charming to the pleasant and attentive young waitress. Her parents start relaxing a little, thinking, "Maybe this time things will be OK." But they still order, as usual, food that can be prepared very quickly. Janie wants the hot dog, but the restaurant only has the jumbo size. Sally knows her daughter can't eat all that and she suggests the hamburger.

Janie erupts. She screams "HOT DOG!" six times at the top of her lungs. Then she pulls her place mat off the table, spilling the water and sending the silverware clattering to the floor. Other people look over with the critical gazes so familiar to these parents. The looks say "What's the matter with you?" "Why can't you control that kid?" and "Why don't you eat somewhere else?" Saying nothing, Bob grabs Janie roughly and leaves for the car. Sally sits there—no longer hungry—trying to decide whether to cancel the order.

The Pleasant Space Cadet

"Mrs. Collins, Sarah is doing about as well as she did last year. She's such a dear! She doesn't cause a bit of trouble, you know, and she's so sweet. But it's just like she's not there a lot of the time. You know, like she's out in left field. Sometimes we'll be doing a class project and she's just not with us. She'll be staring out the window or fiddling with something in her desk. And I don't want to embarrass her by asking her a question, because I really think she wouldn't be able to answer it.

"My guess is she's just a bit of a slow learner. I think she's just immature. She tries, though I can't say she tries real hard. She does seem to try hard for short spurts, but then it's like she's off on a tangent again and, as you know, a lot of her work doesn't get completed. I try not to be too hard on her. I mean, you can't dislike the girl a bit. She's not sassy or argumentative. She always tries to do what I tell her, though she does have a tendency to want to jabber with her friends a bit. But that's normal.

"She's not a bit like Jeffrey was when I had him. No offense, but, as you know I'm sure, Jeff was a much more difficult child. I sometimes felt we should have done an evaluation with her older brother. But not Sarah. She's just a lovely child.

"She'll come along, I expect. She just needs some time to mature."

The Lucky Teacher

It's 90 degrees, mid-May, and only 2:45. School doesn't get out until 3:15. Mrs. Simpson will have to call Jeff's parents again today because he's completed hardly any of his work. He has remained off-task almost all day, and the fact that the air conditioning isn't working made matters considerably worse. All the other children have been more restless and Jeffrey had to watch every movement each of them made.

An impossible task, but he tried. He did not try to do his math or language arts, however. And for the umpteenth time this year he just couldn't work in his small study group without bothering everyone else, so Mrs. Simpson again had to move his desk. The psychologist told her to put him up front by himself, but then he is isolated—the only one in the room not in a foursome. What good does that do for his self-esteem?

Mrs. Simpson had thought fourth-graders were supposed to be easier to deal with. She tried all the things she thought might work: talking to Jeff alone, more positive reinforcement, daily sheets, parent conferences. Some things help for a while—a few days maybe, but then....

The principal, Mr. Stock, is always pushing her to call the parents. What good is that going to do? Besides, their attitude at the last staffing was positively hostile, and Mrs. Simpson felt like she was being blamed for Jeff's attitude, his underachievement and for all his misbehavior. The child is real nice one-on-one, but in class he's a total monster. Mrs. Simpson feels sorry for the fifth-grade teacher that gets Jeffrey next year. At least there's no chance he'll be retained!

The Main Man

"School is so boring! The main crop in Brazil is...? Man, geography is awesome! The main crop in Brazil has got to be jelly beans. That's it! No, it's probably seaweed. Who could possibly care what the main idiot crop of stupid Brazil is?

"Whoa! Wait—hold the phone! There are two people in the world who could care about this earth-shaking question: my teacher, Mrs. Simpson and my Perfect Older Sister who gets straight As and always does everything right and who always needles me when my parents aren't looking. I hate her. Wait til she finds what I put in her bed before school this morning—that'll set her straight! Then, of course, she'll tell and Mom will cry and have a cow and tell Dad when he gets home and he'll probably knock me around again even before his first drink. But, still...it may be worth it.

"It's not even lunch time yet. OK, Brazil. Crops. Think, dummy! Who invented this garbage?! Not only is this junk boring, but Simpson won't even let you move. Once she even put a string around me and my chair and told me I'd get a detention if I broke it. So, naturally, I just had to—nobody's going to pull that on me.... Had to see the old man, but he's pretty cool—most of the times I've seen him, anyway.

"Brazil.... Wonder if I can finish this idiot work sheet before lunch, so I don't have to bring it home and sit at the kitchen table for hours with my mother nagging and Miss Perfect getting to watch TV and laughing at me.

"I'm hungry. Lunch will be great and then recess, where the authorities actually let you move around. Amazing, they're so kind. I may just bump into that brat who always gets the other kids after me. Beat him up some last week, but it didn't help much....

"This chair has a sliver in it.... Oops, Simpson's looking at me. She knows I'm not paying attention to my work again like all the other good little boys and girls. 'Are you with us today, Jeffrey?' 'Are we paying better attention to our work today, Jeffrey?' If it's our work, why doesn't she do it? Better look like I'm doing something. Head down, look at paper, move hand. Oh god, where's my pencil.... Jeez I'm an idiot!

"No I'm not. Once they told me I got 125 on an IQ test. Whatever I'm supposed to have 125 of sure doesn't keep me from getting Ds. D stands for Dumb. Dork. Death. Dope. Dad got Ds too when he was younger. So where does he get off yelling at me all the time?

"Ten minutes til food. CROPS IN BRAZIL! Ten lousy minutes. I can't stand it! When I get older, I'll drive a truck. You sit up real high and you get to keep moving. It's great. I'll take my little sister with me. Sarah's not so bad, and she doesn't do so hot in school either. She doesn't get in as much trouble as me, but the teacher calls her "spacey" sometimes. One kid heard that and started calling her "Spacey Sarah" on the playground, so I pushed him around and made him promise to shut up. Most of the kids at this school are jerks.

"That creep behind me is popping her gum again. Drives me nuts! Sounds like forty bowls of Rice Krispies right in my ear. Then she'll start gabbing to the jerk next to her, but they'll never get in trouble. They're girls. They thought it was real funny the other day when we were having a math quiz and I didn't even know it. It was their fault! If I pulled the stuff they do, Simpson would be on me faster than you can blink.

"Omigosh, here she is! Those are her shoes standing next to my desk. I didn't even see her coming. Snuck right up on me—what was I thinking? Not again.... Are we irritated, teacher? Well folks, due to technical difficulties beyond our control, lunchtime will be delayed indefinitely...."

The Main Man: 20 Years Later

"This guy doesn't look as snobby as most of my customers, but he isn't saying much. Probably thinks I'm not as good as him or something. Some of them don't say a word—then they pretty much stiff you when you get to the airport. Can't even buy a pack of cigarettes with what some of these blowhards give you. Hot-shot business types.

"Last few jobs I've had haven't paid peanuts. No wonder all my credit cards are bumping their limits. If they'd really pay you what you're worth in this stupid country...but my wife doesn't want to hear that kind of talk. No, no, no. Prefers to rag on me about going back to school, so she can live in the style to which she's become accustomed with her daddy. At least this driving beats being in that apartment with her and that crazy kid....

"Her old man's an idiot. Thinks I'm not good enough for her. Maybe a college degree would shut him up, but the thought of going back to school drives me insane. I tried it. One and one-half years of pure hell. They deliberately try to make it as boring as possible.

"Here's the idiot dispatcher again. 'Where are you Jeff?' 'Give me your location?' 'Why is it taking you so long?' Why doesn't he get out here on the road himself with these other maniacs?

"Move over lamebrain! If you weren't so busy gabbing on your stupid phone and trying to show everybody what a big shot you were, you'd be able to see where you're going!

"This guy's a real chatty Cathy—two words so far. How did a jerk like him swing a house like he had? Won the lottery no doubt. Or maybe his daddy bought it for him. I'll tell ya, all I need to do is...."

2

Symptoms

Attention Deficit Disorder has been called many things over the years. Still's Disease and Impulse Disorder were early attempts to describe overly active and impulsive children. Later, the terms Minimal Brain Damage and Minimal Brain Dysfunction scared the daylights out of many parents. Hyperkinetic Reaction of Childhood followed, focusing on the most obvious symptom of the problem, overactivity.

Attention Deficit Disorder was first called by that name in 1980, in what was known as the DSM-III (Diagnostic and Statistical Manual of Mental Disorders, Third Edition). A new definition stated that the core of the problem was a difficulty focusing and sustaining attention.

According to the DSM-III, there were two kinds of ADD: ADD with hyperactivity and ADD without hyperactivity. Both types involved the ADD, or difficulty with attention, but children who experienced ADD with hyperactivity were the overly active, impulsive, often disruptive and "in your face" kind of kids. They were usually boys. ADD-without-hyperactivity children also had problems focusing and sustaining attention, but they were usually mild-mannered souls who presented little in the way of behavioral problems. Some people referred to this second type of ADD as "the pleasant space cadet" syndrome, and these children were often girls. DSM-III also recognized that ADD kids often grew up to be ADD adults, so the term "ADD, Residual Type" was included.

The DSM-III was revised in 1987, and the results of this new edition, DSM-III-R (Revised), were somewhat controversial. Some people felt that DSM-III's ADD excessively deemphasized the hyperactive and impulsive symptoms, so in DSM-III-R the label was changed to the rather awkward "Attention-Deficit/Hyperactivity Disorder." This change recognized the fact that both inattentiveness *and* restlessness were often involved in the condition. But the description of ADHD in the DSM-III-R unfortunately scrapped the ADD-without-hyperactivity subtype. Instead, reference was made to ADD "undifferentiated type," a kind of catch-all category for anything that didn't fit neatly into the ADHD classification.

This problem was remedied in DSM-IV, but the awkward ADHD was retained. ADD without hyperactivity reappeared as the "Predominantly Inattentive Type," a much needed correction that still, however, left us in the clumsy position of having "ADHD without the H." The result has been some confusion with regard to terminology. ADHD remains the technically correct term, but many people (including myself) still prefer the original ADD.

In this chapter we'll examine ADD from three points of view: A) ADD according to the DSM-IV, B) actually living with ADD, and C) ADD as basically a problem of self-control.

A. The DSM-IV Criteria

DSM-IV does represent an improvement in our thinking about Attention Deficit Disorder. According to DSM-IV, several criteria must be met for an individual to qualify as having ADD. Basically, the person must show a pattern of inattention and/or hyperactivity-impulsivity that fits the following criteria:

1. Persistence: the behavior has lasted for at least six months.
2. Early onset: symptoms were present (not necessarily diagnosed) prior to age 7.
3. Frequency and severity: the inattentiveness and/or

hyperactivity- impulsivity are extraordinary for persons of comparable age.

4. Clear evidence of impairment: the ADD behavioral pattern must cause significant interference with a person's ability to function.

5. Impairment in two or more settings: the symptoms cause serious trouble in multiple contexts, including school (or work for adults), home and social situations.

DSM-IV provides two lists, each with nine symptoms. The first list includes manifestations of *Inattention*:

a. fails to pay close attention to details or makes careless mistakes

b. has difficulty sustaining attention in work or play

c. does not listen when spoken to directly

d. fails to finish schoolwork, chores or work duties

e. has difficulty organizing activities

f. avoids tasks requiring sustained mental effort

g. loses things

h. is easily distracted

i. is forgetful

The second list also includes nine symptoms. The first six are signs of *Hyperactivity* and the last three are signs of *Impulsivity*:

Hyperactivity

a. fidgets or squirms in seat

b. leaves seat when remaining seated is expected

c. runs about or climbs in situations where such activity is inappropriate

d. has difficulty playing quietly

e. acts as if "driven by a motor"

f. talks excessively

Impulsivity

g. blurts out answers before the question is completed

  h. has difficulty awaiting turn
  i. interrupts or intrudes on others

Here's how you make the diagnosis. If a child (or adult) qualifies for six or more items on both lists, the diagnosis is Attention-Deficit/ Hyperactivity Disorder, Combined Type. These individuals have trouble paying attention and they are also overly active. This type of ADD is what we used to refer to as ADD with hyperactivity.

If a child (or adult) qualifies for six of the nine Inattentive items, but does not meet six of the nine Hyperactivity/Impulsivity criteria, he or she would be described as Attention-Deficit/Hyperactivity Disorder, Predominantly Inattentive Type. These children are not restless or disruptive, but they do have trouble focusing on tasks, sustaining attention and organizing and finishing things. This type of ADD is what we used to refer to as ADD without hyperactivity.

At this point the observant reader may pose the question: "Wait a minute. There should be one more kind of ADD. What if you meet the Hyperactivity/Impulsivity criteria, but not the Inattentive criteria?" Good question. In fact, the DSM-IV does recognize a "Predominantly Hyperactive-Impulsive Type," but there is some justifiable controversy about whether or not this kind really exists. Is the Predominantly Hyperactive-Impulsive Type a truely separate entity, or is it a kind of byproduct of the structure of the DSM-IV? If you have two separate symptom lists, obviously, you can qualify on one, on the other or on both.

The opinion of many experts is that the Predominantly Hyperactive-Impulsive Type is really the same as the Combined Type, but simply a younger version of it. First of all, the group of children that the Hyperactive-Impulsive Type was based on was a very young group, averaging between four and five years of age. At that age it is very difficult to say that a child is extraordinarily inattentive, so many of these kids would not qualify for six or more items on the inattentive list.

Second, it is hard to imagine a child who is hyperactive and impulsive but who is also focusing and sustaining attention well. If you are fidgety, leaving your seat, running about excessively and "driven by a motor," it is unlikely that you will also be paying attention to just one task. You will more likely be paying attention to one thing after another in rapid-fire fashion. Third, DSM-IV acknowledges that with the Predominantly Hyperactive-Impulsive Type, "inattention may still be a significant feature." If this is the case, you're back to the Combined Type.

B. Another Look: Living with ADD

DSM-IV provides an accurate, but still largely clinical, view of ADD. Symptom lists are a useful and necessary part of diagnosis, but they do not describe what it is like to be—or to live with—an ADD child. Below are descriptions of eight characteristics that usually go along with ADD. These real-life descriptions will give a better picture of how ADD affects a child and his or her family. Our list includes some of the DSM symptoms, but it also includes others that are not mentioned in that manual.

A large percentage of ADD kids have all of the characteristics below. Other children will show only some (we will specifically describe some of the major exceptions later). Children who might qualify for the Combined Type (ADD with hyperactivity) will most often show all of the attributes on our list. On the other hand, Predominantly Inattentive children (ADD without hyperactivity) may fit only items 1, 6 and 8.

The first item below, inattention, is, at the present time, considered the most important or core symptom. Items 2-5 on our list in a sense define the temperament—or personality—that usually accompanies ADD (especially Combined Type or ADD with hyperactivity). You might consider items 6-8, finally, as the results of the other characteristics:

CORE	1. Inattention or distractibility
TEMPERAMENT	2. Impulsivity
	3. Difficulty delaying gratification
	4. Hyperactivity
	5. Emotional overarousal
RESULTS	6. Noncompliance
	7. Social problems
	8. Disorganization

Let's look at each of these characteristics.

1. Inattention or Distractibility

The ADD child has an attention span that is too short for his age. He cannot sustain attention on a task or activity, especially if he sees that activity as boring or semi-boring. Naturally, most ADD children spend a good deal of their time in school, and we hear from them over and over again how "boring" it is. Ask an ADD child what he doesn't like about school, and he may simply say, "the work." It is a significant strain for these children to try to stay on task; they are fighting an invisible problem they can't understand. The stress they experience is considerable and—for someone who has not gone through it himself—hard to even imagine. As they get older, ADD kids often begin to feel stupid, and they are often accused of being lazy. It is obvious that these experiences are going to damage self-esteem.

What often confuses the picture here, however, is that many Attention Deficit children *can* pay attention (or sit still) for limited periods of time. They may be able to do this when they are in situations that have one or more of four particular characteristics. These characteristics are:

1) novelty
2) high interest value
3) intimidation
4) being one-on-one with an adult

This temporary ability of the ADD child to appear normal can amaze people who have seen these kids in their hyperactive mode. It can also produce plenty of missed diagnoses! Examples of these special situations? The first two weeks of a school year (novelty), watching TV or playing Nintendo (high interest value), a visit to a pediatrician's office (intimidation), going to a ball game alone with Mom or Dad (one-on-one), psychological testing (all four!).

Another way of looking at the attention problem is to think of it as distractibility: the ease with which the child can be gotten off task by some other stimulus. ADD kids respond automatically to anything new. Many ADD children can tell you how much it bothers them when the garbage truck pulls up in the parking lot during social studies, when someone's using the pencil sharpener, or when they have their socks on inside out.

Generally, distractors come in four forms: visual, auditory, somatic and fantasy. Visual distractors are things within the child's field of vision that draw his attention away from his work or task. For example, someone walking by will cause him to look up, and then he may not return to his work at all. Auditory distractors are things the child hears that bug him. They can be obvious, loud noises or quieter sounds like the ticking of a clock, someone tapping a pencil on a desk, or another child sniffing. These things may not seem bothersome to you, but they are to the ADD child.

Somatic distractors are bodily sensations that take away the child's attention. We have seen a number of children who complain that when the seam in their sock is not in the right place they can hardly stand it. They become very fidgety and can't concentrate. The same results occur if their stomach is growling, if their seat doesn't feel right, or if they have a headache. Fantasy distractors are thoughts or images going through the child's mind that have more appeal than schoolwork. We all daydream, but hyperactive children are often correctly identified by teachers as daydreaming excessively. The child might start thinking of his new video game, or lunch, or—if he's old enough—about a girl.

Some children may be more vulnerable to certain kinds of distractors than others. Some kids, for example, complain more about things that they hear than things that they see. That's why it helps with the diagnosis if a child can describe in his own words what kinds of things get him off task.

What is the biggest distractor? Very likely human conversation. If your child tells you that she can't concentrate when other children talk around her, this is probably not an excuse; it's a very real problem for her.

2. Impulsivity

The second trait on our list is impulsivity: acting without thinking or doing whatever happens to come to mind without regard for the consequences that will follow. Impulsive acts by ADD kids can range from trivial to extremely dangerous.

We know of several ADD children who caused their homes to burn down. One boy started playing with matches in a wastebasket in his living room. The flames were intriguing, but they soon reached up to the curtains and then spread. No one was hurt, but the house was lost. Another five-year-old ADD child almost drowned when he went to a pool with his father. The father turned away for only a short time, but the child saw the water, saw other kids jumping in, and thought "Fun." Fun—period! His thought processes didn't extend as far as remembering that he didn't know how to swim. He was pulled off the bottom of the pool several minutes later, fortunately still alive.

Other impulsive ADD behavior borders on less damaging mischief. In school situations, teachers will often recognize the ADD child by his tendency to blurt things out in class. Some of the blurting out may be an attempt to correctly answer a question, but the youngster forgets to raise his hand. Other times the child will blurt out things intended to be funny or smart-alec. Many ADD kids attempt to be the class clown, and, unfortunately, some of them are quite clever and really *are* funny. This type of behavior, however, presents the teacher with a major class management problem.

Impulsivity can also seriously impair the social interactions of the ADD child. When frustrated he may yell at other children, and sometimes even physically strike out or push others around in an attempt to get his way. His impatience about having to immediately be the first in line and his tendency to grab things can be constant sources of irritation to other kids.

One writer, Virginia Douglas, used to say that the ADD child had a "stop, look and listen" problem. She meant that the Attention Deficit boy or girl, when entering a new situation, didn't take the time to stop, look at what was going on, listen to what was being said, and then respond appropriately. The ADD child just sort of bombed right in and did whatever came naturally or automatically.

In talking to ADD kids, one readily gets the impression that they do not have a well-developed ability to either visualize consequences or to "talk to themselves" about what is likely to result from some of their actions. This impression is quite accurate. Some ADD kids who impulsively steal, for example, just look at the money laying there and think, "Wow! Neat!" Then they take it. It may occur to them later that their father will almost certainly miss the five dollars that was sitting on top of the dresser in his bedroom, but by then the damage has been done.

ADD kids often lie for the same reason. "Is your homework done?"

Mom asks. "Yes," Junior responds quickly. He wants out of this potential hassle (doing homework) *now*, and he doesn't think of what will happen later when he is caught. Parents are often amazed and mystified by this phenomenon. They can't imagine anyone being so "stupid" as to lie—not just once, but repeatedly—"knowing" he will certainly be caught later.

3. Difficulty Delaying Gratification (Impatience)

A third ADD trait is difficulty delaying gratification. You might think of this one as simply a bad case of impatience. To parents it often feels like the child is saying, "I want what I want when I want it—which is NOW! If you don't give it to me I'll have a temper tantrum or badger you to death until you do give it to me!"

When an ADD child gets an idea in his head about something he wants, he can be remarkably persistent in pursuing it. This kind of behavior often makes shopping with him a miserable experience. Unless you're at a store that has nothing of interest to the youngster, he will see a million things and want all of them in sequence. Difficulty delaying gratification makes some parents feel defeated before they even leave home, because they think that just about any shopping trip is going to mean buying the kid something. Mom and Dad may have long ago given up any desire to put up with the embarrassment of horrible tantrums in public.

At school, difficulty with delay can manifest itself in a number of ways. The child may shove others in order to be first in line, or run down the hall bumping into people to be the first one out for recess. In schoolwork, impatience can show itself in hurried, messy work. To the child the task is simply to "get this stupid stuff out of the way as soon as possible," rather than to do a good job on it. This attitude can mean not reading directions and doing a lot of work the wrong way.

Difficulty with delay can also result in sloppy handwriting. Since many ADD children have trouble with fine motor skills, it is sometimes hard to tell if they are just rushing, if their sloppy work is the result of a problem with fine visual-motor coordination, or if it is some combination of both.

Impatience can also mean that birthdays become a royal aggravation. The ADD child gets overly excited waiting and wants his presents early.

The times around Christmas and the holidays also become difficult for the same reasons, and it certainly doesn't help that everyone else is excited at the same time.

Some Attention Deficit children even have trouble with soiling or wetting because of difficulty with delay. This idea sounds strange, but it does happen. The youngster is out playing and having a good time. He feels the need to go to the bathroom. You would think that with difficulty delaying gratification he would be more in a hurry to go to the bathroom, but unfortunately it doesn't always work out that way. What happens instead is that the child *can't put off the next few minutes of play*. He doesn't want to take the time out. The urge to go builds, he keeps repressing it, and then—in a moment of physical exertion—he loses control and soils or wets. Even after this, some kids will continue to play because they still don't want to go in!

If you think of this kind of mentality, you can easily imagine why one of the words that frequently comes out of the mouths of ADD kids is "BORING!" Imagine you are always thinking about what the next exciting thing to come along is going to be. In the meantime you feel like you are just sitting around and the minutes are crawling by. Things would seem pretty boring to you, too.

4. Hyperactivity

Hyperactivity is a probable symptom of ADD, especially in our younger, pre-adolescent children. Hyperactivity means gross-motor restlessness, not just fidgetiness. Parents will describe their child as being always on the go, or "he looks like he's driven by a motor." Being around this constant activity can be very draining and very irritating for parents. Repeated—but useless—suggestions to "Sit still!" or "Calm down!" will often be heard around the house.

Even among the children who are hyperactive, the hyperactivity will usually greatly diminish by adolescence. This fact explains why people used to think that hyperkinesis would be outgrown. The typical reduction in activity level with age doesn't mean, however, that restlessness and other ADD symptoms are gone; these characteristics usually continue into adulthood.

In addition, hyperactivity itself is *not* constant. Combined Type children can sometimes sit still in situations that are new, fascinating, somewhat scary or one-on-one. There are only a few ADD children who can never sit still at all.

ADD girls tend to be less hyperactive (and less impulsive) than ADD boys. Studies have shown that among normal babies in a hospital nursery, boys in general move around more than the girls, so it isn't surprising that ADD kids follow suit. But not all ADD children are hyperactive, as evidenced by the DSM-IV criteria for the Inattentive Type. This diagnosis is meant for children who have difficulty concentrating but who do not present a lot of behavioral problems. These children do exist—some boys as well as girls, but among ADD kids they are in the minority. They also often fall through the cracks in a school system because they don't aggravate anyone very much. As many writers have noted, disruptive behavior "drives" referrals.

5. Emotional Overarousal

Another rather odd but interesting quality that often accompanies Attention Deficit Disorder is an intensity of feeling that often goes way beyond the normal. The child, it seems, cannot experience just a little bit of emotion. It always has to be a lot, and the ADD youngster will usually "broadcast" the feeling—those around him will be very much aware of his state. Emotional overarousal is not mentioned on the DSM-IV lists, but it probably should be.

Perhaps the two most common emotions involved in this regard are 1) happiness or excitement, on the "positive" side, and 2) anger, on the negative side. A happy ADD child is frequently overly excited. He will get into what we call the "hyper silly" routine, especially in unstructured groups with other children. He'll run around frantically, talk loud, act goofy and generally make a fool out of himself. While witnessing this display his parents may be mortified and other children may look at him funny. Who doesn't know what's happening? The ADD child himself. ADD kids are notoriously insensitive to social cues. They don't notice the displeased expression on someone's face, pick up on the negative tone of voice, or even hear the words spoken.

As many parents know, one of the least effective adult tactics in these situations is to plead or yell "Calm down!" That suggestion is like throwing gasoline on a fire. Usually the child needs to be removed from the situation for a while.

When angry, on the other hand, ADD children may produce fabulous temper tantrums. These tantrums sometimes appear like insane rages, way beyond the degree of frustration most people would express. Because of moments like these, some parents have wondered if their ADD child was psychotic. However, the rage may subside as quickly as it started, and then the ADD child may be off to some pleasant, new encounter, leaving an exhausted and bewildered parent in his wake.

Although emotional overarousal with ADD children is often thought of in terms of these two extremes—excitement and anger—recent research strongly suggests that other emotions can be exaggerated as well. New studies of ADD kids have found that by the time they are teens, 30 percent of ADD children may also meet DSM criteria for an anxiety disorder. Another 20 percent may also meet DSM criteria for depressive disorder, and perhaps 10 percent may meet criteria for bipolar disorder. These psychological problems all involve, to varying degrees, the exaggeration of certain negative emotions.

Some ADD kids, for example, experience extreme separation anxiety. They have a hard time leaving their home or parents. Others experience sadness—and in older children, depression—to a greater degree than normal. Fortunately, these periods of depression or sadness do not last so long in the younger children; mood changes are typical of ADD kids. However, as the child gets into adolescence a more pervasive depression is a serious risk, especially if the Attention Deficit Disorder—with all its primary and secondary symptoms—is not being treated effectively.

What about guilt? ADD children probably can have fleeting moments of guilt, but—according to most parents—this is not one of the emotions they tend to feel too intensely. If the ADD child is also depressed or anxious, however, it is more likely that guilt, as well as lower self-esteem, will be present. Of course, many parents of ADD youngsters wish their kids felt more guilt! In fact, these parents often worry that their child doesn't have a conscience.

6. Noncompliance

ADD children have a hard time following the rules and they often present significant discipline problems, especially Combined Type kids. This fact prompts some adults to say, "We've got to teach them the rules." Believe it or not, knowing the rules is not the problem. During quieter times ADD kids can remember and recite the rules, but in the heat of battle they tend to forget them. Emotional overarousal, hyperactivity and impulsivity take over. ADD is not a problem of knowing what to do, it's a problem with *doing what you know*. Performance, rather than knowledge, is the issue.

Some ADD noncompliance involves aggressive behavior. The ADD child is often pushy with other children and is usually terribly intolerant of siblings. He can create an awful amount of domestic turmoil. Mom and Dad are often torn between their desire to treat their children fairly and equally and their knowledge that the ADD child does in fact start most— though not all—of the fights around the house. Other aggressive, noncompliant behavior includes arguing and yelling.

Noncompliance is the reason that 50 to 60 percent of ADD kids also qualify for a DSM diagnosis of Oppositional Defiant Disorder (ODD). ODD children (at younger ages mostly boys and ADD Combined Type) are negative, defiant, hostile and argumentative. These kids lose their tempers easily, seem to have a chip on their shoulders, like to annoy others, and blame everyone else for whatever goes wrong. As you can easily imagine, younger children who are ADD and ODD often turn out to be CD (Conduct Disorder) as teenagers. CD teens have advanced to nastier, much more noncompliant and much more dangerous kinds of behavior. CD kids violate age-appropriate norms. For example, they often smoke, drink, use illegal drugs and engage in sex at very early ages. Conduct disordered children have very impaired conscience development, and they may hurt other people physically, steal, vandalize property or even torture animals. Many of them will turn out to be antisocial personalities as adults.

After reading a discussion like this about noncompliance, some people react this way: "Is there now a 'disorder' for everything?! What happened to the old notion of responsibility for one's own behavior? Must we always be making excuses for the unruly, disruptive, harmful and even illegal behavior of obnoxious people?" This kind of reaction is common these days. People worry that we are trying to "psychologize" or rationalize away willful and injurious behavior. It is important to keep in mind that the terms ADD, ODD and CD (known as the disruptive behavior disorders) are descriptions of behavior. They are not to be used as excuses for anything.

Noncompliance, of course, can also be passive and not particularly harmful to anyone other than the passively noncompliant person herself. This is especially true when the Inattentive Type of ADD (ADD without hyperactivity) is involved. Because of their inattentiveness, general disorganization and forgetfulness, these ADD kids don't clean their rooms, forget to feed the dog, and don't do their homework. One motto of our parent support groups is "Don't ever ask an ADD child to do three things in a row." You're lucky if she finishes one! A parent may ask a child to take out the garbage. She agrees, which may be unusual in itself—and heads off to get it. On the way, however, she passes the TV. That's it—the garbage is forgotten.

7. Social Problems

For too many ADD children, peer problems are a big part of their lives. It has often been said that ADD with hyperactivity (Combined) kids will often be *rejected*, while ADD without hyperactivity (Inattentive) children will be *overlooked*. The result is often heartbreak for the child's parents.

Most Combined Type ADD kids have a difficult time getting along with other children, especially those who are the same age and sex. The ADD child's interpersonal problems usually come from being too intense, bossy, aggressive and competitive. ADD kids "suffer" from what is often referred to as "L.F.T.": Low Frustration Tolerance. Most of these youngsters hate losing, and they may resort to cheating, fighting or changing the rules in the middle of a game in order to get their way.

One fascinating recent study asked the question, "How long does it take to create a negative impression that lasts?" The study was conducted with ADD children at summer camp, and the answer to the question was three hours! It only took three hours to establish a bad reputation that lasted for the whole summer. How can a child so rapidly guarantee his reputation as a bad apple? The answer to this question was simple: aggressive behavior. Push, bite, bully, hit and generally be loud and obnoxious.

Aggressive behavior often results in an ADD child's being isolated or frequently playing with children several years younger than himself. The reasons for the isolation are obvious. But why do ADD kids play with younger children? We'll explain that in Chapter 4.

Unfortunately, interpersonal problems are very difficult to change, especially the bad reputation of the rejected child. This reality is especially discouraging because one of the strongest predictors of adult success in life is one's social skills. Making matters much worse is the fact that social skills training for ADD kids (Combined Type) doesn't work very well— at least as it has been tried so far.

On a happier note, many Inattentive Type ADD children get along just fine with playmates. Often these children are very easy-going, pleasant and somewhat passive—the opposite of the "in-your-face" type of ADD child.

8. Disorganization

If you had all the seven of the ADD characteristics mentioned so far, you would probably have trouble with organization, too. Attention Deficit children are often disoriented and forgetful; they lose track of time and they frequently lose things as well.

ADD children are not just forgetful—they are *amazingly* forgetful. What drives many parents crazy is an ADD child who doesn't do his homework. What really drives them nuts, though, is an ADD child who does his homework and then loses it before he even gets a chance to turn it in! Where did it go? It's on the floor in the back seat of the car or perhaps under the bed. Many times the homework actually got to school in the youngster's notebook. But it was a math paper and it got filed under social studies, so it didn't resurface for three weeks.

There seems to be a psychological law which dictates that trouble concentrating leads consistently to forgetfulness. ADD kids forget what they studied just last night for today's spelling test. They constantly lose their schoolbooks, their clothes, their new watch and even their toys. One nine-year-old boy came in one day and mentioned he had played a little league game the day before. When asked the score, the boy said, "It was 17 to 2." When asked next who won, he said he didn't remember! Normally one would recall vividly either getting trounced by—or, on the other hand, trouncing—another team.

An ADD child may also have a poor sense of time and place. She can never seem to get home on time, even if she has a watch. Some of this disorientation, of course, is due to the problem of delaying gratification— the child doesn't want to leave what she's doing and go home. But she also just doesn't pay much attention to time. This trait is painfully obvious in the morning when Mom, Dad and the rest of the family are trying to get out the door. Early morning chaos is one of parents' biggest complaints; everyone leaves the house and starts the day in a bad mood.

Family members find that the ADD child is always borrowing their things, and then innocently losing them. Fathers will go through many sets of tools before an Attention Deficit son grows up and leaves home. Some ADD kids are "prowlers" and "hoarders." They seem to be constantly snooping around the house, and they may actually steal other people's things with no consideration of giving them back.

As mentioned earlier, ADD Combined Type children will likely fit all eight of the characteristics just mentioned. Those who are of the Inattentive variety, however, will show only items 1 (inattention), 6 (noncompliance—more the passive rather than the defiant kind) and 8 (disorganization). Combined Type children (ADD with hyperactivity) are often noticeable and diagnosable as early as age two or three. What stands out at these very young ages, of course, is not inattention but disruptive behavior. Preschool ADD children are obvious primarily because of excessive (for their age) impulsivity, impatience, emotional overarousal, hyperactivity, noncompliance and social aggressiveness.

Inattentive (ADD without hyperactivity) kids, on the other hand, don't usually appear out of line until they hit school, where their daydreaming, forgetfulness and inability to finish things become more of a problem. Even in the early grades, however, these children are too often overlooked because they cause little or no trouble.

C. ADD and Self-Control

Another way of looking at ADD, and an idea that is apparently catching on, is the notion that Attention Deficit Disorder is fundamentally a deficit in one's ability to self-regulate or self-control. Proposed by Dr. Russell Barkley in *ADHD and the Nature of Self-Control*, this point of view suggests that the basic problem is one of "behavioral disinhibition."

According to this point of view, a person with ADD has trouble *not* responding to the newest, most interesting, most pressing or most fascinating (prepotent) stimulus that comes along, *especially when he should be doing something else*. If you are taking a casual stroll through the forest, for example, it's OK to bend down to examine a bug, watch a hawk soaring high above, or even wander off the path to follow a green leopard frog. If you are sitting in a classroom taking an ACT test, however, it's not OK to daydream about your girlfriend, watch a squawking crow flying by the window, or become irritated by your neighbor's sniffling and walk out of the room (this has happened!).

Barkley proposes that people with ADD have trouble holding back and waiting before making some kind of internal or external response. As mentioned earlier, Virginia Douglas used to call this a "stop, look and listen" problem. Barkley takes the idea farther, however. Because the ADD individual responds impulsively, he says, he does not take the time or get a chance to use four "executive functions" that are the essence of self-regulation. These executive functions involve the ability to calm down and think things over—even if it's only for a second or two. The executive functions include working memory (holding relevant facts in your mind), internal speech (talking to yourself), emotional regulation (calming down or motivating yourself), and reconstitution (creating a useful solution or response). People with ADD not only do not use these executive functions well in the first place, they also do not get a chance to practice and hone their "executive" skills over the years.

An example will help. Imagine two high school sophomores who live in Chicago. Fred has Attention Deficit Disorder; Mark does not have ADD. Both are finishing their supper at 6:45 p.m. on a dark, cold Tuesday night in February. Both boys are enthusiastic Chicago Bulls fans and there is a game on at 7:30. Both Fred's and Mark's mothers remind them that they have homework and both boys head upstairs to their bedroom desks to get started (a minor miracle in itself).

At 7:15 the mothers check in on their sons. Mark is working hard on his algebra and Fred is on his computer playing his favorite fighter pilot game. His homework is untouched.

What happened? Let's do a slow-motion replay of each boy's mental processing during the minutes right after dinner. Fred, who is ADD, went up to his room intending to do his homework, but his first reaction upon sitting down at his desk was a strong emotional revulsion toward the idea. He then glanced at his computer, thought about the fighter pilot game, and started playing. What he did was an automatic, impulsive response more than a real "decision." The game was fun—a lot more fun than homework—and Fred would probably go on playing it for hours if not interrupted.

Mark also went up to his room intending to do his homework, *also felt revulsion* at the idea when he sat down, and—like Fred—also glanced at his computer and thought about the fighter pilot game. But then he stopped (behavioral or response inhibition) and thought a little bit. He remembered (working memory) that he had algebra, Spanish and a lot of history to do—and there was a Bulls game on at 7:30. "I'll never get the homework done by then," he thought to himself (internal speech), "but I'd hate to miss the game." While controlling his distaste for the schoolwork in front of him (emotional regulation—calming down), he recalled that the last time he had not done his algebra homework he had wound up embarrassed in front of the whole class. "I don't want that to happen again!" he thought (emotional regulation—motivation).

Then he had an idea (reconstitution). He would ask his mother to tape the Bulls' game and make her swear not to tell him the final score. He would then watch the taped replay after finishing his work. It would be his reward (motivation), in a sense, for getting his work done.

The difference between the two boys is clear—and sad. You can see that ADD involves a difficulty being constructively oriented toward the future and engaging in goal-directed activity. As Ned Hallowell, the coauthor of *Driven to Distraction*, says, "When you're ADD there are only two kinds of time: now and not now. I have a final exam next week. Not now!"

So perhaps the new name for ADD should be "BID: Behavioral Inhibition Disorder." For many years the core trio of ADD symptoms has been considered to be hyperactivity, impulsivity and inattentiveness. Hyperactivity (Hyperkinetic reaction of childhood) and inattentiveness (Attention Deficit Disorder) have had their turn. Maybe it's time for impulsivity to take center stage.

Barkley's newer view of ADD is both provocative and enlightening. Unfortunately, the new theory also complicates things a bit, because it only refers to Combined Type ADD. Inattentive children, according to Barkley, "show a deficiency in focused or selective attention that is not related to problems with behavioral inhibition and self-regulation." Are the Inattentive and Combined Types different parts of the same continuum, or are they totally different entities? At this point, the jury is still out.

3

School, Home and Friends

When they all are present, the symptoms of ADD can cause a child problems in all areas of his or her life. As you may remember, the DSM-IV requires that some kind of impairment be present in at least two settings. With the Combined Type of ADD, however, impairment often exists in *all* settings. In this chapter we'll examine how ADD traits can affect a child at school, at home and in social situations.

School: Combined Type (ADD with hyperactivity)

If you maliciously set out to produce an environment that could drive an ADD child crazy on a daily basis, you probably couldn't come up with anything worse than school. School requires that the youngster not only sit still but also concentrate on material that he usually finds uninteresting. *Boring* is one of the most common words used by ADD children to describe school.

Because of his difficulty with rules and self-control, the Combined kind of ADD child is often a significant negative force in the classroom. He will stand out like a sore thumb, and all the other children will be aware of who he is and how much trouble he gets into. He will often fall into a vicious cycle with his teacher: he acts up, she tries to control him, he resists by acting up more, she attempts to exert more control, and on and on. By April, the hostilities can be extreme, and by that time the parents are also likely to be involved in the confusion.

Even though his IQ can be the same as his classmates, the ADD child's academic performance will be inexplicably uneven, causing adults to comment, "He can do it if he really wants to!" He may be accurately accused of daydreaming when he is distracted by internal stimuli. At other times he may blurt out appropriate answers (but without raising his hand) or clown around by making jokes or silly noises.

Actually, most ADD children want to do well just as much as other kids do, and they can have spurts when they indeed do well. But because they are continually bumping their heads against an invisible concentrational and motivational problem, these kids will not be able to sustain their effort.

Some ADD kids have been known to have an entire year where they did not do all that badly. When this occurs, it is usually due to a very positive "teacher interaction" effect. Bobby, for example, gets Mrs. Smith in the third grade. She likes him, and she is willing to put up with a certain amount of goofing up. Bobby also likes her and is willing to work for her more than he usually does. The year goes fairly well, and Mom and Dad start thinking Bobby is finally "maturing."

Unfortunately, fourth grade rolls around and Bobby gets Mrs. Hammond. Mrs. Hammond thinks ADD is a fabricated diagnosis and says she "doesn't believe in it." She doesn't particularly like Bobby, and early in the year he impresses her as being kind of a brat. Bobby reciprocates, and in a short period of time problems start up again.

What do we know about the IQs of ADD children? Some people tend to associate ADD with giftedness. Certainly there are Attention Deficit children who are gifted, but this is not typical. In general, ADD kids are about as smart as anyone else. That means some are quite bright, most are average, and some are of below-average intelligence. The problem, though, is that—whatever their IQ—ADD youngsters can't use all of it because of their difficulty paying attention.

With regard to learning disabilities, it's a different story. ADD kids as a group do have more of a tendency to have a learning disability in addition to their ADD. In the general population, perhaps 10 to 15 percent of all children have learning disabilities. In the ADD population, this figure is more like 30 to 40 percent. Attention Deficit children, therefore, often have two handicaps to deal with.

The result of all these problems is that ADD kids will usually be significant underachievers. From a very early point in time they find that they do not like school. A typical conversation with an ADD child during a diagnostic evaluation may go something like this:

> "What do you think of school?"
> "I don't like it."
> "What don't you like about it?"
> "It's boring."
> "What's boring about it."
> "The work."
> "What's your favorite subject?"
> "Recess."

Some people believe that a child's "academic self-concept"—or what he expects of himself in school—may be formed very early, perhaps by the third grade. If this idea is true, it is a frightening notion, because early in their academic careers ADD kids may decide that school is not the place for them to be.

School: Inattentive Type (ADD without hyperactivity)

The Inattentive Type of ADD child will show many of the same problems as the Combined Type—minus the disruptive behavior. These children are often, but not always, girls. They may quietly fade into the background of the classroom, and no one seems to notice them. If you watch closely, however, you will see a little girl in trouble. She is dreamy and detached. She does not finish her work on time or at all. She is not really following what is going on in class, but it's easy to miss her inattentiveness because she is polite, tries to be cooperative, makes little noise and causes no trouble.

Inattentive ADD children are often seen as simply being slow learners, in spite of the fact that most have average or above-average intelligence. Their forgetfulness and disorganization, however, are seen as signs of limited intellectual ability rather than as signs of ADD. The presence of a learning disability or anxiety can further this mistaken impression of the problem. Due to their quiet and gentle natures, though, in the early grades these children often are not recognized as needing diagnosis and treatment.

Home: Combined Type (ADD with hyperactivity)

Let's imagine that the ADD boy we described in the first section of this chapter didn't have such a good day at school. It would be nice if he could come home, put his feet up, and relax a little. Unfortunately, where Attention Deficit is involved things don't usually work out like that.

An ADD child will constantly bewilder his parents: they just can't understand what makes him tick. He will often become the black sheep of the family, just as he may have been the black sheep of the classroom. He will often be the source of constant disruption, and will produce what seems like an endless flood of noise. Sibling rivalry with ADD children is unusually intense, with the ADD child most often being the instigator of the trouble. He is extremely jealous of siblings, sometimes correctly perceiving that they are liked more than he is.

General discipline is almost always a problem for parents with their ADD offspring. Nothing seems to work as it did with the other children. One study showed that out of every ten interactions between ADD children and their parents, nine were negative and only one positive. This sad statistic obviously does nothing for anyone's self-esteem, and it produces consistent aggravation for the entire household.

At home the ADD boy or girl won't remember the rules or his chores. When asked to do even minor things, he may produce a major tantrum. He is usually sloppy, his room is a disaster area, and he doesn't follow through. Asking the child to do several things in sequence is usually a lost cause. After requesting that a youngster turn off the TV, hang up his coat, and come to dinner, for example, parents may return ten minutes later to find the child standing immobile—coat in hand—staring at the TV.

As the years go on, both the child and his parents can experience a continual drop in self-esteem and an increase in depression. As we have mentioned, the very first person in the family to get clobbered by the existence of an ADD child is not the child: it is the mother. Mom gets the brunt of the difficult child's behavior. And since we still live in a society that tends to blame parents for everything their kids do, the parents —and especially the mother—will constantly be trying to figure out where they went wrong with this kid.

Home: Inattentive Type (ADD without hyperactivity)

In general, the Inattentive ADD child at home is not an aggressive disruptor or noise-maker. She may, in fact, have a fairly mild-mannered disposition and be fairly easy to get along with. Some of these children are actually too passive. They may appear unmotivated and slow to process information. Often you find they are not listening to you even when you are speaking right at them. They are amazingly forgetful and absent-minded. They have trouble getting organized and following through on activities like getting up and out in the morning, doing homework or completing their chores.

Inattentive Type kids, though, do all this quietly and passively. They will not intrude so much on their parents' senses or consciousness. Mom and Dad may have to track their little daydreamer down to find out what she has or has not accomplished. These children are also more passive in sibling rivalry, but occasionally they can put up a first-class fuss when they feel they are being treated unfairly or abused. Parents who tend to be well-organized themselves, or those who lean toward the perfectionistic, can certainly find Inattentive kids very frustrating, even when making noise or causing major disturbances are pretty much absent in the child's behavior.

Peers: Combined Type (ADD with hyperactivity)

As if these problems weren't enough, when the rambunctious type of ADD child goes out and plays, he will encounter further difficulties. His frequent lapses in self-control make it hard to engage in games that require following rules and restraint. The ADD child suffers from a major case of "low frustration tolerance." Everything is a big deal to him, and he is extremely competitive, often trying to modify or create rules to serve his goal of winning at all costs.

As mentioned before, this Attention Deficit youngster will often be bossy and sometimes physically aggressive. Parents of ADD kids are often quite distressed by their child's treatment of playmates who come over to the house. The hyperactive and impulsive child has a very difficult time sharing and does not pay much attention to what the other child wants to do. After a difficult few hours, many of the playmates don't want to return again. The ADD youngster finds that they do not reciprocate by calling to invite him over. It is not unusual for Attention Deficit kids to be left out of birthday parties that would usually involve their entire class from school.

Adding to the child's woes is his tendency to get overstimulated in groups and to act "hyper" and silly, making stupid noises, poking people and being a general nuisance. Since ADD kids are notoriously insensitive to verbal and nonverbal social cues, they will not realize how poorly they are coming across. Adults who try to tell the child to "calm down" in these situations find that their words are like throwing gasoline on a fire. You must take the child out of the situation for a while to calm him down.

Though you wouldn't expect it with all these problems, ADD children often initiate interactions with other kids, but often in a negative or irritating way. One little third grade ADD girl would kick all the boys in the shins in the coat room at the end of the day. It was kind of her way of saying, "See you later, have a nice evening," but the effects were obviously detrimental to her chances of getting along with anybody.

When the inevitable fights and arguments do occur, ADD children always blame the other kids for the problem. Parents waste their breath trying to point out to the child what he may have done to cause the trouble, even though the parent may have seen the whole thing.

The result of all these social difficulties is that the hyperactive child either winds up isolated or frequently plays with younger children. The cause for the isolation is obvious, but why do ADD kids wind up with younger playmates? There are several reasons. First, the ADD child's maturity level is usually several years less than his actual chronological age, so he fits in better in that respect. Second, he will usually be physically larger than the younger children, so they will let him be the boss. This suits the ADD child just fine, since he will be much less frustrated if he always gets his way. This arrangement often suits the younger children just fine, too, because they find the ADD child entertaining and fun. He always seems to be coming up with something interesting to do. It may not be legal, but then again it's safe, because if they get caught, the older kid usually takes the rap!

This is not to say that it is bad for hyperactive kids to play with younger children. That is certainly preferable to having nobody to play with. Some of these ADD kids can also get along better with older, or opposite-sex, kids. The acid test of the social skills of an ADD child, however, is his ability to get along with same-age, same-sex children.

Peers: Inattentive Type
(ADD without hyperactivity)

Inattentive ADD children do not make bad impressions on other kids. They frequently make *no impression at all* on other kids. They are simply overlooked. Instead of being pushy and aggressive, they hold back and remain on the fringe of activities— only joining in when they are invited.

Still, when they do join an activity, forgetfulness and daydreaming may put them in embarrassing situations. One little boy was playing left field during a baseball game, but he became distracted by a family of geese walking off to his right. As he meandered in their direction, a triple was hit to his left. It took quite a bit of teammates' screaming to bring him back to the game and to his job of retrieving the ball.

Many Inattentive ADD children, on the other hand, are just fine playmates. They are easy-going, listen fairly well, accomodate others' interests and often let others direct their play. As opposed to the Combined Types, ADD Inattentives may have an advantage when it comes to social skills training. Which is easier to overcome: a bad reputation or no reputation? The answer is the latter. ADD children with no black marks against them socially can often be trained to join activities successfully.

4

Growing Up ADD

As they progress from infants to adults, ADD children will show different characteristics and different behaviors at different stages of their development. After all, life makes special demands on children depending on their ages. Ages 3 and 4, for example, require mastering self-care skills, such as getting dressed, tying shoes and brushing teeth. Ages 8 and 9 ask that you make and keep same-sex friends, clean your room and finish your homework. The interaction of ADD symptoms with life's demands will produce a constantly changing picture as the child grows up. Unfortunately, ADD will interfere with many developmental tasks, and as you get older, of course, life almost always demands more and more self-control.

Not all Attention Deficit children will show every single one of the characteristics or problems we are about to mention. The developmental course we will first describe represents what you might expect in the growth of a "typical" child with Combined Type ADD, where no diagnosis or effective treatment has been undertaken. Then we will take a look at the case of Sarah, a girl who grew up with undetected Inattentive Type ADD.

Developmental Course: Combined Type (ADD with hyperactivity)

Infancy

The infant signs listed here correlate to some extent with ADD, but they are not as reliable as those indicators that will be described later. There is a tendency for "ADD-to-be" infants to show more of a negative response to new situations and to simply spend more time in negative moods. (Apparently some people can be born crabs!) They can also show overly intense emotional reactions, disturbed sleep patterns, and feeding difficulties. Allergies are more frequent in ADD children, and the babies sometimes make strange, repetitive vocalizations. Finally, a few of these babies will physically resist affection and cuddling, almost as if they feel it is too restraining.

Keep in mind that these infant "signs" should be taken with a grain of salt. Many ADD kids were wonderful babies.

Toddler Years

More reliable indicators of ADD occur when the kids get to be toddlers. In fact, many experts believe that it is possible to identify 60 to 70 percent of ADD children by ages two to three. The predominant indicators, though, will not include short attention span, because few two-year-olds concentrate on anything for very long.

Instead, noncompliance can become more of a problem and stubbornness may be extreme. If the child is a firstborn (and ADD kids do tend to be firstborn), it is difficult for parents to tell if this is just the "terrible twos" or if the child is just "all boy." The child may walk early and always be on the go. Many of these children are accident prone, due to the hyperactivity, impulsivity and frequent coordination difficulties that many of them experience. They often stop taking naps at an early age—much to the chagrin of the mother—and are very demanding of attention, not playing well alone. If there are siblings, sibling rivalry and jealousy can be constant and extremely intense.

Ages Three to Five

As the ADD child gets older, noncompliance in public can become more of an issue, very often creating extremely embarrassing situations for the parents. Many families simply stop going out much, or even taking vacations, because of the awful scenes they have been through in cars, restaurants and motels.

Peer problems can also emerge as the children graduate from parallel play to more interactive play, where the situational demands to share, listen and get along are greater. Phone calls from preschools and kindergartens can begin about the child's misbehavior, often producing the beginning of "phone phobia" for mother. It is not unusual to find ADD kids who have already been "kicked out" of one or more preschools, often because of their aggressive behavior and difficulty complying with the normal routines.

At this age it also now becomes more obvious that discipline doesn't work with the ADD child as it does with other children, and frustrations may inspire "insane" fits of temper totally out of proportion to the actual difficulty. Hostile destructiveness is not uncommon in these children, but they can also break things or take them apart simply out of impulsive curiosity.

Another interesting correlate of ADD, which is often overlooked, is that household pets, such as dogs and cats, will consistently avoid a young ADD child. Animals naturally avoid repeating painful experiences.

At this point, too, Mom and Dad will start arguing more about how to handle the child, causing increased marital friction on a regular basis. The fact that these kids often respond quite differently to their fathers than to their mothers usually doesn't help the situation. A number of studies have shown the divorce and separation rates to be higher in families that have ADD kids.

Ages Five to Twelve

Now the ADD child hits the "big time" in school. Demands to sit still and concentrate usually increase dramatically in first grade, and thus school complaints also become more frequent at that time. Some kindergartens, however, seem to consider themselves junior versions of Harvard Law

School, and they put considerable pressure on the children for self-restraint as well as academic performance. When this is the case, many of the ADD children will start having serious problems in kindergarten.

Retention may also be considered around this time because the "child is so immature." Retention should be given careful thought, however. Holding a child back can be a big mistake unless a complete ADD evaluation (see Chapters 7 and 8) is done. If the problem is primarily ADD and nothing is done about it, many of these ADD kids will provide just as much trouble the second time around in first grade.

In the first, second and third grades, LD problems may begin to emerge, since a large portion of ADD children will also have a learning disability. It is very common for ADD kids to have major problems with handwriting, and for many of them this isn't just because they rush their work. It's also because their fine motor coordination isn't that good. Math seems to involve an unusual amount of sustained concentration, so it is often an area where many ADD children have difficulty.

Socially, the child may be more of a loner, and acting out can increase, such as lying, fighting and stealing. Lying often is related to unfinished schoolwork. Trends toward acting out are worrisome because we know that about 25 percent of our ADD children are at serious risk for later developing "conduct disorders"—problems that involve more serious, age-inappropriate and precocious activities that are sometimes illegal.

During the grammar school years the child is now old enough to know something is wrong. His self-esteem may begin to suffer. Even though everything that comes out of his mouth is an attempt to blame parents, teachers or other kids for his problems, he is aware enough to sense inside that something is wrong with him. He won't, of course, have the slightest idea of what it is, and may simply begin to feel that he is simply dumb, mean or weird.

Adolescence

Attention Deficit Disorder and adolescence don't mix too well. It's true that many ADD children will simmer down some in terms of gross motor restlessness (hyperactivity), but much of the time ADD in the 13-to-19-year-old crowd means "adolescence with a vengeance"!

By the time the ADD youngster is an ADD teen, many families are totally fed up and at the end of their rope after years of frustration. Other family members, especially fathers, can themselves get mad at the drop of a hat and at times outdo the child's tantrums. Parents get especially frustrated with arguing. For years the ADD child has always had to have the last word, he can never take "no" for an answer, and he will argue endlessly over the slightest things. People who have lived in a home where this routine has occurred regularly develop an ability to sense a blowup coming, giving them an aggravating, disheartening and sickening feeling.

As for student life, many ADD teenagers are sick of school by the time they hit high school. Academically they may be behind their peers because of all the years when they couldn't concentrate enough to be able to learn what they were supposed to. Tackling high school courses with this shaky base—on top of a residual attention problem—is extremely difficult. Many of these ADD kids long ago internalized the notions that they were "stupid" or "lazy," although they usually don't say this out loud. Most will graduate, but they will have paid a price.

Difficulties with peers can continue in adolescence, but they may not be as bad outwardly as they were when the child was younger, more aggressive and bossier. Isolation, however, is frequently a problem, or the teen may go through a series of short-term relationships that just never seem to last. A frequent concern of parents is that their teenager does have friends but the parents either don't like them or rarely get a chance to meet them. There is a danger that an unsuccessful ADD teen will hang out with the "burnout" crowd—those kids who also don't like teachers, school and parents.

As you might expect, there is also research evidence that ADD teens are not as good drivers as their non-ADD counterparts. (Non-ADD teens, of course, especially males, are not such good drivers in the first place!) Imagine an ADD adolescent driving to the store to get an exciting new CD. He approaches a light that just turned yellow. Impulsivity, difficulty delaying gratification, emotional overarousal and noncompliance might all conspire here to produce a dangerous situation. Driving performance is usually not such a horrible problem that one should keep these kids off the road, but many parents try to get to the car keys first when they're going out together.

Yet the picture is not all bleak for many ADD teens. Some of them will experience a noticeable "mellowing" as they get older. Some of them are smart enough to do well in school and go on to college. Some of them have friends who enjoy their exuberance and their ability to be the life of the party. Some will go on to find jobs where their intensity will be an asset. Parents find, though, that ADD teenagers always seem to keep them somewhat off-balance.

Adulthood

We now know that ADD is not outgrown and that there are people who are ADD adults, or what is sometimes referred to as "ADD, Residual Type." Though this fact is discouraging, the situation is not all bad. Symptoms like concentration difficulties, emotional overarousal and even some forms of impulsivity can continue. On the other hand, even though some symptoms continue, they do tend to "mellow," being less severe than in the person's younger years. Gross motor hyperactivity will diminish quite a bit, perhaps partly because the adult has many more pounds to maneuver around. And a few lucky ADD people—probably less than 25 percent— will show no symptoms as grown-ups.

Though the symptoms lessen, secondary problems that were not part of the original ADD picture may now have come along for the ride. "Growing up ADD" does not do a lot for one's self-esteem, especially when 80 to 90 percent of the feedback you get from your parents and teachers is negative. This type of history can lead to depression and a generally gloomy outlook toward life and other people. The ADD child usually had to sit through at least 12 years of education, which required that he do two things daily that he was never very good at: 1) sit still and 2) concentrate on things that were normally quite boring.

One significant blessing for many ADD adults is that there is no more school! Unless, of course, by choice, but now there's a difference: if you are ADD, you choose to attend school and you are no longer going there primarily for the benefit of your parents or for the society in which you live. You may now choose something more interesting *to you*, and—as we have seen—interest value can help both attention and motivation considerably.

An ADD adult, on the other hand, may choose not to go to school anymore and may instead pick an occupation that better suits his or her skills and temperament.

The personalities of some ADD adults may actually make them more effective in their work. Although difficulty paying attention will never be an asset no matter what you are doing, some of the other ADD "symptoms" may actually help a person in some kinds of work. If you take someone who is reasonably intelligent and has good social skills, his intense energy level, strong emotions and aggressiveness (appropriate) can certainly help him in certain jobs. Some of these individuals will be good entrepreneurial types and may succeed at starting their own businesses. They will do better in a situation where they don't have to have a boss. Others may do well at outside sales, where they can drive around or travel, meet different people and use their energy making sales. The bad news for ADD salespeople? From time to time they are required to sit down at a desk and write their weekly or monthly activity or expense report.

There is research evidence that ADD adults both switch jobs more often and tend to have part-time jobs more often. These findings may be due to the unfortunate fact that the general socioeconomic status of ADD adults is lower than that of their family or peers. Perhaps ADD individuals feel a need to supplement their incomes—or simply to expend more of their excess energy.

The outlook here is not all bad. Most ADD children, in spite of the fact that they maintain some of their symptoms, will grow up to be employed, married, physically normal and self-supporting adults. And the problems that they do maintain can be treated. For more on ADD in adults, see Chapters 17-19.

Developmental Course: Inattentive Type (ADD without hyperactivity)

Sarah's mother always said she was an easy baby. She seemed to have a very pleasant, calm temperament, smiling often and enjoying the presence of other people. Her developmental milestones were normal. Sarah walked at about twelve months and was putting a few words together just after age two.

During her preschool years, Sarah presented no particular problems. Her mother went back to work when Sarah was about three. For about three to four weeks, however, Sarah had trouble separating from her Mom when dropped off at daycare. She would not tantrum, but she would cry and be reluctant to go inside. This reaction, of course, made her mother feel guilty about going to work. She would stew about her daughter during the day and sometimes even call the center. At those times she would be told that Sarah was "doing fine."

Socially, Sarah seemed to enjoy the presence of other children, but she also seemed somewhat passive and hesitant. When first introduced to a new group of kids, she would just watch and watch, standing off to the side. She obviously enjoyed watching the children, though, because she would smile and laugh at the children as they played. Gradually Sarah would get more involved, especially if she were not forced to do so prematurely. Fortunately, her parents and teachers appreciated the fact that it was not a good idea to push her in this regard.

Sarah loved kindergarten, and she especially loved her teacher, Mrs. MacArthur. The feeling was reciprocal, because Sarah was also one of Mrs. MacArthur's favorites. She kept telling Sarah's parents that their little girl was "so sweet!" Sarah, in fact, was a sweet kid. She always seemed to be in good spirits, rarely got mad and never caused any trouble. She was always willing to help and cooperate with any agenda. And Sarah seemed to be loosening up a bit socially; she now had two good friends.

Grammar School

In first grade things went OK, but not quite as well. According to her teacher, Sarah sometimes appeared a little "slower than the other children." She had trouble keeping her pencils and papers in order, and she often appeared to lose things for no apparent reason. Her teacher also commented that Sarah "was not always with the rest of the class." Sometimes she would be looking out the window and at other times she seemed to be lost in a daydream.

For a while in November, she resisted going to school again. She had trouble leaving the house to catch the bus. When her Dad asked her if she liked school, she said yes, but without as much enthusiasm as she had shown before. This stage quickly passed and Sarah's parents were reassured that there was a lot of variation among first graders. Sarah was a lovely child, and she certainly would come along just fine.

Second and third grades, however, were worse. Teacher comments about disorganization and being unable to focus on the task at hand continued. Yet as soon as any teacher uttered these criticisms, the words were followed with the comment, "But don't worry, everything will be fine. She's such a sweet girl."

Sarah *was* still a sweet girl. At home she gave her parents little trouble, except for the fact that she couldn't seem to remember anything and was always losing things. Fortunately, Sarah's parents were not obsessive-compulsive types, and their daughter's pleasant disposition made it hard to get mad at her. But she'd forget to feed the dog, leave her toys outside, and it was dreadful trying to get her up and out in the morning.

As grammar school progressed, Sarah stumbled along. Once letter grades appeared on the report card, she got mostly Cs, with an occasional D or B. Teacher comments about inattentiveness, disorganization and problems completing work continued. All her teachers liked her, though. They all felt she wanted to cooperate and her failings were simply due to some kind of absentmindedness. Sarah was never a behavior problem, and she seemed to get along well with the other children.

Junior and Senior High

In junior high, things worsened considerably. Now Sarah had seven different teachers, a locker and lots of homework. Her organizational skills, which were never strong, were now simply overwhelmed. She brought the wrong books to the wrong classes. She lost her assignments. Term papers and other long-term projects were forgotten until the last minute. Her parents were now beginning to wonder if their daughter wasn't being just a little bit obstinate. Arguments about school and schoolwork increased. Homework took three to fours a night to complete, and even then the work was hurried, messy and full of careless mistakes.

In eighth grade something happened that changed Sarah's life. Her English teacher asked her to read a poem in front of the whole class. She wasn't crazy about the idea, but she walked up to the front of the room.

While she was reading, however, she began feeling short of breath and she started sweating. Her hands began to shake and she could hardly hold the paper. Her voice shook. She wanted to run away, but she couldn't. She felt like a total fool.

Finally, the teacher, in a kind voice, asked what was the matter. Sarah said she didn't know. The teacher told her she didn't have to finish. Sarah sat down, completely humiliated. She couldn't look at anybody. After class her teacher tried to talk to her, but Sarah hurried away.

Sarah had been blindsided by her first panic attack, induced by a fairly common fear, the fear of public speaking. She hoped at first that it had just been a bad day. But the next time she had to read or speak in class, she panicked again. From then on she dreaded going to school, horrified by the thought that she might be called on to once again make a fool out of herself in front of everybody.

Sarah's anxiety added to her inattentiveness. Her grades dropped further in high school. Now she was getting Cs, Ds and Fs. Her parents were more frustrated with her. They were always asking her what was the matter, but Sarah simply said she didn't know. Her anxiety generalized into social situations. She was now afraid to speak up in any group, and never wanted to be the center of attention. Speech class was total terror. She feared people would hear her voice quaver, or see her hands shake. She couldn't drink coffee in front of anyone or even hold a soup spoon. She only brought things for lunch like sandwiches, which she could grab with both hands, or else she just didn't eat.

As Sarah's anxiety increased and her school performance got worse, her self-esteem fell apart. She became more and more depressed. She had little contact with friends. Finally, her parents took her to see a psychologist. This event was even more embarrassing. Though Dr. Walker was a very nice woman, Sarah said very little and she did not mention her problem with anxiety. The psychologist concluded the girl was depressed, and she recommended counseling and medication.

Sarah started seeing Dr. Walker weekly. She also began taking a medication which Dr. Walker described as an "SSRI" antidepressant. After a month or so—to her surprise—Sarah did start feeling better. She also began feeling less anxious, which puzzled—and relieved—her. One day she actually gave a speech at school without any symptoms of panic.

Finally, Sarah told Dr. Walker about her problem with panicky feelings during social situations and public speaking. Dr. Walker explained that the medication might actually help with this anxiety as well as with depression—which was exactly what was happening.

But Sarah's schoolwork continued to be a problem. Her grades had improved to Cs with an occasional D. She still hated homework and long-term assignments were torture as usual. Dr. Walker and her parents felt she was brighter than these grades indicated, so psychological testing was ordered. Laura came up with a full-scale IQ of 123. She was bright!

So why the average to below-average grades? No one could figure it out. The focus on depression, and later on anxiety, had helped to cover the existence of Inattentive ADD.

Sarah muddled through two years at a community college; her grades didn't improve. By that time she was sick of school and wanted to do just about anything else. She started working at a fast food restaurant. Although the work was boring and the manager sometimes got after her for forgetting some of her jobs, it was still better than school.

Eventually Sarah married Mark, one of the managers at the restaurant. Although he was almost ten years older than she, they had one thing in common: they were both shy. Sarah had stopped taking the SSRI antidepressant and a good deal of her social anxiety had returned, but she was out of school and at the restaurant she avoided doing the cash register. Mark understood her reluctance.

At first, being married didn't seem so bad. Mark and Sarah agreed that she could stay home for a while and not have to work. Knowing little or nothing about birth control, Sarah had two babies in just under three years.

Conclusions?

Among the many conclusions that can be drawn from the above developmental histories, several stand out.

First, Inattentive ADD children are usually hard or impossible to distinguish from non-ADD preschool kids. All preschoolers show short attention spans.

Second, disruptive behavior (restlessness, running excessively, noisiness, blurting out and interrupting) "drives" referrals for evaluation. In other words, the ADD kids most likely to get picked up early will be the Combined Type children—the ones that are always "in your face." ADD without hyperactivity youngsters, like Sarah, are too often either diagnosed later or never evaluated at all.

Third, the older an ADD child gets, the more likely he or she will also develop another psychological disorder. Sarah eventually had trouble with anxiety and then depression. Anxiety and depression are what are often called "internalizing" disorders—they do not directly bother anyone other than the person afflicted with them. Combined Type (ADD with hyperactivity) children, however, are prone to not only internalizing disorders, but also "externalizing" disorders (those that do bother others), such as Oppositional Defiant Disorder or Conduct Disorder.

Why isn't there a separate section on the developmental course of the Hyperactive/Impulsive Type of ADD? Because many people, as we mentioned before, feel that this "type" is really an artifact of the DSM-IV structure, and that it really only fits preschoolers. It's hard to find a preschooler in the first place who qualifies for six out of nine DSM-IV inattentive symptoms. As they become older, these children will most likely become the Combined Type of ADD.

5

Causes

What causes ADD? First, we should clarify the question. What we are really asking is this: What could cause a consistent behavioral pattern characterized by inattentiveness, impulsivity and hyperactivity? Or, if we look at ADD as a problem with self-control, we are asking, What could cause continual problems with response inhibition and the four other executive functions (working memory, internal language, emotional regulation and reconstitution)?

Questions about cause can also be answered in different ways or at different levels. Is ADD hereditary, learned or some combination of both? Is ADD caused by "chemical imbalances" or structural differences in the brain? What about brain injury or impaired fetal development?

Heredity vs. Learning

We have known for some time that ADD is a disorder that has a strong hereditary component. ADD, in other words, is not something you learn as you grow up. Many studies have shown that relatives of children with ADD, as a group, have a much higher incidence of ADD themselves. The average school-age child, for example, has about a five percent chance of being ADD. If we know, however, that a particular child has an ADD sibling, that child's chances of being ADD go up to 30 percent. Another recent study found that if a parent had ADD, the risk of one of their children being ADD is just over 50 percent.

Adoptive studies also show a strong tendency for ADD to be inherited. Biological parents of ADD children show a much greater prevalence of ADD themselves than do the adoptive parents of ADD children. (It's nice to know that parents can't catch ADD from their kids!)

Other support for the largely hereditary nature of ADD comes from studies of twins. Monozygotic twins come from exactly the same egg (which divides in two), so they are identical. Dizygotic twins, on the other hand, come from two different eggs. If a characteristic is largely inherited, you would expect that, if one of two monozygotic twins has it, the chances are the other one will have it. On the other hand, if one of two dizygotic twins has a particular trait, the chances should be less that the other one also has it.

This is exactly what happens with ADD. If one monozygotic twin is ADD, the chances that the other will also be ADD are about two out of three. If one dizygotic twin is ADD, however, the chances that the other will also be ADD are about one out of three.

How do children inherit certain traits from their parents? From high school biology classes, you may remember Mendel and his peas. Or, more recently, you may remember the movie involving a semi-mad scientist supposedly reconstructing dinosaurs from the DNA in blood that had been stored for millions of years in a mosquito.

Children receive thousands and thousands of genes from their parents. These genes carry instructions for how to make a human being, and they also carry instructions that determine the many specific hereditary traits (height, IQ, skin color) that human beings have. The genes are arranged in long chains on rod-shaped, miscroscopic bodies called chromosomes. In humans there are 23 pairs of chromosomes. Each pair of chromosomes has one chromosome from the father and one from the mother.

Genes don't always do their work correctly, and when "errors" occur, serious problems can sometimes result. Errors in single genes, for example, are known to cause about 4,000 hereditary diseases. These include cystic fibrosis and Huntington's chorea, a severe, degenerative neurological disorder. Other disorders can occur when there are problems with several genes at the same time. These are called "complex genetic disorders," and they often interact with environmental factors to produce certain results. Most psychiatric problems, cancer and heart disease fall into the category of complex genetic disorders.

It is likely that ADD falls into this last category as well. Most experts feel that several of the 100,000 or so human genes will eventually be implicated in ADD, rather than just one. Researchers are hot on the trail of genetic variations or abnormalities that tend to run in families where ADD is present. By taking blood samples from parents and children, you can actually look at the chromosomes and the genes to see if there might be common genetic defects that occur in these families but not in non-ADD subjects. Already certain genes are being examined that have something to do with the functioning of the neurotransmitter dopamine in the central nervous system. We have known for some time that dopamine-transmission problems are often involved in ADD and that stimulant medications tend to help by improving dopamine transmission.

The identification of the different genes that are involved in producing ADD will have a number of different implications. First of all, certain patterns of genes may produce certain types of ADD. Perhaps we'll find that there is not only an Inattentive subtype, but also an anxious subtype, an aggressive subtype, a bipolar-ADD subtype and/or a depressed subtype. Second, identification of genes may point the way toward different treatments. For example, certain people may have a problem with dopamine reuptake in the synapse, while others may have a problem with dopamine reception in the post-synaptic neuron. We know that Ritalin and Dexedrine work somewhat differently in regard to dopamine. Perhaps genetic mapping will eventually be able to tell us what medication would be best for a particular ADD individual.

Genetic research, however, often gets ahead of actual treatment. Simply knowing which genes do what does not automatically lead to an effective way of dealing with a problem. Nevertheless, genetic research is an exciting new development in the field of Attention Deficit Disorder.

ADD and the Brain

To say that a disorder is hereditary—or largely hereditary—does not really explain what is causing the problem right this instant. It simply means that whatever is directly causing the problem can be passed on from generation to generation. There's another important question: "What is going on in this person right now that produces ADD symptoms?"

Today more and more people are referring to ADD as a "neurobiological" condition. That's because more and more research is pointing out that problems with attention, impulse control, activity level and self-regulation result from the inadequate functioning of certain areas of the brain. One of the areas of the brain that appears to be frequently involved in ADD is known as the "prefrontal cortex."

Several lines of research have implicated the prefrontal cortex:

1. Glucose metabolism studies (PET scans) have shown that these prefrontal areas of the brain are actually *underactive* in subjects with ADD.
2. The prefrontal areas of the brain are dopamine-rich areas, and we know that our most potent anti-ADD medications (the stimulants) *enhance* dopamine functioning.
3. Recent neuroimaging studies have suggested that these brain regions are *smaller than normal* in persons with ADD.
4. The prefrontal cortex is known to be associated with both *behavioral inhibition (the ability to stop, look and listen) and the other four executive functions* mentioned earlier.

People often wonder "Why in the world would you give a stimulant medication to a hyperactive person?" Now you can begin to understand the reason: with ADD parts of the brain (prefrontal cortex) that play a significant role in regulating a person's activities are actually *underactive*. These parts of the central nervous system, in other words, must be stimulated in order to do their job right.

Imagine, for example, that the governor of a state was lazy, drank constantly and spent all day in bed. The state itself would be a mess. People would fight, rob each other, not pay taxes. The schools, police, post office and other services would be terribly inefficient. Social, economic and political chaos would result and everyone would be miserable.

But imagine you could get that ruler out of bed, take him over to the window and say, "Look what's going on out there!" Perhaps you could stimulate him to do his job better, with the result that the state would become more orderly. Crime would drop, people would pay their taxes, the mail would get delivered, and generally people would be a lot happier.

The evidence suggests that something analogous to that occurs in the central nervous system of persons with ADD. Deficiencies in the prefrontal cortex (and its connections with other brain centers) result in a kind of "lazy governor," with the result that the ADD individual's activities are random, unfocused, disorganized, sometimes too aggressive and frequently overly emotional. The person does whatever he or she feels like doing at the moment. Self-restraint and future goals are sacrificed. Stimulant medications, however, can stimulate the lazy governor (prefrontal cortex) in the brain to do its job right, with the result that the activities of the ADD person become more focused, organized and purposeful.

So our thinking at the present time is that ADD has something to do with a predominantly inherited inability of the prefrontal areas of the brain to do their job of self-regulation correctly. Yet heredity may not be the whole story for everyone who has Attention Deficit Disorder. Studies have also shown that ADD can be related to biological hazards that can affect a child before, during or after birth. Identifiable risk-factors include maternal smoking, maternal alcohol use, prematurity and low birth weight. These hazards may somehow impact the prefrontal areas of the developing brain in the fetus. Brain injury to children and adults has also produced symptoms that are very similar to ADD (sometimes referred to as "secondary ADD"). We know these dangers contribute to ADD much less than heredity, but unlike genetic causes, they are for the most part preventable.

ADD and Bad Parenting

There are plenty of bad parents in the world. Some are grossly negligent, some are sexually or physically abusive and some are just plain mean. It is highly unlikely, though, that any of them ever singlehandedly caused

ADD in one or more of their children. Children do not learn to be ADD. You can certainly cause psychological problems in your kids by bad parenting, but ADD won't be one of them.

Unfortunately, this notion—"screwy parents make screwy kids"—is still one of the most widely held views of child-rearing in our society. This notion might be called the psychological, psychogenic or family dynamic theory of ADD, and it produces a great deal of unnecessary guilt in parents of ADD kids. In our schools the psychogenic view is still the predominant theory regarding childhood emotional and behavioral problems. Parents of ADD kids find it overtly—as well as subtly—expressed in the comments and reactions of friends, pediatricians, psychologists, teachers and relatives at the annual family picnic. The message is something like this: "If you would only set firmer limits on that little brat of yours, he would act like a normal child." Or if you drank less or argued less or spent more time at home, etc., etc.

Many of us parents, of course, blamed ourselves for our ADD child's behavior long before anyone else did. This is especially true of mothers, who initially bear the brunt of the problem. It's important to remember: ADD is primarily hereditary. And the other factors that may also cause ADD—or something like it—are biological hazards, not bad parenting.

Bad parenting, however, can affect an ADD child in two important ways. First, *bad parenting can aggravate ADD*. Some ADD symptoms tend to mellow with age. But inconsistent parenting, abuse or a chaotic home life can aggravate inattentiveness, impulsivity, aggression, emotional overarousal, hyperactivity and disorganization. This problem is made more difficult because many parents of ADD children are ADD adults, and it is often hard for them to be reasonable and consistent. That is why the treatment of an ADD child—to be effective—often must involve the concurrent treatment of the parents.

Second, *bad parenting can contribute to comorbidity*. Look at what are called the externalizing and internalizing disorders, for example. On the externalizing side, we know that marital instability and poor parenting can "facilitate" the metamorphosis of Oppositional Defiant Disorder into Conduct Disorder, which in turn can result in an adult version of the problem known as Antisocial Personality Disorder. On the internalizing side, anxiety and depression will at least be exacerbated—if not caused—by a parent who is constantly nagging, lecturing or screaming at a child.

The moral of the story is this: your parenting weaknesses didn't cause your child to be ADD. On the other hand, if you have an ADD child, you'd better work hard on your parenting defects, because life is demanding a lot more of you than it does of the average parent.

What Doesn't Cause ADD?

Contrary to Ben Feingold's claims, diet does not produce Attention Deficit Disorder. Systematic research has consistently failed to support the idea that artificial colorings, flavorings or natural salicylates are the nutritional troublemakers that produce ADD or LD in a majority—or even a significant minority—of children. It may be true, however, that there is a very small group of kids that is diet-sensitive in some ways, so parents' claims to that effect should never be taken lightly.

Also, contrary to popular belief, sugar doesn't cause hyperactivity either. Some interesting studies have shown that a child who ODs on sugar may actually become more lethargic for awhile—and also spacier. In other words, too much sugar reduces hyperactivity but also hurts concentration. However, many mothers steadfastly claim that their ADD child goes crazy after too much sugar intake. There may be a small subset of ADD children for whom this is true, contrary to what large-group studies have found. If your child has this reaction, limiting sugar intake certainly makes sense. Make sure, though, that it's the sugar that made her hyper, and not the situation—such as a wild and crazy birthday party!

In a way similar to the dietary effects we just discussed, allergies may aggravate ADD, but they don't produce Attention Deficit to start with. A child who is allergic and feeling sick is very likely to be more irritable, oppositional and generally out of sorts. Unfortunately, studies have shown that ADD children are more prone to allergies than the rest of the population. So it's quite possible for a child to be ADD *and* allergic. Allergies can complicate behavior, and so can some of the medications used to treat them.

Does lead cause ADD? The jury is still out. If there is a relationship between elevated body lead and ADD, the association is probably small.

Unfortunately, the research examining the issue has failed to control for heredity, and has also not studied groups of children who have been carefully diagnosed as ADD.

People often ask: "Why is there so much ADD around now compared to previous years? Is there some new factor that is causing a dramatic increase in its prevalence?" The best answer is probably that ADD has always been around, and it's probably always been around to the same degree it is now. The reason it's being diagnosed more is due to a tremendous increase in public awareness of the problem. And our best evidence suggests that ADD is *not* being overdiagnosed.

6

Predicting the Future

A number of studies have shown that parental stress is often based
more on parents' worries about how their child will turn out than on
what is actually going on right at the moment. When Johnny flunks his
spelling test, refuses to do homework, lies or pushes his sister to the floor,
Mom and Dad frequently entertain disturbing fantasies about their son's
never being able to hold a job, living at home his whole life, or winding
up in prison. These worries vary from parent to parent, but they often take
a very extreme form—*imagining the worst.* Such mental predictions make
parents very upset.

Raising an ADD child is difficult enough without having unnecessary
worry add to your burdens. Although ADD is a serious problem, the future
is usually not so bleak. The human mind, however, has a terrible propensity
for automatically and repeatedly coming to the worst possible conclusions
about all kinds of things. Since we all seem to be natural worriers, it would
be very helpful to look at some of the factors that can help us predict how
ADD kids will turn out as adults. Our goal here is to think as realistically
as possible about a child's future. On the one hand we don't want to dread
the future, but we also don't want to be naive.

Research on Attention Deficit Disorder has come up with a number of factors that have been shown to be related to adult outcome. Some of them overlap. Some of these factors are under a parent's control; others are not.

I. Socio-economic Status (SES)

Higher is better. That may sound a little funny, but for a long time we have known that higher SES is correlated with better health—both physically and mentally. There may be several reasons why a higher family SES leads to a better outcome with an ADD child. Perhaps parents in higher socioeconomic brackets are better educated and therefore more aware of potential problems. Perhaps they are more willing to seek assistance in evaluating difficulties with their children. In addition, these parents will be more able to afford diagnosis and treatment, and to be able to sustain these efforts over the many years necessary with an ADD child.

Finally, as we mentioned earlier, there is some association between ADD and prenatal, perinatal or postnatal difficulties. The child whose parents are in a higher economic bracket is less likely to experience danger here because his medical care is likely to be of higher quality.

On the other hand, children forced to grow up under conditions of urban poverty experience many risks that can aggravate ADD and worsen prognosis. Population density, inadequate housing, limited access to health care and other resources, high rates of crime, exposure to biological hazards, and family instability can all increase the risk for mental health problems.

2. IQ

Higher is better. A bright ADD child has a distinct advantage over his less intelligent counterparts. Superior intelligence can go a long way toward compensating for many different handicaps, including attentional problems as well as learning disabilities. Since the worst place—in a sense—for an ADD child to be is school, and since performance in school is very much related to brain power, it is easy to see how a higher IQ can contribute to better prognosis.

Imagine two different ADD children for a moment. One has an IQ of

100, which means exactly average and is the equivalent of the 50th percentile for his age group. The second ADD child has an IQ of 130, which is classified as "superior" and means this child is smarter than about 97 percent of his own age group. (Keep in mind that an IQ is not a perfect pinpoint type of score, but only an estimate of the child's overall ability.)

Let's suppose, further, that these two children are in the same third-grade class and they are both given the same math problem to do. Being ADD, they both have a fairly low frustration tolerance, so let's also assume both of them can work on a problem for a maximum of seven minutes before getting frustrated and quitting. The ADD child with the 130 IQ finishes the math problem in four minutes, feels good about his accomplishment, and receives praise from his teacher. The ADD child with the 100 IQ is capable of doing this particular problem in *ten* minutes, which exceeds his frustration tolerance. After seven minutes of working, therefore, he gives up, starts bothering the child next to him, and gets in trouble with the teacher.

Quite different outcomes. Although the example is somewhat oversimplified, it gives a fairly clear idea of the advantage IQ can provide. Multiply these experiences hundreds of times every year for each child, and you can easily imagine the effects on self-esteem.

One caution with bright ADD children: these kids are often overlooked. There is a myth that you can't be ADD and also get good grades. Bright ADD children can sometimes coast through the K-5 years with excellent grades. After all, the brighter you are, the more interesting school is and the more you can be successful (and get positive feedback). Even troublesome ADD behavior can be somewhat subdued when a child is interested in what he is doing. But come junior high and high school, you often see our smart ADD children start to slip. Why? More *homework* and more *organizational skills* are required.

3. Aggressiveness

More is worse. A large percentage of ADD children are overly aggressive in social situations. Physical aggression—especially in younger children—may occur as well as just plain bossiness. Aggressive behavior is fairly common in two-to-three-year-olds, so it doesn't always mean there is an unusual problem. Aggression (hitting, kicking, biting, spitting) is much more of a concern when it continues to age five and beyond.

Aggressive behavior does two things: it gets a youngster into trouble with adults, and it turns off a child's peers. Aggressive behavior—much more than simple inattentiveness—generates referrals for evaluation. In a sense response this is good, because possible ADD may be discovered. But this kind of behavior is still a big worry. Prognosis is especially poor if the aggressiveness does not moderate with age, and also if it turns into more serious forms of antisocial behavior in adolescence. Oppositional Defiant behavior, for example, which is usually more reactive than aggressive, may evolve into Conduct Disorder, which is defiant, aggressive and mean. ADD/CD kids are a big worry—and their behavior is hard to change.

Aggressive behavior also makes an unfavorable impression on one's peers, producing a "bad reputation" that is very hard to modify. And studies have shown that bad reputations can persist in people's minds even though the initial behavior that produced the reputation has changed for the better.

4. Hyperactivity

More is worse. Just as with the level of aggressiveness, the child who is extremely active will run into more problems than his less active counterparts. Although most hyperactive children can sometimes sit still in situations that are novel, interesting, intimidating or one-on-one with an adult, there are a few ADD children who can literally never sit still. Some, for example, cannot sit through a children's TV program where only a short attention span is required. Others cannot stay focused during preschool or kindergarten activities, which are short as well as fun. As was mentioned earlier, most hyperactivity will be "outgrown" by adolescence, but those few kids who don't outgrow it are in for more problems.

Ironically, there may be an instance where being less hyperactive is a drawback of sorts. This has to do with the Inattentive Type of ADD. Since these children are often not as active as the Combined kids, and are more the "pleasant space cadet" type, they do not come to the attention of the adults who might be able to evaluate and help them. Therefore as they grow up, they run into more and more problems, their self-esteem drops and they are more vulnerable to anxiety and depression. But nobody does anything about it because these children are "internalizers"—they are causing little trouble for anyone else.

5. Social Skills

More interpersonal competence is obviously better. Social skills and social status are extremely critical factors in determining a child's future happiness. Study after study has shown that a person's social skills play a major role in his adjustment. These studies have been done in many areas, not just with regard to ADD. One study, for example, looked at people diagnosed with schizophrenia and the simple trait of "likeability." The study found that the likeable schizophrenics had a much better prognosis than the obnoxious schizophrenics. This research is interesting and somewhat disheartening with respect to ADD, because Combined Type kids engage in a lot of abrasive behavior. It is hard to feel compassion for—or to want to help—someone who turns you off all the time.

We become very concerned about an ADD child if she has not developed some reasonable social abilities and does not have some friends by the age of ten. By this time it's getting late. If she is still isolated, or arguing and fighting a lot with peers, she is in trouble. Playing with younger children (which many ADD youngsters do), though, is still preferable to playing with no one at all.

Oddly enough, some ADD characteristics can, off and on, be assets for some children. The hyperactive older child can sometimes be the "life of the party." He may be enjoyed for his overarousal and high energy level, provided these qualities do not reach ridiculous proportions. Also, there is sometimes a fine line between bossiness and leadership. Some ADD children are capable of getting their way in a not-so-abrasive manner, and this can be an asset. Maybe they'll run their own company someday!

6. Early Diagnosis

The earlier the better. Detecting just about any problem at the earliest possible stage, whether it's astigmatism, cancer, a learning disability or Attention Deficit Disorder, is always preferable. Young children are still very malleable; if their ADD is picked up in the preschool years and dealt with properly, these kids have a good chance to develop fairly normally and avoid some major self-esteem problems. Remember that we think we can detect 60 to 70 percent of ADD children by ages two to three (usually the Combined kind of ADD). Trying to treat a 17-year-old ADD child for the first time is often very difficult because the child is so much more likely to be resistant, and to have adapted—for better or worse—to the way he is.

There is another reason early detection is better. Though we don't know for sure, our hope is that if we can pick up ADD early and treat it appropriately, we may be able to prevent—or get rid of—certain comorbid problems. For example, perhaps parent training and marital counseling for Mom and Dad might prevent some children from making the ADD-to-ODD-to-CD progression. In other children, treating ADD early and thus preventing school failure may very likely prevent later anxiety, depression and poor self-esteem.

7. Family Strength/Psychosocial Adversity

This prognostic dimension can be looked at in two ways: parental psychopathology and family strength.

Parental psychopathology: this is simply a rather fancy way of saying that the better put-together Mom and Dad are emotionally and behaviorally, the better off the child will be. It does not mean that Mom and Dad cause ADD. But if parents are fairly reasonable, competent and intelligent—even though not perfect—the child will obviously be better off. Unfortunately, it is often hard for parents to show these qualities for two reasons: the stress the ADD child creates and the fact that biological parents of ADD children have a tendency toward having certain types of psychological problems themselves.

Family strength: this dimension is closely related to the first. Healthy parents also make for a more stable family. A strong family unit can do a lot in helping an ADD child develop more normally. If the child feels the parents and siblings are "on his side" and care about him, his self-esteem will suffer much less from the inevitable batterings he will receive. If Mom and Dad can negotiate their differences in a democratic and satisfactory way—especially as regards the ADD child, and if the family allows for open expression of thoughts and feelings, the child will be better off.

One final but important sign of family strength that is very often overlooked is shared fun. It is unfortunately true that when there is an ADD child in a family, family fun is dangerous. Sibling rivalry, for one thing, can ruin many an outing. But the family that regularly plays together is always better off. Keep in mind that some of the best times are one-on-one—one parent with one ADD child. One sure strength of ADD individuals is their ability to have fun!

8. Comorbidity

By the time they are in their teens, 50 percent of our ADD children will be what is sometimes referred to as "squeaky clean" ADD, that is, the only psychological problem they have is ADD. The other 50 percent, however, will have at least one other psychological condition in addition to their ADD. It doesn't take a rocket scientist to figure out that the more problems you have, the poorer the prognosis is going to be. These additional problems, which can also vary in their own degree of severity, include conduct disorder (in children and teens), antisocial personality and substance abuse (in teens and adults), anxiety, depression, learning disabilities and bipolar disorder.

To make matters worse, it is not unusual for an ADD person to have *three* diagnoses. For example, a not uncommon pattern involves ADD, bipolar disorder and substance (alcohol *and* drug) abuse. These individuals are very difficult—though not always impossible—to treat successfully.

Tom Brown, a clinical psychologist from Yale University, has suggested that there might be certain kinds of comorbid anxiety that may actually counteract ADD to some extent and improve prognosis. For example, ADD involves impulsive behavior and difficulty with self-restraint. An overly anxious person is the opposite. She is always thinking "What if this happens or what if that happens?" Anxious people are often cautious, reserved and even inhibited. It's not hard to imagine the anxious tendency counteracting the impulsive tendency, thus reducing chaotic behavior, poorly-thought-out decisions and obnoxious statements.

9. Overall severity of ADD

Attention Deficit comes in different shades of gray that range from mild to severe. The DSM-IV simply requires that an individual qualify for six out of nine items from the Inattentive list and/or six of nine items from the Hyperactive/Impulsive list to be classified as ADD.

Severity of ADD, however, might very well affect ultimate outcome. Think of severity in three ways. First of all, Combined Type is, by definition, more severe than Inattentive Type because the diagnosis requires that symptoms from two lists be present rather than just one. The caveat here, of course, is that outcomes with Inattentives are frequently affected negatively by the fact that the diagnosis is either missed or very late (see item 6, Early Detection). And comorbidity can complicate things as well.

Second, the DSM-IV list says nothing about severity. To qualify on a particular item you must show that characteristic more often than the average person your age. But even so, all professionals know that within the ADD population traits such as forgetfulness, distractibility, losing things, noisiness and hyperactivity itself can vary a lot. There are some rating scales that have been developed that include not only the DSM-IV items, but also a severity rating for each.

Third, severity can be measured by how many of the DSM items you qualify for. Nine out of nine on both lists might very well be different from six out of nine on both.

ADD is a serious matter that doesn't go away. Perhaps the discussion above will help you feel more reassured about your child's future. On the other hand, it may point out areas that need some work.

Part II

Diagnosis

7

Information Collection

The diagnosis of Attention Deficit Disorder has a catch to it. An ADD evaluation is different from diagnosis in physical medicine, or even from diagnosis with other types of psychological difficulties. The first reason for the catch is that there is no specific test for ADD. There is no one physical, neurological or psychological test that can prove or disprove the existence of ADD. It would certainly come in handy if there were!

The second reason diagnosing Attention Deficit is tricky is that, oddly enough, the face-to-face interview with the child in the office is often one of the least helpful parts of the evaluation process. Studies have shown again and again that *80 percent of ADD kids will sit still in a doctor's office*—no matter how they behave the rest of the time. Why? Because the situation is usually fairly intimidating to a child, it may be somewhat new or interesting as well, and sometimes it is one-on-one.

There is no way to tell how many times frustrated mothers have told a doctor or mental health professional how difficult and impossible their child's behavior was, only to have the doctor or professional dismiss the possibility of ADD simply because the child sat still in the office.

Making the child interview even less helpful is another problem:

many Attention Deficit children are lousy historians. They cannot accurately recall and/or describe their past experiences; other ADD children can recall past events well enough, but they are defensive and—at least initially—unwilling to admit any problems.

The result is that the diagnostic process must involve a lot of information-collecting from sources in addition to the child. The child must be seen, of course, but what is needed primarily is detailed information about the child's school, home and social functioning. This information should include a careful developmental history as well as a thorough description of the parents' primary concerns. Information about a child should be gathered from multiple sources—parents and teachers are especially important.

Who can competently conduct an evaluation for Attention Deficit Disorder? Any mental health professional or physician *trained and experienced in the evaluation of ADD*. A pediatrician could do the diagnosis if he or she had the proper amount of time as well as expertise, and so could a psychiatric social worker or psychologist. A physician is not necessary for the diagnosis by itself, though a physician does become necessary when medication is being considered.

The Diagnostic Process

The evaluation for ADD should involve the following steps. In most cases the evaluation should take approximately three to four hours of a professional's time. Psychological testing is a different process, which we will discuss later.

1. The Parent Interview

An interview with the parents comes first (unless the child is thirteen or older) to cover the presenting problems, developmental history and family history, and to plan the rest of the evaluation procedures. Parental concerns should be compared to the DSM-IV criteria for ADD, the other ADD characteristics mentioned in Chapter 2, and the DSM-IV criteria for possible comorbid conditions, such as ODD, CD, depression and anxiety.

A number of structured interview formats are available to help accomplish the objectives mentioned above. Barkley's *Clinical Interview-*

Parent Report Form (from *Defiant Children, Second Edition: A Clinician's Manual for Assessment and Parent Training*) is useful in this regard. This form covers ODD and CD symptoms first before getting to ADD, in order to give parents a chance to "simmer down" before talking about the possibility of Attention Deficit Disorder.

The Diagnostic Interview Schedule for Children (DISC) is also popular with mental health professionals. All childhood disorders in the DSM-IV are included. To speed up the interview process, key features of each disorder are inquired about first. If the key features are not there, the interviewer then flips to the next diagnosis.

The child's parents are the most vital source of information. They should be taken very seriously and approached with a nonjudgmental attitude. The evaluator must keep in mind the fact that—if the child is ADD—the cause is not faulty parenting, but rather an inherited condition.

There are several reasons why it isn't always easy to remember this fact. First, many parents are so stressed by their child's behavior that they do not exactly make the best impression on the diagnostician. They can come across as angry, hysterical, depressed or worse, and therapists with a strong leaning toward family dynamic theory will often conclude, "No wonder the kid's having such a rough time—I'd be hyperactive myself with parents like these!" Many parents, however, will accurately report that they were not so emotionally disturbed—and even considered themselves fairly normal—before this child arrived on the scene.

Second, there is evidence that the biological parents of hyperactive children as a group show a higher incidence of certain other psychological problems. These problems can include alcoholism (and/or drug abuse), depression, sociopathy, anxiety and, of course, ADD itself. Many of these parents have more than one of these difficulties (comorbidity), which can make the diagnostician's job of relating to them even more difficult.

Third, there is a higher incidence of marital dissatisfaction, separation and divorce in families where there is an ADD child, so the couple may disagree and argue during the interview about the child as well as other issues. If only one parent is willing to come to the session, it will almost always be the mother, and she may show the effects of the stress resulting from living with not only one, but two, ADD people—her son and her husband. Adding to the potential for marital discord in the therapist's office is the fact that many ADD children respond quite differently to their fathers than to their mothers (usually in the fathers' favor), which, unfortunately, makes some Dads belittle their wives' opinions and comments.

The first topic covered with the parents is what brings them to the office. A general question about presenting problems should be asked initially and then, if ADD is suspected, more specific inquiries into other possible symptoms that may not have been spontaneously mentioned, such as emotional overarousal or difficulty delaying gratification. When Combined ADD is involved, the presenting problems that parents mention usually focus on such issues as school underachievement, domestic difficulties involved in living with the child, social problems and other kinds of disruptive behavior. With Inattentive kids, problems are less obvious and parents are often more bewildered. Their complaints focus more on disorganization, amazing forgetfulness, inability to finish things and general "spaciness."

Following a detailed analysis of the presenting problems, a developmental history should be taken. A number of structured developmental history forms are available. These include the *Conners-March Developmental Questionnaire* and Goldstein and Goldstein's *Childhood History Form for Attention Disorders*. When an ADD screening is being done, this history should involve more than just the usual developmental milestones, such as when the child walked and talked. Since many experts feel that ADD symptoms can appear in 60 to 70 percent of hyperactive kids around the ages of two to three (usually ADD *with* hyperactivity), the interviewer should specifically inquire about the development of the ADD symptoms listed before, such as impulsivity, hyperactivity, impatience, emotional overarousal, noncompliance and social aggressiveness.

Few parents will report a problem with short attention span in preschoolers, since preschoolers are supposed to have short attention spans. What the interviewer is trying to focus on is *age-inappropriate* behavior. This data is not always easy to obtain, especially when the ADD child is a firstborn (as many are!) and the parents may have little perspective on what is normal for different ages.

Information about pregnancy, labor and delivery are also relevant, since there is a possibility that in some situations prenatal, perinatal or postnatal injury to the brain may produce ADD or something akin to it.

Infant characteristics are not reliable predictors, but there are significant mild correlations between ADD and infant temperaments involving negative responses to change or new situations, more time spent in a negative mood (including colic), and exaggerated emotional responsiveness. After three to six months the list of ADD infancy correlates can include resistance to cuddling, high activity level, sleep and feeding disturbances, and monotonous, ongoing vocalizations or crying. Keep in mind, however, that these are not definitive signs for ADD.

After taking the developmental history, a family history should be explored due to the hereditary nature of Attention Deficit Disorder. Because of the preponderance of males with this problem, the father is usually "picked on" first with a question such as "How did you do in grammar school?" The focus here is often limited to things like concentration, grades and misbehavior, because it is often difficult for people to remember that far back (especially males). The mother is then asked similar questions (keep a look out for the possibility that Mom was an Inattentive Type). It is a good idea to explain to the parents why these questions are being asked, because this is often the first time many parents have ever even heard the notion that their child's problems may be hereditary rather than a result of faulty parenting methods.

Next, inquiries about other relatives, including siblings, are often helpful. The interviewer is looking for signs of ADD or residual ADD symptoms, as well as signs of depression, substance abuse, anxiety, sociopathy and psychosis. In very large families, reports of a few relatives with these problems should be temporarily taken with a grain of salt.

Finally, the initial parent interview should conclude with a cooperative planning of the rest of the evaluation and—if ADD is suspected—some way for the parents to learn more about this disorder (seminars, books, videos, support group meetings, etc.). This educational component is an extremely helpful part of the diagnostic process, because many parents will almost be able to make the diagnosis themselves after hearing more about the common problems and typical developmental course of untreated

ADD. In addition, many of the fathers—and some of the mothers—will recognize themselves in the descriptions. This awareness may lead to the possibility of their being treated for adult ADD.

Education about ADD should be done only if ADD is strongly suspected after talking with the parents and reviewing the results of the rating scales. The evaluator should also inform the parents about the possibility of ADD look-alikes as well as comorbid disorders. It is helpful to keep in mind that the factors that often discriminate ADD (Combined Type) from other disorders are early onset and consistent, chronic course.

2. The Child Interview

The interview with the child comes next. The goal of interviewing the child is to rule out more serious disorders, such as psychosis, to see how willing the child is to talk, to get as much information as possible about how the child perceives his school, home and social life, and to begin to build a good relationship, which may be necessary for later work.

As mentioned before, when interviewing the child for the first time, *the diagnostician should not expect to see hyperactive/impulsive symptoms in the office*. There certainly are some little ones who cannot sit still and who will be in constant motion and/or constantly chatty. These children will appear only about 20 percent of the time, but they are much more likely to be ADD.

One good way to begin the session with a child is to say in a matter-of-fact way something like, "I assume this wasn't your idea to come here." This tactic is especially good for older children and teens. Most kids do not want to see any doctor, and this statement lets them know it's not unusual to feel that way. This introduction often helps the child talk more freely. Most children will talk, though with widely varying degrees of accuracy and truthfulness. It is important that the interviewer not try to be too friendly—ADD children will frequently become very suspicious of an adult who seems too syrupy or condescending.

Older children can sit and talk for 45 minutes to an hour, and many will open up quite a bit when talking with an adult who is sincerely trying to understand them. Many of these children are so used to being criticized that being treated with respect is a refreshing experience for them. With smaller children, having them draw or play while they talk is often useful, though the session may still have to be kept shorter, perhaps limited to half an hour.

When a child is too defensive to be able to tolerate sitting and talking about problems, several options are possible. One is to begin by talking about enjoyable topics or strengths; one little boy warmed up considerably while discussing fireworks. Some children are actually quite interested in the school information collected, such as their old report cards or achievement test scores. These items can often be discussed fruitfully.

Toward the end of the session, the child is told just what the rest of the evaluation process will involve. Some of the older children may even have some say in the design of that process. Some children, for example, are resistant to doing school questionnaires because they don't want anyone at their school knowing they are seeing a "shrink." Other children may be interested in doing psychological testing if they think it might reveal some of their strengths.

There are a number of child self-report forms available that children can fill out (if they are old enough), and these can later be used in a semi-structured interview format. Children usually under-report their own disruptive (externalizing) behavior, so parents and teachers are better sources in that regard. Parents and teachers, on the other hand, often miss childhood symptoms of anxiety and depression (internalizing disorders), which children themselves can often report more accurately.

3. Rating Scales and Questionnaires

Structured rating scales that screen for ADD as well as possible comorbid conditions are an essential part of the evaluation. Rating scales can ask a large amount of questions in a relatively short period of time. A child's scores can then be compared to norms for his age group. Questionnaires are often filled out, returned and scored before the first parent interview, which gives the evaluator useful information and ideas as to what issues need to be pursued further. Rating scales often provide large graphs which are helpful in explaining diagnostic results to parents. There are a number of good rating scales that are useful in ADD evaluations. Different professionals have their preferences.

Rating scales are often referred to as either "broad-band" or "narrow-band." Broad band scales cover a wide range of possible problems, so they provide a kind of overview of a child's functioning. Narrow band scales are used when the evaluator wants to look more closely at a potential problem area, such as ADD itself or possible comorbid conditions.

Two popular broad band scales are the Achenbach Child Behavior Checklist (CBCL) and the Behavior Assessment System for Children (BASC). The Achenbach is well-normed, easy to score (if you can computer-scan it), and good for comorbidity. The scales, however, are somewhat prone to false negatives (they may miss a real diagnosis) and take a while for diagnosticians to master. The CBCL offers parent, teacher and child versions, and it has a number of subscales:

> Aggressive Behavior
> Delinquent Behavior
> Anxious/Depressed
> Somatic Complaints
> Social Problems
> Attention Problems
> Thought Problems
> Withdrawn

The BASC is also well-liked and its scores correlate well with those of other diagnostic scales. The BASC has parent, teacher and child versions, as well as a list of subscales that is similar to the CBCL:

> Hyperactivity
> Aggression
> Anxiety
> Depression
> Somatization
> Atypicality
> Withdrawal
> Attention Problems
> Social Skills

The popular Connors Rating Scales-Revised (CRS-R) have both

broad-band and narrow-band features. While the CRS-R focuses extensively on ADD, it also has subscales such as Oppositional, Cognitive Problems, Anxious-Shy, Perfectionism, Social Problems and Emotional Lability. There is no separate scale for depression. The Conners series includes parent and teacher versions and an adolescent self-report form.

When using the Conners Parent scale, it is beneficial to have the mother and father fill out separate questionnaires. One reason for this is that ADD children often behave much better with their fathers, who are sometimes seen as more intimidating and less familiar. In one's future work with the family it is worthwhile to be aware of such a difference between parents.

Also popular with clinicians for ADD diagnosis are the ADD-H Comprehensive Teacher/Parent Rating Scales (ACTeRS) and the Attention Deficit Disorder Evaluation Scale (ADDES) series.

Barkley's Home and School Situations Questionnaires are useful information-gathering devices which approach the problem from a somewhat different angle than the instruments just described. The Home Situations Questionnaire—filled out by the parents—lists sixteen different situations, such as "When at meals" or "When playing with other children." The parents indicate if this situation is a problem —yes or no—and, if yes, how severe it is on a scale from one to nine. The suggested cutoff for ADD here is simply more than 50 percent of the items checked "Yes." The severity ratings are used only to provide more clinical information. As with the Conners Questionnaire, it is often productive to have mothers and fathers make separate responses.

The School Situations Questionnaire includes twelve items, such as "When arriving at school" and "During individual task work." The response format and scoring are the same as the Parents form. The School Situations Questionnaire has one limitation: it can only be used prior to junior high (sixth grade). When a child has many teachers, as in junior high or high school, no one teacher has access to all the information necessary to fill out the entire form.

Other narrow-band instruments can help appraise certain other diagnoses and/or comorbid possibilities. These rating scales include the following:

Depression

Child Depression Inventory (CDI)
Hamilton-Depression Scale (HAM-D)
Schedule for Affective Disorders and Schizophrenia (K-SADS)

Anxiety

Children's Stress Scale
Children's Manifest Anxiety Scale

Obsessive Compulsive Disorder (OCD)

Leyton Obsessional Inventory
Child Yale-Brown Obsessive-Compulsive Scale (CY-BOCS)

Tics/Tourette's

The Motor tic, Obsessions and compulsions, Vocal tic Evaluation
    Survey (MOVES)

4. School Information

The collection of information (present and past) from school, such as grades, teacher observations, achievement test scores and current placement is time-consuming, but very important. Attention Deficit is a condition that starts early in life, so most ADD children will have had problems with school for a long time. Preschool problems are usually behavioral. Primary grade problems will often involve both behavioral and academic concerns.

A priority is collecting previous grades—and actual report cards, if possible—all the way back to kindergarten. Many parents save report cards, and they are helpful not only for the grades themselves, but also for the teachers' comments. With ADD children, comments related to the basic symptoms are frequent and reappear year after year. These persistent observations can include "always wandering around," "bothers others," "blurts out answers," "too easily gotten off task," and so on.

The grades of an ADD child can be extremely variable. ADD children in junior high (grades 6 through 8), for example, will often get—on the same report card—one of every possible grade, from A to F. This variability is due to the teacher and subject-sensitivity of the ADD child, who can often function well if she likes the teacher and the subject, but who can go the opposite direction if she doesn't. It is also not unusual for grades to vary tremendously for the same subject for the four quarters of the school year. This inconsistency drives parents and teachers crazy, prompting them to come up with many creative theories. In addition, since underachievement is a hallmark of the ADD child, the child's grades will usually not match her ability level.

Achievement test scores are also gathered, going back in time as far as possible. The interpretation of these can be somewhat difficult. Achievement tests are group-administered, and ADD children usually do more poorly in a group than in a one-to-one situation. With many ADD children, therefore, the achievement test scores will not measure up to overall ability. If the child can remember taking these tests, it is often helpful to ask her if she recalls really trying hard to do her best, or if she blew the tests off by impulsively guessing or by making designs on the computer answer sheets.

On the other hand, some children produce achievement test scores that are *better* than the child's grades for the same subjects. This unusual finding is reassuring, and the reasons for the discrepancy should be carefully explained to both parents and child. Achievement test scores that are better than the child's grades may indicate that *the child is learning the material*, even though her grades are not good. Both parents and child will be glad to hear this!

The achievement scores are more useful for clinical information than for determining the existence of Attention Deficit Disorder. Since there are many more ways to artificially lower test scores (illness, bad mood, distractibility) than there are to artificially raise them (cheating), a fairly safe assumption is to take the achievement scores to be a *minimum* estimate of the child's actual achievement—and perhaps of her ability as well.

As part of the evaluation, the child's current placement in school should also be noted. If the child is in special education, psychological testing and staffing reports are collected.

Questions About Diagnosis

1. Are physical and/or neurological exams necessary?

Just as there is no definitive psychological test for ADD, there is also no definitive physical or medical test for Attention Deficit Disorder. A urinalysis, blood work-up, MRI or CAT scan won't do the job. A recent physical exam and medical history, however, can give us important information relevant to possible ADD and its treatment:

- Is the child in general good health?
- How well is he sleeping and eating?
- Is his sensory apparatus intact?
- Does the child suffer from other physical conditions to
      which ADD kids are prone, such as allergies, otitis media,
      enuresis or encopresis?
- Are there other physical causes (recent head injury, toxic
      poisoning, CNS infection) for the "ADD" symptoms?
- Are there other physical tests that should be done?
- Are there contraindications to medication use for ADD?
- Are other medications being used (Theophyline, pheno-
      barbital, dilantin) which might aggravate ADD symptoms?
- Are there signs of physical abuse?

In diagnosing ADD a neurological exam is not essential, although some people—who perhaps still think in terms of "minimal brain damage"—feel that a referral to a neurologist is necessary. A neurologist can often pick up what are called "soft" neurological signs, such as fine motor coordination problems, motor overflow or perseverative behaviors. These signs, however, are only correlates of ADD, and they can appear in non-ADD children as well.

The same is true of the EEG (electroencephalogram). Though some ADD children will show some EEG abnormalities, most ADD children have normal EEGs. The test cannot prove that ADD is or is not there, so the EEG is not routinely done for ADD evaluations. However, if other problems are suspected or present, such as seizures, chronic and severe headaches, or a recent onset of concentrational difficulties, the EEG may be useful.

Keep in mind that a physician or neurologist certainly can diagnose ADD. To do this, the doctor must have three to four hours available and must be willing to do a careful history, a detailed analysis of the presenting complaints, a child interview, the gathering of school data, and the collection of appropriate parent, teacher and child rating scales.

2. It is true there is no psychological test for ADD, but perhaps one-third of ADD children also have a learning disability or two. What about psychological testing to evaluate LD as well as intellectual potential?

Sometimes the intellectual potential (IQ) of the ADD child and the possibility of learning disabilities—in addition to attentional problems— need to be evaluated. As far as other personality tests are concerned, projective tests are not particularly helpful in this regard and are not able to discriminate ADD in the first place. Vague comments about low self-esteem or hostility to authority figures are not especially useful.

The intelligence tests normally used are the Stanford-Binet, the Wechsler Intelligence Scale for Children, or the Wechsler Adult Intelligence Scale (for older teens). A knowledge of the child's intellectual ability is important for several reasons:

A. The IQ tells us what we can reasonably expect from the child and to what extent he is underachieving.
B. The IQ is a necessary part of the definition of LD.
C. IQ is a major prognostic indicator with ADD.
D. Higher IQ levels can modify the ADD symptom picture by inhibiting hyperactive behavior to varying degrees at school.

Unfortunately, IQ tests for ADD children can be notoriously inaccurate. One little boy, for example, scored a Full Scale Wechsler IQ of 133, and then three years later he produced an 81. As we mentioned before, you should consider the higher score more accurate, since there are many more ways to artificially lower an IQ score.

Some writers have suggested that Wechsler scores may contain a "distractibility factor" that is reflected in the Arithmetic, Digit Span and

Coding subtests. Such a factor, if it exists, would certainly be important in evaluating the ADD child. While we do look at this trio of subtests, and many ADD children do drop in them, the three subtests do not powerfully discriminate ADD children from non-ADD kids. Although these subtests do load together in factor analytic studies, the deficits in these scores do not necessarily reflect a concentrational problem.

Since 35 percent or more of ADD children may also have learning disabilities, these deficits should be separately evaluated. Difficulties involving visual and auditory perception, short-term memory, math computation, and expressive language difficulties are unfortunately common. Handwriting problems are very frequently encountered with ADD children, though it is initially difficult to determine whether or not their sloppy written productions are due to the child's impatience with schoolwork (rushing) or to a fine visual-motor coordination problem.

As many writers have pointed out, the field of learning disabilities is an important part of American education, but it continues to be a service category characterized by inconsistency and disagreement. One useful model used to define the presence of a learning disability is the standard score model, though it is far from universally agreed upon by school districts in this country. With this method, a learning disability is said to exist when there is a variation of more than one standard deviation (15 points) between an IQ test score and two other standard scores: 1) an individually administered achievement test score and 2) a related processing score from an individually administered test. The scores must all be standard scores with a mean of 100 and a standard deviation of 15. A child with a Wechsler IQ of 103, for example, who scores a 78 on a reading decoding test and a 75 on a test of auditory memory could be classified as learning-disabled.

Some common individually administered achievement tests are the Wide Range Achievement Test, the Peabody Individual Achievement Tests, and the Woodcock-Johnson Psychoeducational Battery. Tests of processing abilities, such as perception, sequencing and memory, include the Detroit Tests of Learning Aptitude and the Illinois Test of Psycholinguistic Abilities.

A unique problem arises when we consider testing ADD children: to what extent will the ADD itself artificially lower the test scores? What if the child is hyper and distractible and blurts out poorly conceived responses? We may get an IQ that is 25 points lower than it really is. Then we'll have an inaccurate view of the child's potential, and the youngster will almost certainly not qualify as learning-disabled.

It appears there may be two "kinds" of ADD children here. The first kind of child is capable of responding well in a one-on-one situation where feedback of one sort or another comes every few seconds. These kids do well and enjoy the testing experience. They are usually fairly bright and their scores are more likely to be accurate.

The second kind of ADD child retains ADD symptoms, such as distractibility and impulsivity, even in the testing situation, so that the scores become suspect. Although a competent examiner can observe these interfering behaviors during testing, it is hard to predict which children will show them. Valuable testing time may be wasted and meaningless scores produced.

There are two possible solutions to this problem. First of all, children who have a history of retaining ADD symptoms even in one-on-one, novel, interesting or intimidating situations *should not be tested right away*. If the evaluation shows they are ADD, and medication is going to be considered for them, a better plan is to first start and adjust the medication carefully, using school performance as the criterion. Once the medication dose and response are satisfactory, the child should then be tested *on the medication*. The hope here is to knock out as many ADD symptoms as possible during the testing, so that more accurate IQ and achievement test scores are elicited.

A second—and probably less feasible—solution is this: children who can inhibit their ADD symptoms and maintain their self-control in unique, intimidating and one-on-one situations might be tested without medication. This procedure still carries some risk, so the testing psychologist may be instructed to discontinue if he feels that too much ADD-like behavior is present, and that this behavior might artificially lower the child's scores.

3. What about the use of "continuous performance tests" (CPTs) as part of the diagnostic evaluation?

In recent years there has been a tremendous increase in the use of CPTs in the diagnosis of ADD. These tests can be given in paper-and-pencil forms or on a computer. A child may be instructed, for example, to click a button only when he sees a certain symbol on the screen. If he sees the symbol and clicks, he gets one right. If he sees the wrong symbol and clicks, he commits what is called an error of "commission"—thought to be related to impulsivity. If the child sees the right symbol and doesn't click, he commits an error of "omission," less typical with ADD kids.

Computer CPTs are handy because they are easy to give, short (20 minutes or so) and can be scored immediately. CPT scores also tend to correlate with certain ADD symptoms. If a child does poorly on the CPT, in other words, he is likely to be ADD.

What if, on the other hand, a child does well on the CPT. Does this mean he is not ADD? No. CPTs often have a problem with what are known as "false negatives." Thirty percent or more of children who are truly ADD will "pass" the CPT test.

Why does this happen? The CPT tests aren't perfect, of course, but motivation may be another factor. As with psychological testing, some ADD kids may find a continuous performance test novel and fun, and—in a sense—they "get up for it" and do OK. So if a child passes the test, you still can't be sure that he is not ADD.

So why use CPTs? Some people feel that some of the newer versions, which focus on scoring only errors of comission, may be more accurate with ADD subjects because they provide a measure of a primary ADD symptom: impulsivity. Other people feel that the CPTs add little to diagnosis other than a kind of false aura of technological sophistication, almost as if there were a test for ADD. In any case, these tests should never be used by themselves to make a diagnosis.

8

Putting the Data Together

A DD is not an all-or-nothing disorder: it comes in varying degrees of severity. ADD also comes in different types: Combined (ADD with hyperactivity) and Inattentive (ADD without hyperactivity). And ADD can appear along with other syndromes, such as Conduct Disorder, Oppositional Defiant Disorder, anxiety disorders and mood disorders.

Since there is no one definitive diagnostic procedure or test for ADD, the final determination of whether a child qualifies for this diagnosis must rely on an integration of all the data collected. The following questions help make sense out of this mass of information. The diagnostician should keep in mind that, in addition to a making a statement about the presence or absence of ADD and other problems, he is also attempting to describe a profile of strengths for this particular child.

Integration of the Data

Question 1: Does the child qualify for six or more out of the nine items on one or both of the DSM-IV symptom lists for Inattention and for Hyperactivity/Impulsivity?

Inattention:

a. fails to pay close attention to details or makes careless mistakes

b. has difficulty sustaining attention in work or play

c. does not listen when spoken to directly

d. fails to finish schoolwork, chores or work duties

e. has difficulty organizing activities

f. avoids tasks requiring sustained mental effort

g. loses things

h. is easily distracted

i. is forgetful

Hyperactivity/Impulsivity:

Hyperactivity

a. fidgets or squirms in seat

b. leaves seat when remaining seated is expected

c. runs about or climbs in situations where this is inappropriate

d. has difficulty playing quietly

e. acts as if "driven by a motor"

f. talks excessively

Impulsivity

g. blurts out answers before the question is completed

h. has difficulty awaiting turn

 i. interrupts or intrudes on others

Do the presenting complaints show a pattern that is persistent and which started early in life? Are the frequency and severity of the symptoms such that they are extraordinary even for the age of the child, cause significant impairment in the child's life, and cause impairment in two or more settings?

We also like to match the presenting problems with the eight ADD characteristics listed in Chapter 2. Although this list overlaps to some extent with the DSM list, it also includes items that are a little different but which many parents can relate to easily. These items include difficulty delaying gratification, emotional overarousal, noncompliance and social aggressiveness. As a kind of "macro-problem," school underachievement is usually a significant issue as well. Correlates of ADD are also examined, such as allergies, fine and gross motor coordination problems and enuresis.

Question 2: How does the developmental history taken from the parents match the typical course of untreated Attention Deficit Disorder (Chapter 4), whether it is the Combined or Inattentive kind? Answering this question involves looking for the manifestations of the symptoms listed above, but also being aware of how the picture changes with age. Early hyperactivity, for example, will simmer down quite a bit by adolescence. Self-esteem issues do not become significant until after age eight or so. Inattentive kids do not show many problems until they hit the primary grades. Retention in school is common in the early years, but has been known to occur with some ADD kids as late as junior high school.

Question 3: Who else in the family has Attention Deficit Disorder and/or the other conditions that often accompany ADD? An important indicator here is what we often call the "chip-off-the-old-block syndrome." A father may say, for example, that when he was in grammar school, his performance and behavior were very similar to his son's. If this observation is offered without much doubt or hesitation, we consider it evidence for genetic transmission. If a child is ADD, the chances that one or both parents are also ADD is 40 to 50 percent. A previously diagnosed ADD sibling is also a red flag and raises the chances of ADD in the child being evaluated from about five percent to about 30 percent. The possibility of an ADD mother also cannot be forgotten, especially since the true sex ratio with ADD is at this time unclear.

Question 4: Is the information from the child consistent with ADD symptoms? Some ADD children can and do describe typical symptoms in their own words. Those problems most often described accurately include distractibility, boredom and sometimes emotional intensity. Other ADD traits may not be mentioned because the child sees them as weaknesses, such as hyperactivity or problems getting along with other children.

Other ADD children reveal symptoms verbally but indirectly, saying they hate school "because of the work" or consistently blaming other people—teachers, playmates, parents—for whatever problems they have. Some of our "ADD suspects" will show hyperactive and impulsive kinds of behavior in the office, such as fidgeting, walking or running around, speaking rapidly and loudly, interrupting and being distracted by the various objects in the room. As mentioned earlier, these children have a higher probability of being ADD.

Question 5: Does the child score above the cutoffs for ADD on the structured rating scales? Are more than 50 percent of the situations checked as problems on the Home and School Situations Questionnaires? How severe are the ratings?

Question 6: Does the school and achievement testing information support the notion that the child is not working to capacity? To what extent might learning disabilities account for this underachievement if it exists?

Question 7: Do the parents—after becoming more familiar with ADD through an educational seminar, book, audio or video—feel that their child could be Attention Deficit? Many of the parents who say "That's my kid!" are correct. Remember that parents have many more images and recollections about their child than they could ever share with any diagnostician in three or four hours. When Mom and Dad encounter two hours or more of an educational program about ADD, they can match more of their many thoughts and memories with the program.

Two cautions are important here. First, the fact that true ADD is not caused by faulty parenting is an appealing idea to parents, and it may bias their perceptions. Second, the possibility of comorbidity and ADD look-alikes must be kept in mind.

Comorbidity and ADD Look-Alikes

Recent research on Attention Deficit Disorder has confirmed and clarified what we have suspected for some time: ADD is often accompanied by other psychological problems. By the time they are in their teens, 50 percent of our ADD children (whether they are boys or girls) will also qualify for one or two other DSM-IV diagnoses. These diagnoses will fall under the categories of disruptive disorders, anxiety disorders, mood disorders and learning disabilities. The other 50 percent of our ADD children will be what is sometimes called "pure" or "squeaky-clean" ADD: they will have ADD and nothing else.

Below are listed the possible comorbid disorders and the approximate *percentage of ADD children* who will show that problem (whether it's diagnosed or not) by their mid-adolescent years. If the percentages differ for boys and girls, this difference will be indicated.

Most of these comorbid disorders are to some extent "ADD look-alikes." They share common characteristics with ADD and, consequently, they can sometimes be mistaken for ADD. After all, concentration impairments can accompany many childhood psychological problems, including depression and anxiety. Disruptive behavior, on the other hand, is central to ADD, ODD and CD. It is therefore important to keep in mind the different diagnostic possibilities:

1. ADD exists by itself
2. Another disorder exists by itself (without ADD)
3. The two disorders exist together
4. No disorder exists

Oppositional Defiant Disorder (Boys 60 percent; girls 30 percent): ADD and ODD show a tremendous amount of overlap. ADD kids can be obnoxious due to their hyperactivity and impulsivity, but they don't—at least initially—mean to irritate you. ODD children, on the other hand, have their primary problem with authority. They are negative, defiant, resistive and deliberately (not so much forgetfully or impulsively) disobedient. Like ADD children, ODD kids have bad tempers, argue and blame others for their own mistakes. Unlike ADD youngsters, though, ODD children are spiteful, vindictive and purposely try to irritate other people. ODD usually starts at home, then it may transfer to school. Unlike ADD kids, therefore, ODD children focus appropriately, complete schoolwork and show few behavior problems in the early grades.

Conduct Disorder (Boys 25 percent; girls 8 percent): CD may be the modern euphemism for juvenile delinquency. ADD kids don't want to irritate you, but they do. ODD children do want to irritate you and they become very good at it. CD kids want to hurt you or others. They don't care if they make you angry, and they are more aggressive than ODD children. CD youngsters threaten, bully and fight. They can be physically cruel to people as well as animals. CD kids steal, force others into sexual activity, set fires and destroy property. They frequently break rules by staying out too late, running away or skipping school. ODD children often "graduate" to CD as the years pass. Conduct Disorder children are not good treatment candidates. Ironically, they are better treatment candidates if their CD isn't their only problem! If their difficult behavior is also related to another disorder which is more treatable, such as ADD, depression or bipolar illness, the prognosis is better.

Multiple Anxiety Disorders (30 percent): ADD boys and ADD girls both show a strong tendency toward anxiety problems, and when they do have such a problem, these kids often have *more than one anxiety disorder*. In addition to ADD, for example, they might show two of the following: separation anxiety, generalized anxiety disorder (formerly overanxious disorder of childhood), and Obsessive-Compulsive Disorder (OCD). Social phobia and panic attacks may develop in older children. The characteristic of emotional overarousal, mentioned earlier, can certainly affect the ADD child's experience of anxiety as well as anger.

Major Depression (20 percent): An episode of Major Depression is characterized primarily by a period of two weeks or more in which an individual shows a depressed mood and/or a drastically reduced interest in just about everything. This episode must be a major alteration in the person's usual way of functioning; it involves symptoms such as a change in weight, fatigue, restlessness, increased or decreased sleeping, feelings of worthlessness, poor concentration and thoughts of death. In children and adolescents the depressed mood may show itself primarily as irritability.

Bipolar Disorder (10 percent): The category of Mood Disorders above includes depressive—or "unipolar"—disorders. Unipolar depression means that only one side—or pole (depression)—of a problem is shown. Individuals with "bipolar" disorders, on the other hand, experience both extremes—highs and lows—of mood and behavior. These variations come in several different forms, but in general a person with a bipolar disorder will experience, in addition to periods of depression, distinct periods of an abnormally elevated, expansive or irritable mood (lasting at least one week). Severe versions are known as "manic" episodes, and less severe are called "hypomanic."

A true manic episode is very disruptive to an individual's work, social life and family life. Oddly enough, though, the person experiencing the episode feels fine. Manic individuals not only feel fine, they feel *wonderful* and can't fathom why others are concerned about them. Their self-esteem is grandiose, they sleep much less, they can't shut up, and they often get involved in pleasurable but dangerous activities, such as spending too much money or promiscuous sex.

Like a manic episode, a hypomanic episode is also a distinct period of elevated mood and increased mental and physical activity, but hypomania is not as severe or as disruptive as mania. A hypomanic episode can rapidly escalate within a day or two and last for several weeks to several months. It may be preceeded or followed by a depressive episode, but hypomanic periods are usually shorter—and they start faster—than depressive episodes.

Distinguishing what is ADD and what is bipolar—or both—is a serious and difficult problem. Making a correct diagnosis is critical because some of the medications used to treat ADD (stimulants and tricyclic antidepressants) can actually bring on manic or hypomanic episodes in people who are bipolar alone, or bipolar plus ADD. Until recently the general consensus was that bipolarity didn't usually show itself until adolescence or later. Today, some experts are talking about bipolar preschoolers and preadolescents. As you saw before, the percentage of ADD kids that are also bipolar has been estimated to be 10 percent. If you go the other way, however, some authorities believe that well over 90 percent of bipolar kids may also qualify for ADD! Bipolar children, for example, can also be hyperactive, impulsive, deny having problems and show poor concentration skills.

How do you tell the two apart? Here are several suggestions:

1. The moods of bipolar kids cycle more slowly than those of ADD children. These moods may involve longer periods of dysphoria that alternate with floaty, dreamy, spacey times bordering on euphoria.

2. Bipolar temper tantrums are much worse than those of ADD children. These tantrums, sometimes referred to as "affective storms," can last for hours, use up an amazing amount of energy, and often have an overly dramatic quality to them.

3. ADD destructiveness is usually due to inattention or impulsiveness. Bipolar destructiveness has more of a deliberate and purposeful quality.

4. ADD tends to mellow somewhat with age. Bipolar moods and behavior tend to get worse.

5. Family history: with bipolar youngsters look for a family history of bipolar disorders.

6. Nightmares and gory dreams may be more characteristic of bipolar kids.

7. Medication response: stimulants may worsen behavior of bipolar children, while mood stabilizers (e.g., lithium, Tegretol) help. Mood stabilizers do little or nothing for ADD.

Keep in mind that many children can be *both* ADD and bipolar. This differential diagnosis remains a difficult one.

Tic Disorders (10-15 percent): Tics are sudden, short-lived and repetitive motor movements (eye blinking, shoulder shrugging, facial grimaces) or vocalizations (throat clearing, grunting, sniffing). Tics can occur in complex forms, such as repeating phrases or engaging in repetitive grooming behavior. These impulses are usually experienced as irresistible, although sometimes a person can temporarily suppress them. They also happen less during sleep. When tics do occur, they are usually only mild to moderate in severity. Tic symptoms usually diminish—and sometimes disappear entirely—during adolescence and adulthood.

When both motor and vocal tics have been going on for some time and produce marked distress, Tourette's Disorder may be diagnosed. While only a small percentage of ADD children will also have Tourette's, it has been estimated that 60 percent of Tourette's children will qualify for ADD. Differential diagnosis here is important because it has implications for medication treatment. Recently, with increased media exposure, tic disorders have become more well known and understood, but they may also have become more feared. It is important to keep in mind that tic disorders are rarely incapacitating, and when they coexist with ADD, the ADD is most often the biggest problem.

Sleep Disorders (30 percent): Most parents of ADD children are very aware of the fact that their children are not good sleepers. Getting these little devils to bed at night is often a bigger chore than raising the Titanic. As ADD children become older, getting them up in the morning also becomes harder and harder because they didn't go to bed in time to get enough sleep. As a matter of fact, a number of years ago one theory had it that ADD was caused by sleep deprivation. Although this belief is not accurate, sleep deprivation may have a significant impact not only on ADD but also on comorbid disorders such as anxiety and depression.

Learning Disabilities (Boys 25-35 percent; girls 15 percent): Distinguishing between ADD and LD is a difficult—and not always possible—task to accomplish. The two categories often overlap. Perhaps 35 percent of ADD kids will have a learning disability, and 25 percent of LD children may have ADD. And many children have one handicap and not the other.

Learning disabilities that often accompany ADD include reading problems (dyslexia), difficulty with math computation and story problems, strong aversions to handwritten assignments, and what are sometimes called "nonverbal" learning disabilities. LD problems cause achievement in one or more academic areas that is much lower than what would be expected based on intellectual ability. Learning disabilities are chronic, invisible (like ADD), unrelated to IQ and seen more often in boys.

There are several ways of attempting to distinguish Attention Deficit from learning disability. The first is the developmental history. Most LD-only children will not show at age two or three the ADD symptoms of hyperactivity, impulsivity, emotional overarousal, social aggressiveness and so on. Some LD-only children, though, may show these behaviors after years and years of academic frustration.

Second, if the child's IQ and achievement test scores are not discrepant and are considered valid, LD may be ruled out by definition.

Third, if from the early school years on, there are consistent comments about distractibility itself and short attention span, one leans toward ADD as the diagnosis. LD-only children are more prone to looking distractible when working on tasks that involve their weak areas; on other tasks their attention may be normal.

Finally, a medication trial will often eliminate a lot of ADD symptoms. If a medicated child is able to function fairly normally in an academic setting and no longer underachieves, it would appear that the problem was ADD alone. No one believes that medication will help with a true learning disability.

Idiosyncratic Patterns

Several factors can make substantial changes in the typical ADD symptom picture and may, consequently, cause a diagnosis to be missed in a genuine ADD child. These factors include the following:

1. *Good social skills.* A significant number of ADD children—even Combined Types—will get along well with their peers. The kids will have friends, will not be overly bossy, and may not show the usual low frustration tolerance in competitive situations. In some of these children some of the ADD symptoms are moderated just enough to become social assets. Bossiness, for example, may become leadership, or excessive energy may make the child "the life of the party."

2. *High IQ.* ADD children who are smart enough can not only succeed in school, but may also actually enjoy it. Because of their academic success and the reinforcement they receive from parents and teachers, very bright ADD kids may *inhibit* inappropriate behavior while at school. However, many of these youngsters will go off like rockets when they come home, and lots of ADD symptoms then make family life miserable for the rest of the evening. This kind of behavior pattern often leads evaluators to conclude incorrectly that the parents or the family itself is the problem.

3. *Shyness.* From the earlier descriptions of ADD children (especially the Combined Type), these kids sound anything but shy. Instead, they seem indifferent about how others see them and they come across as socially boorish. We now know, though, that about 30 percent of our ADD children will also experience anxiety problems. Some ADD kids are extremely concerned about the opinions of others. In public these children inhibit their hyperactive/impulsive behavior, but—like the high IQ child—they usually show their ADD symptoms at home. In some of these children shyness has been aggravated by difficulties with coordination, speech or learning disabilities that made these kids targets of ridicule from peers.

4. *No siblings, or one-on-one preschool situation with parents.* In some ADD children, problems do not appear until the child reaches the primary grades. These kids, of course, may be Inattentive Types. Others, however, show a developmental history that seems to lack parental reports of extreme hyperactivity, impulsivity, emotional overarousal, and so on

during the child's preschool years. Sometimes the reason for this apparent absence of symptoms is the lack of siblings at home during these years; the youngster may have been an only child, or perhaps the sibs were either much older or were not born yet. *Lack of sibling rivalry and a one-on-one (or one-on-two) situation with parents can moderate ADD symptoms considerably.* The lack of competition, in addition to having reasonably competent and attentive parents, can produce fairly normal behavior, at least for a while.

5. *Inattentive Type.* ADD without hyperactivity is still overlooked too frequently. As we mentioned before, the last diagnostic manual (DSM-III-R) eliminated this category entirely. When hyperactivity is not a problem in the early years, other possible ADD characteristics, such as emotional overarousal and social aggressiveness, are also moderated quite a bit or are just plain nonexistent. In this case, the diagnostic evaluation must focus heavily on the existence of characteristics such as major concentration difficulties, disorganization, forgetfulness, passive noncompliance and inability to finish things. Inattentive children may not be disruptive, but they are still unsuccessful and they are still suffering.

The Post-Diagnostic Interview

Once all the information has been collected, the child and parents have been interviewed, and the evaluation has been completed, it's time to explain the results to everyone. Many ADD children, of course, are not super-interested in talking about something called ADD, but it's important to try to explain the problem (*their* particular version of ADD) and the treatment to kids as best one can. These days there are a number of books for children that describe ADD (Combined or Inattentive) from a child's point of view.

Parents, however, are *very* interested in hearing what the problem is. Not too many years ago, when a therapist explained ADD to Mom and Dad, it was usually the first time the parents had heard about such a problem. Today all that is different. Now therapists must keep in mind that most parents have been "educated" about ADD through newspapers, magazines, television and radio. ADD or ADD is a household word and parents may think they know a lot about it.

Mom and Dad's store of "knowledge," however, may include a lot of good—as well as a lot of inaccurate—information. Before trying to explain the problem and its treatment, therefore, it is helpful if the therapist firsts asks what the parents (and the child) have already heard about ADD (one little lad, for example, was mixing up ADD and AIDS). The evaluator must listen carefully and sympathetically to whatever is said before attempting to correct or reinforce any piece of information.

The post-diagnostic interview is also the time to prepare the parents and child—and to motivate them—for the treatment plan. A number of issues need to be understood from the beginning. ADD, for example, is a chronic problem that is not outgrown. Treatment, therefore, also needs to be "chronic." You don't necessarily need to come in weekly, but you also shouldn't stop entirely. Continuing education for parents and child about ADD is critical. Mom and Dad might consider joining a support group. Medication and treatment need to be explained over and over. Drug treatment, for example, is actually very safe and very effective, but it can sometimes take a while to find the right medication for a particular child. Other issues such as social skills and educational underachievement may need to be addressed.

The post-diagnostic interview lays the groundwork for the future. With good treatment, parents and child may be able to look forward to reasonable success and happiness. With poor or no treatment, the coming years will bring increasing failure and dissatisfaction.

Part III

Treatment

9

Education About ADD

Educating anyone affected by ADD in a major way is critical, especially today when there continues to be an explosion of good and bad information about Attention Deficit Disorder through media channels. It's amazing how many people really believe that television and newspapers are a public service.

Parents should become "experts" in ADD, and the ADD child should be given information about the disorder that is presented in language and concepts that are appropriate to his age.

In addition, teachers, mental health professionals and pediatricians must have a good working knowledge of the facts about basic symptoms, developmental course, causes, prognosis, diagnosis and treatment. Siblings, grandparents, certain friends and babysitters should also come to know more about this disorder if they have regular contact with the ADD child.

Issues that need to be understood involve specific facts about Attention Deficit Disorder, from symptoms to side effects possible with certain medications, to reasons for various interventions selected with the child. If an ADD girl is going to a special education class, for example, she should know that it is to work on her writing and math skills. She should also know how long she is likely to be in the class and what the criteria are for getting out of it. Education about some of the emotional issues that come along with ADD treatment should also be discussed. If, for instance, a teenager is doubting the need to continue taking medication (after a good friend of his recently refused to take pills anymore), it is helpful for him to have some objective person—preferably outside the family—who can listen to the him first and then carefully provide some needed answers to questions and other information.

Parents should, of course, first become educated about ADD and then help to pass along information to their child as the youngster becomes able to understand it. A good guideline or checklist for the kind of information that Mom and Dad need to assimilate is the Table of Contents of *All About Attention Deficit Disorder*. From the definition of ADD to diagnosis to adult ADD, all the information is important. This information must be gone over again and again, since it is impossible to learn it all the first time around. Although this field is not known for sudden or dramatic changes, one must also be on the lookout for new developments.

20 Question ADD Multiple Choice Test

What is your ADD IQ? See how many questions you can answer correctly on our ADD Multiple Choice Test. Be careful, because some items may have more than one correct answer, or no correct answers. The correct answers are provided in the section following the test.

1. The Combined Type of ADD used to be known as

      a. Undifferentiated ADD

      b. ADD without hyperactivity

      c. ADD with hyperactivity

      d. Hyperkinetic reaction of childhood

2. The Inattentive Type of ADD used to be known as

      a. Oppositional Defiant Disorder

      b. ADD without hyperactivity

      c. ADD with hyperactivity

      d. Conduct Disorder

3. As an ADD child grows older and matures, his symptoms *usually* will

    a. get worse
    b. get better
    c. disappear
    d. stay the same

4. ADD can be diagnosed as young as

    a. adolescence
    b. first grade
    c. junior high
    d. the preschool years

5. The most useful test for ADD is

    a. a genetic blood test
    b. an EEG
    c. a urinalysis
    d. the Wechsler IQ test

6. ADD can be diagnosed by a

    a. neurologist
    b. psychologist
    c. physician
    d. mental health professional

7. An ADD evaluation should take approximately

    a. 15 minutes if the child is hyper
    b. one hour under most circumstances
    c. three to four hours
    d. 10 hours or more

8. In a doctor's office, the ADD child will usually

    a. show his ADD symptoms quickly

    b. sit still

    c. not leave his mother's side

    d. tear the place apart

9. ADD children usually respond better to their

    a. fathers than to their mothers

    b. mothers than to their fathers

    c. babysitters than to their teachers

    d. none of the above

10. Research has shown that ADD is a primarily

    a. learned or acquired as the child grows up

    b. hereditary

    c. caused by high levels of lead

    d. caused by diet

11. If a child has a sibling who is ADD, that child's chances of also being ADD are

    a. zero

    b. 100 percent

    c. 70 percent

    d. 30 percent

12. The chief problem with social skills training groups is

    a. poor design

    b. ADD kids don't like them

    c. lack of generalization

    d. trainers don't like ADD kids

13. Stimulant medications have been known to help with

    a. sports
    b. school
    c. peer relations
    d. compliance with parental requests

14. The best antidepressants for ADD symptoms are the

    a. SSRIs
    b. tricyclics
    c. both SSRIs and tricyclics
    d. neither

15. The approximate percentage of ADD kids who cannot take stimulants due to side effects is

    a. 3 percent
    b. 10 percent
    c. 25 percent
    d. 50 percent

16. The best seat placement for an ADD child in a classroom is usually

    a. in the back of the room
    b. in the front of the room
    c. with a group of children who also are ADD
    d. by the window

17. The best treatment(s) for ADD include

    a. dietary adjustments
    b. behavior modification
    c. vitamins
    d. medication

18. ADD adolescents and adults are also likely to experience problems with

    a. depression
    b. anxiety
    c. learning disabilities
    d. psychosis

19. Research has shown that, compared to non-ADD controls, individuals with ADD

    a. drink more
    b. smoke more
    c. eat more pasta
    d. drive more carelessly

20. Alternative treatments for ADD are not recommended because

    a. they can waste valuable "growing-up" time
    b. they have not been proven effective
    c. they can be costly
    d. the people advocating them are dishonest

The Answers!

Now, so as not to keep you in suspense, here are the correct answers. The correct responses for each question have been put in bold.

1. The Combined Type of ADD used to be known as

    a. Undifferentiated ADD
    b. ADD without hyperactivity
    c. **ADD with hyperactivity**
    d. **Hyperkinetic reaction of childhood**

2. The Inattentive Type of ADD used to be known as

    a. Asperger's syndrome
    b. **ADD without hyperactivity**
    c. ADD with hyperactivity
    d. conduct disorder

3. As an ADD child grows older and matures, his symptoms *usually* will

    a. get worse
    b. **get better**
    c. disappear
    d. stay the same

4. ADD can be diagnosed as young as

    a. adolescence
    b. first grade
    c. junior high
    d. **the preschool years**

5. The most useful test for ADD is

    a. a genetic blood test
    b. an EEG
    c. a urinalysis
    d. the Wechsler IQ test

6. ADD can be diagnosed by a

    a. **neurologist**
    b. **psychologist**
    c. **physician**
    d. **mental health professional**

7. An ADD evaluation should take approximately

    a. 15 minutes if the child is hyper

    b. one hour under most circumstances

    c. **three to four hours**

    d. 10 hours or more

8. In a doctor's office, the ADD child will usually

    a. show his ADD symptoms quickly

    b. **sit still**

    c. not leave his mother's side

    d. tear the place apart

9. ADD children usually respond better to their

    a. **fathers than to their mothers**

    b. mothers than to their fathers

    c. babysitters than to their teachers

    d. none of the above

10. Research has shown that ADD is a primarily

    a. learned or acquired as the child grows up

    b. **hereditary**

    c. caused by high levels of lead

    d. caused by diet

11. If a child has a sibling who is ADD, that child's chances of also being ADD are

    a. zero

    b. 100 percent

    c. 70 percent

    d. **30 percent**

12. The chief problem with social skills training groups is

    a. poor design
    b. ADD kids don't like them
    c. **lack of generalization**
    d. trainers don't like ADD kids

13. Research has shown that stimulant medications can often help with

    a. **sports**
    b. **school**
    c. **peer relations**
    d. **compliance with parental requests**

14. The best antidepressants for ADD symptoms are the

    a. SSRIs
    b. **tricyclics**
    c. both SSRIs and tricyclics
    d. neither

15. The approximate percentage of ADD kids who cannot take stimulants due to side effects is

    a. **3 percent**
    b. 10 percent
    c. 25 percent
    d. 50 percent

16. The best seat placement for an ADD child in a classroom is usually

    a. in the back of the room
    b. **in the front of the room**
    c. with a group of children who also are ADD
    d. by the window

17. The best treatment(s) for ADD include

    a. dietary adjustments
    b. **behavior modification**
    c. vitamins
    d. **medication**

18. In addition to ADD, ADD adolescents and adults frequently experience problems with

    a. **depression**
    b. **anxiety**
    c. **learning disabilities**
    d. psychosis

19. Research has shown that, compared to non-ADD controls, individuals with ADD

    a. **drink more**
    b. **smoke more**
    c. eat more pasta
    d. **drive more carelessly**

20. Alternative treatments are not recommended because

    a. **they can waste valuable "growing-up" time**
    b. **they have not been proven effective**
    c. **they can be costly**
    d. they were shown on TV

So, what's your ADD IQ? Our suggestion is this: if you have an ADD child, you should score 85 percent or better (17-20 items correct) on the test. Wouldn't it also be nice to give this multiple choice test to your child's teacher, pediatrician, therapist or grandparent? Think about the possibilities!

ADD Myths and Misconceptions

Some of us used to believe, long ago, that with the development of our support groups throughout the country, there would come a day when myths and misconceptions about ADD would disappear. Then ADD children and adults would be recognized, diagnosed and treated properly.

In the last ten years there has been a tremendous amount of progress. More people understand ADD than ever before and more ADD kids and adults are being treated appropriately. However, we still live—and we will always live—in a society that values two often contradictory things: science and entertainment. Science and careful research provide and improve useful information about the diagnosis and treatment of ADD. Much of the information about ADD found in newspapers, magazines, radio and TV, however, is there simply to grab attention, stimulate controversy and entertain.

As a parent or professional, therefore, your education about Attention Deficit Disorder had better come from somewhere else. Keep in mind that media channels are never going to consistently provide accurate information about ADD. Here are some of the myths and misconceptions you may regularly run into:

General Myths and Misconceptions:

1. ADD kids are always hyperactive
2. ADD is due to faulty parenting
3. ADD will be outgrown
4. ADD is caused by brain damage
5. ADD is caused by diet or allergy
6. ADD must be diagnosed by a physician (or neurologist); schools can't diagnose ADD
7. ADD is a fabricated diagnosis—all kids are like that
8. ADD kids respond well to social skills training
9. The most essential part of ADD diagnosis is talking to the child in the office
10. ADD will always show up during psychological testing
11. ADD boys outnumber ADD girls by about 10 to 1

Medication Myths and Misconceptions:

1. Stimulants are dangerous and frequently cause terrible side effects
2. Stimulants are addictive to ADD kids
3. Stimulants stunt growth
4. Stimulant meds have opposite effects on ADD vs normal children
5. Stimulants can't be used after mid-adolescence
6. Ritalin causes brain damage and Tourette's
7. Teachers shouldn't have to learn about different ADD medications and their effects
8. Ritalin is the only game in town

Can you explain what's wrong with each of these statements?

Controversial and Idiosyncratic Therapies

One of the problems with the fields of physical health and mental health is trying to determine what kinds of treatments work with what particular problems. Unfortunately, you often hear of many different kinds of treatments that—according to some people—"work" for many different kinds of problems. In the areas of psychology and psychiatry especially, there are many more claims of effectiveness made than there are legitimate approaches.

This proliferation of claims is partly due to the fact that "placebo" effects are more rampant in mental health fields than in physical medicine. Placebo effects occur when someone apparently "gets better" because he thinks (or his parents think) he is being treated with an effective procedure. Placebo effects usually don't last very long, and with Attention Deficit these effects occur less often than they do with other psychological problems. In research studies, for example, placebo effects with anxiety disorders can run as high as 40 to 50 percent. With ADD, however, these "artificial" effects usually don't exceed 10 percent.

Adults who are constantly frustrated by ADD kids often are anxious to climb on a new treatment bandwagon. And for a while, these adults may see a new treatment as being helpful when in fact it isn't really changing anything. Parents who are willing to go to the trouble of trying some new kind of diet, for example, may also inadvertently do other things (such as using more positive reinforcement) that may help their child do better for a while. Or, because of all the effort they have put in, parents may *see* their child as doing better when in fact his behavior may not be much different.

How can you tell if a particular "treatment" for ADD is likely to be a waste of time? Generally, unless you're willing to read all the literature and go to all the conferences on the subject, it's quite difficult. You almost always have to rely on someone else's opinion. If you're a parent, you pretty much have to rely on the professionals; and even if you're a professional, you still have to rely on other professionals.

Fortunately, professionals write a lot and fight a lot. They don't always agree with one another. What is good about this squabbling is that if somebody comes up with a new treatment idea, they had better be able to prove that it works and the new idea had better be able to stand the test of time. Other professionals—even those who didn't develop the idea—must also come up with the same opinion.

All this arguing back and forth is published in professional journals. Not newspapers and magazines and television, but professional journals. All this disagreement may sound tedious and petty, but it serves a purpose. After a while it's possible to get a sense of the "state of the art" and to learn what works and what doesn't. According to scientific literature that involves carefully designed and controlled studies, those strategies that stand the test of time will be recommended. Other approaches will fall by the wayside or will eventually fall into the "Controversial and Idiosyncratic Therapies" category.

How do you know if a proposed treatment falls into this category? It's not always easy to tell, but there are several ways. One is that the theoretical basis of the method doesn't fit with modern scientific knowledge. Another way to tell is that the technique may be claimed to be effective for a broad range of rather poorly defined problems. In addition, adverse effects of the new method are often minimized, since the therapy may emphasize "natural" methods such as diet, vitamins or bodily manipulations. Finally, the "publication" of the therapy may appear in the media rather than in scientific journals, and later controlled scientific studies that don't support the method will be discounted due to "bias" or the alleged unwillingness of the scientific community to accept new ideas.

What are the controversial and idiosyncratic therapies as of now? To date, there are no reliable indications that such approaches as biofeedback, a food-additive-free diet, dietary supplements, elimination of sugar, megavitamin therapy, patterning or treatment of alleged vestibular dysfunction have any benefit above minor placebo effects.

An Open Letter to Individuals Proposing New Treatments for ADD

Dear Mrs. Franklin,

Thanks for sending me your packet of information on NewLife dietary supplement. As a clinical psychologist working with lots of ADD children, I am frequently contacted by people seeking my thoughts about specific ways of treating and managing Attention Deficit Disorder. At this moment I am responding to several requests for opinions.

Since there are so many ADD children and since so many people are, unfortunately, skeptical about medication treatment, interest in ADD treatment alternatives continues at a high level. Just a few weeks ago our local newspaper had another article about ADD and alternative/adjunctive treatments. Those of us who work with ADD children and their families are obviously very concerned with determining what constitutes valid treatment and what does not.

For me to recommend a particular approach to my clients, the procedure needs to have been somehow scientifically validated. In a business where both anguish and hope run high (parents rarely give up!), enthusiastic anecdotal information about a multitude of possible treatment approaches—or adjunctive treatment approaches—is, unfortunately, easy to come by. This makes things very confusing for parents who are trying to do the best thing for their children.

It's the replicated, "scientific" testing of a particular treatment that we need before we can recommend it. A method has to be proven, and then proven again and again in both research and practice. This proof has been provided, for example, for medication therapy in well over two hundred controlled studies. Medication treatment is not perfect, but it is very good. Try as they might, however, researchers and therapists are still having a hard time getting social skills training for ADD kids to make much of a difference. No matter how much these people want this training to work, when they examine their results critically, they have to admit that social skills training—as we've been doing it—doesn't work well with ADD children. (There are some suggestions, though, that social skills training may work better with non-ADD kids.)

That's the main reason we haven't done social skills training for ADD children in our practice. It isn't right to charge money for something that has not been proven to work. Believe me, I could have sold hundreds of concerned parents on the idea of this kind of group for their youngsters, simply because social relationships are such a big problem for ADD kids and also because it's so easy to make social skills training sound good to Mom and Dad. And since parents tend to be very forgiving as well as hopeful, it's quite possible they might have felt the groups made a difference even when they really didn't.

But listen to some of the mental health professionals who have been working like dogs over the past ten to fifteen years trying to get social skills training to work. Some of them are almost heartbroken that the early hopes for this training were smashed on the rocks of objective research. But these individuals haven't given up; they're still looking at other possibilities. Maybe, some of these researchers say, instead of elaborate attempts at setting up training groups, we need to just find our ADD child one friend. Maybe we can then show that that approach works.

I don't think many people realize how particular scientific researchers are about how their studies should be conducted. These people could qualify as having Obsessive Compulsive Disorder! But careful researchers take their precautions and go through all their tedious designs because— as your letter mentioned about the "Hawthorne" and "Rosenthal" effects— people are funny. Reasonable adults, if they are not careful, can come up with conclusions that are not warranted—especially if these conclusions are *what they want to believe.*

Good research, therefore, requires painstaking design and effort. Allow me to point out some of the requirements needed for a study to demonstrate that a particular strategy works for ADD kids:

1. Selection of subjects. For a study to have relevance to ADD, the subjects must be carefully selected ADD subjects—not just "problem" children. If we're talking about concentration, for example, can NewLife help concentration *in ADD children*?

2. Double blind studies are necessary. What does this mean? It means more painstaking precautions. Both the subjects (the kids) and those giving them the supplement cannot know if it is the real deal or a placebo. This means placebos must be developed that look like the real thing. This is super tedious (not to mention expensive), but in med studies this is exactly what is done. Why? Because people are forever hopeful, and in "open" studies (where everyone knows what's given to whom) reported results average 20 percent greater than in blind studies! In the NewLife study which you sent to me, I believe, the average changes in the Achenbach scores were actually less than 20 percent.

3. A control group is necessary. This is a group that does not get the treatment. The control group is matched to the treatment group and also followed over time. Why? To "control" for Hawthorne—or placebo—effects. Sometimes—as was the case in the Hawthorne study—just the very fact of doing some kind of intervention makes for certain reported changes, whether or not the actual treatment does any good.

4. Finally, a study has to be replicated by someone else. And then by someone else after them, until we have little doubt about what's going on. When people get enthusiastic about some tactic, they tend to find results that they want to find. But we can't, in good conscience, recommend an approach to parents until we know it has been proven to work.

Again, thanks for sending me the packet. I would certainly take another look at NewLife—or any other approach to ADD—when it has been repeatedly shown to be effective under the research conditions listed above. Though meeting these criteria is a time-consuming grind, I think we owe it to our children—and their parents—to recommend only what we know will help.

Parents have two critical—but limited—resources. One of these is money. Treatment can be expensive. Things like diagnosis, comorbidity, medication, tutoring, counseling and books can eat up a lot of dollars (as well as gas). Most families don't have a lot of money to throw around.

But a second important resource is time. As you know, the outcomes for untreated ADD are scary. We must do the best we can *as soon as we can* for our kids by using what we know works. Otherwise, a valuable piece of growing-up time may be robbed of its full potential and untreated ADD allowed to do further damage.

Sincerely,
Thomas W. Phelan, Ph.D.

10

Counseling

The issue of counseling for Attention Deficit Disorder has many sides to it. Who is going to be counseled, children and/or parents? Are ADD children good counseling or psychotherapy candidates? What about counseling for comorbid conditions, such as anxiety or conduct disorder? How do education about ADD and counseling work together?

Counseling for ADD Children

There is some controversy about counseling with ADD children. Many people feel that ADD kids are very much in need of counseling or psychotherapy. After all, these children are problems to themselves as well as to others, and the prognosis for untreated ADD is guarded.

Just because a strategy looks like it's needed and appears logical, however, doesn't always make it a good idea. Two factors make counseling with ADD children difficult. First of all, the very characteristics that make children ADD can also make them poor candidates for counseling. Are you a good counseling candidate, for example, if you don't want to see the therapist, blame everyone else for your problems, don't pay attention well during a session and, finally, forget everything that was discussed after you get home? Probably not.

Second, research has shown that the core symptoms of ADD, impaired concentration, impulsivity and hyperactivity, do not respond to counseling or psychotherapy. Many parents have learned this lesson the hard way: "He's seen Dr. Matthews every week for the last two years, but he's just as disorganized and restless as he was to begin with!" It's very hard to do something verbally to an ADD child in a doctor's office that is going to change his behavior during the other 167 hours in the week.

Yet it is important for ADD youngsters to see some professional periodically as they are growing up. The visits certainly do not need to be weekly and what is actually done may not really qualify as counseling or psychotherapy in the strict sense. The "counselor" is really more of a monitor or treatment supervisor, and he or she may serve several functions. These include moral support, continuing education about ADD, mediation and the fine tuning of the overall treatment plan.

In a world that seems to be continually critical of his every action, an ADD child's having someone who listens sympathetically and points out his good qualities can be like a breath of fresh air. A good relationship with the doctor also helps the child cooperate with the treatment. The therapist can also help educate the child about Attention Deficit as much as is possible. In fact, it is often better if this information comes from an outsider rather than from one of the youngster's parents. From time to time the counselor may also help mediate disputes between the child and his parents, disputes which can cover issues such as homework (at age 10), the use of the car (at age 17), or chores (at any age).

How can you determine the extent to which an ADD child can benefit from this kind of supervision/monitoring/counseling process? Several factors can give you a rough idea. First of all, the age of the child is important; a twelve-year-old is much more likely to benefit than a six-year-old. Second, how well does the child relate to or get along with this particular professional? Some kids see the visits as simply another embarrassing admission that there is a problem. Other children see the therapist as the only person who ever treats them nicely. Third, how defensive or open is the youngster about discussing his problems? Some kids wouldn't touch these personal topics with a ten-foot pole ("Everythings just great—can I go now?"), while others are much more candid with a sympathetic adult.

Another consideration which can affect decisions about counseling with an ADD child is the extent to which comorbid conditions are present. Some comorbid conditions can improve the likelihood of counseling being useful, while others reduce this potential for benefit. The DSM-IV disorders that may actually improve therapy prospects include depression and the anxiety disorders. We have known for some time that these conditions can respond quite favorably to talking therapies (as well as certain medications). On the other hand, the disorders which make for poorer therapeutic prospects include Oppositional Defiant and Conduct Disorders. Even though ODD and CD kids still need therapeutic monitoring and supervision, these children are very tough to talk with profitably.

Counseling for the Parents

Educating people about ADD can evoke a good deal of emotion in the recipients of this new knowledge. Reliable information about Attention Deficit will affect people's thoughts not only about the disorder, but also about themselves as well as about the whole treatment procedure. Learning the facts about ADHD, therefore, is going to be intimately involved with—and sometimes indistinguishable from—psychotherapy or counseling, especially for parents.

A good example of this information/therapy mixture is what we sometimes call the "No-fault" idea about ADD. When a professional explains to you that ADD has a hereditary base to it that no one in the family—child or parent—could have changed, this person is essentially saying that ADD is no one's fault. The "no fault" idea has two major implications. The first is that Mom and Dad no longer need to crucify themselves with guilt about what they think they did to produce this troublesome behavior in their offspring. The guilt parents feel, however, is tenacious. It doesn't just suddenly evaporate, so the job of counseling is to learn, practice and reinforce correct ways of thinking until these new ideas become habitual. Less painful feelings will then come along for the ride.

The second implication about attributions of fault is that the ADD isn't the child's fault either. He did not grow up with the goal of torturing his parents at every opportunity, and he was not put on earth to make them miserable. Here this no-fault idea can reduce the amount of anger that parents feel toward their little ADD youngster, but it won't get rid of all the anger. Most ADD kids are still too irritating too much of the time.

The no-fault idea, however, is not to be used as an excuse by any child for his behavior. Suppose one day our young ADD lad is sitting on top of— and pounding on—his little sister. His parents confront him. He responds by saying, "What can you expect? I can't help it 'cause I'm ADD and have a problem with emotional overarousal, impulsivity and low frustration tolerance!" This self-serving proclamation doesn't cut the mustard. It's an excuse and is irrelevant. Discipline should follow.

Another example of education and counseling working together has to do with parents' perceptions of their ADD children as well as with the problem of self-esteem. During a session with Mom and Dad, for example, a therapist may pose this question: "You have two children, a son who is a sophomore in high school, not ADD and who is getting straight As. You also have a daughter in seventh grade who is ADD and who is getting straight Ds. Which of your children is working harder?"

The parents may, of course, suspect a trick, but they usually respond by saying their non-ADD son is working harder. The therapist then explains that this answer is not correct. Why? For a very simply reason: what is harder to do, get up every morning and do something that you love, or get up every morning and do something that you hate? The answer, obviously, is the latter; it is much harder to force yourself to repeat an activity that you despise. Mom and Dad are told that, yes, their non-ADD sophomore is working hard and is a wonderful child. But their ADD daughter *has to go to school*, and what is required from her every day is a kind of courage that her brother has never experienced. Parents are taught to look at the world through the eyes of their ADD offspring, rather than seeing reality only from the perspective of frustrated parental expectations.

This same idea can be communicated to the ADD boy or girl. The message may go something like this: "Look, I'm not here to feel sorry for you. You have ADD and it's your job to handle it as well as you can. But I'll tell you one thing, I'll give you credit for guts. I know how much you dislike school, but you still go every day and do most of what you're supposed to. It takes a lot of effort to do something that you hate all the time."

After parents are taught to begin to see their ADD child a little differently, they need to learn to apply this same reasoning to themselves. They also didn't ask to have an ADD child and they certainly didn't ask for all the extra work, aggravation and heartbreak that goes along with that. Yet they, too, continue to do what must be done from day to day just helping to keep the kid afloat. This includes the mundane operations of driving, cooking, laundry and purchasing necessities like toothpaste and clothes. The job also includes the harder tasks that go along with having a handicapped child, such as going to staffings, seeing counselors and putting up with large doses of embarrassment at family picnics. No one will give any parent a medal for doing these things, but perhaps they should.

The stress of raising—and of just living with—an Attention Deficit child takes a lot out of a parent, especially a mother. As mentioned before, parents of ADD children, as a group, show a higher incidence of problems such as depression, alcoholism, antisocial personality, anxiety disorders and adult ADD. These problems are not all caused, of course, by the existence of the ADD child. The list sounds pretty dreary, but keep in mind that any one parent isn't going to have all these problems and some parents will have none of them.

When Mom and/or Dad does have one of the problems just mentioned, however, counseling as well as medication are often indicated. Treatment can help immensely with a parent's individual adjustment and also help stabilize the marriage and the family, thus providing more support and structure for the ADD child. One of the biggest oversights in treating ADD kids is *not treating the psychological problems of the parents*. Too many therapists tiptoe around Mom's depression or Dad's drinking, with the result that the effectiveness of treatment is reduced considerably.

Many adults find a form of counseling known as "cognitive therapy" especially helpful. Cognitive therapy is based on two principles. First is the idea that one's emotions are greatly affected by how one looks at things. Second is the idea that when a person is extremely upset about something, it is usually true that her thinking is distorted in some way. With cognitive therapy a person takes a long hard look at how she thinks about the world, life and herself. In the process she attempts to make her thinking and perceptions more realistic. With the help of a therapist, many parents are able to "rethink" things and sort of get back to reality, with the result that they may gradually train themselves to feel better.

Cognitive therapy certainly doesn't take away all the pain, but it can make quite a dent in it. Certain medications can also help Mom or Dad with problems such as depression, anxiety and ADD itself. Most parents are quite ambivalent about the idea of *their* taking medication—just as they were when they first considered it for their child. As often happens with the children, though, the effects of medications such as antidepressants, minor tranquilizers or stimulants can be truly amazing. A good therapist will carefully explain the possible benefits as well as possible side effects of the different drugs available before a trial of any one medication is begun.

Marital Counseling

Most ADD children place a constant burden on the relationship between Mom and Dad. As mentioned earlier, the divorce and separation rate is higher in families that have ADD children, especially when the child presents disruptive behavior problems. The higher rate results not only from the stress of having an ADD child, but also from the problems (listed above) to which parents of ADD kids are more vulnerable. Marital vulnerability is also aggravated by the tendency of ADD children to respond differently to their mothers than to their fathers.

Fortunately, research has shown that marital counseling can be of significant help. One method that is often helpful involves a combination of cognitive therapy and negotiation training. This approach involves several steps.

Step 1: Evaluation. The therapist first meets with the couple to get a picture of the "state of the union" and to find out how interested and willing each person is to work on the relationship. This joint session is often followed by individual sessions to explore issues in more depth and to cover problems that each person may not be comfortable discussing in front of his or her spouse. During the evaluation process, therapist and clients determine what issues are causing the most trouble. One or more of the "big ten" is usually involved:

1. Communication
2. Management of children
3. Money
4. Sex
5. Social life
6. Work and work schedules
7. Fun (or lack of it)
8. Alcohol and drug use
9. Jealousy
10. Values and religious beliefs

Step 2: Introduction to cognitive therapy. Couples are trained in ways to think about themselves and their spouses more realistically. These methods include learning how to stop blaming one other, learning how to stop blaming oneself, understanding how to take responsibility for one's own anger, anxiety or depression, and becoming more adept at not making mountains out of molehills (also known as "awfulizing").

Step 3: Negotiation training. Many—if not most—couples are not very skilled when it comes to discussing disagreements and then coming to some resolution. (Having an ADD child running around the house wreaking havoc a good deal of the time doesn't help either.) Unfortunately, many men and women fall into the "avoid it or argue about it" routine, and significant problems can go untouched for years.

Attention to and assistance with basic negotiation procedures is necessary. The therapist can help a couple master some straightforward, though difficult, communication/negotiation methods, such as:

1. Agreeing on a time and place to talk
2. Defining the problem to be discussed clearly (one at a time, please!)

3. Allowing each person to express his or her opinion without being interrupted

4. Listening sympathetically, rather than simply preparing a rebuttal

5. Generating possible solutions

6. Agreeing on something to try out

Step 4: Getting it together. After having explained their positions and after learning some new ways of thinking and talking, Mom and Dad can get on with the job. The job is to think straight and negotiate fairly. Any problem identified by either party must be dealt with; if it's a problem to one, it's a problem for both. The therapist comes along for the ride to try to prevent anyone from lapsing back into tactics such as repetitive arguing, reliving the past or treating a spouse like an idiot. Marital counseling is hard work, but it can do a lot of good for the entire family.

There's more to dealing with ADD than education about ADD, counseling and the supervision/monitoring of therapy. Medication is usually very helpful, but so is *training*, for both parents and kids. In the next two chapters we'll look at the issue of training parents in the behavior management of ADD children. Then we'll examine the difficult job of training ADD kids in self-control and social skills.

11

Behavior Management: Ages 2-12

M anaging the behavior of an ADD child is a daunting task. As a matter of fact, just living with an ADD child is a daunting task. In a very real sense, you must be a "professional parent," otherwise these children will take you to the cleaners. There are a number of discipline programs available for children in general, but some of them are not intended for ADD children. Attempting to use "discipline" programs that involve *only* attempts at talking to, listening to, or negotiating with young ADD kids will drive you crazy.

Fortunately, research has shown that training parents to better manage their young ADD charges works. Parent training helps parents feel more reasonably in control and raises their self-esteem. It also helps the ADD child learn better self-control and helps stabilize family life. Although we can't prove it yet, we also hope that teaching parents effective management techniques will help reduce the possibility of an ADD child's later developing comorbid disorders, such as ODD, CD, anxiety or depression.

In this chapter we will describe some general principles and some specific methods for managing the behavior of ADD children between the approximate ages of two to twelve. These methods were developed largely with ADD children, and they can be used at home and at school. For parents and teachers, however, one chapter is too short to learn everything necessary to start doing things differently and effectively. For more complete coverage of behavior management principles and techniques, readers are referred to one of our companion books, *1-2-3 Magic: Effective Discipline for Children 2-12*. The "1-2-3" can be used with average as well as difficult kids; the techniques you will find there are kind and effective, but they are also hard-boiled and no-nonsense.

Thinking ADD: ADD Kids Are Not Little Adults

It's important when dealing with ADD children—and other children as well—to keep your thinking realistic. This means, for example, "thinking ADD." Thinking ADD means *not expecting* a regular dose of normal, age-appropriate behavior from your ADD child. Thinking ADD means expecting regular doses of hyperactivity, noise, disorganization and intense sibling rivalry, while at the same time trying to manage these problems as best you can.

Realistic thinking—or thinking ADD—also means not getting caught up in what we call the "little adult" assumption. The little adult assumption is the idea that kids are just smaller than we are, but they have hearts of gold and they are basically reasonable and unselfish. If your child is not doing his homework, for example, you simply sit him down and explain to him the three golden reasons why he should do his homework: 1) he will learn more, 2) it will make you and his teacher happy, and 3) he will grow up to be a responsible and successful person.

If he is a little adult, the child, after receiving this wealth of wisdom, will respond by saying, "Gee, I never looked at it like that before," and he will immediately go to his room to complete his work.

Or, imagine your ADD monster is torturing his little sister for the fortieth time since they got home from school. In an aggravated voice, you ask him how he would feel if someone did that to him all the time. He says, "You know, you're right, I wouldn't like it very much. How insensitive I've been," and he stops the teasing—permanently.

This script would certainly be nice, but it doesn't happen. Kids are not little adults. Parents and teachers who believe—or want to believe—the little adult myth, however, are going to rely heavily on words and reasons in dealing with kids and trying to change their behavior. But words and reasons are going to be miserable failures much of the time. Often talking will have absolutely no impact at all, like "water off a duck's back." Other times words will take parent and child through the Talk-Persuade-Argue-Yell-Hit Syndrome.

What exactly is that? Let's say your child is doing something you don't like, such as being too aggressive with the dog. You try telling your son why he shouldn't treat the dog like that (e.g., the dog won't like him, the dog might bite, etc.). The boy doesn't respond, so you start trying to persuade him to see things your way. When persuasion fails, you start arguing. Arguing leads to a screaming match, and when that fails, you may feel there is nothing left to do but hit. Actually, 90 percent of spankings and other kinds of physical abuse of children are simply parental temper tantrums. The parent loses control because he is going out of his mind with frustration. He may also have no idea what else to do.

Unfortunately, ADD kids are probably more physically abused than other children are. Part of the reason for this, of course, is that ADD children are obnoxious more frequently than other children. The other culprit, however, is the little adult assumption—the misguided parental hope that words and reasons will always be sufficient to change a child's behavior.

How do you get rid of this mistaken notion? You start by changing your thinking about children. This may sound a little strange at first, but instead of thinking of your kids as little adults, you think of yourself as a "wild animal trainer." Parents of non-ADD children sometimes have trouble with this idea; parents of ADD kids do not!

Thinking like a wild animal trainer does not mean using whips, guns or chairs. It does not mean being harsh or abusive. What a wild animal trainer does is choose a method—which is largely nonverbal as well as gentle—and repeat it until the "trainee" does what the trainer wants.

If you have an ADD child, you must become a professional parent, in many ways like the professional wild animal trainer. You need to think of yourself as a trainer, not as a persuader. You must know 1) what mistakes to avoid, 2) the two major categories of problems you will encounter with your children, and 3) how to handle each type of problem.

The No-Talking, No-Emotion Rules

The two biggest mistakes that parents and teachers make in dealing with children are 1) too much talking, and 2) too much emotion. We just examined the reasons why all the talking is bad. Too often talking either doesn't work or it takes you through the Talk-Persuade-Argue-Yell-Hit Syndrome.

What's wrong with too much emotion? Here's the basic reason: when they are little, kids feel inferior. They feel inferior because they are inferior. Little children can be cute and nice and lovable, but they are also smaller, less privileged, less intelligent, less skillful, less responsible and less of just about everything than their parents and older kids are. This "inferiority" bothers them a lot. Children prefer to see themselves as powerful and capable of making some mark on the world.

So what's the point? The point is this: one way that kids feel powerful is by getting their big old parents and teachers all upset. This proclivity of kids does not mean they have no conscience or that they are all going to grow up to be criminals. It's just that having all that power temporarily rewards—or feels good to—the inferior part of the child.

So a corollary of what we are saying is this: if you have a child who is doing something you don't like, go ahead and get real upset about the misbehavior on a regular basis and—sure enough—he'll repeat it for you. There are other discipline systems other than 1-2-3 Magic, but you can ruin any of them by talking too much and getting too excited. These two mistakes, of course, usually go hand in hand, and the emotion involved is usually anger.

Some parents can turn off the talking and the emotional upset like a faucet, and others (who may also be ADD) have to work like dogs to get the job done. Most parents have to remind themselves over and over that talking and arguing and yelling and screaming and hitting don't help. These tactics only blow off steam for a few seconds. If a parent finds that he can't shake these habits, some sort of counseling may be helpful.

Two Categories: "Start" and "Stop" Behavior

When you are having problems with your kids, these problems, in general, come in two different forms. The children are either 1) doing something you want them to stop or 2) they are not doing something you would like them to start. Therefore we call these two kinds of things "Stop" Behavior and "Start" Behavior. The phrasing may be a little awkward, but it helps you remember that there is a difference.

Stop behaviors include the frequent, minor everyday hassles kids get into, such as arguing, whining, fighting, pouting, temper tantrums, disrespect, yelling and so on. Each transgression by itself isn't so bad, but add them all up and by the end of the day a parent may feel like leaving town permanently.

Start behaviors include things like cleaning rooms, homework, practicing musical instruments, getting up and out in the morning, bedtime and eating. In these cases you want the child to do something that is positive or good.

The reason for distinguishing between these two kinds of behaviors is this: you will use different tactics for each category.

- For STOP BEHAVIOR you will basically use
    the 1-2-3, or "counting," procedure.

- For START BEHAVIOR you will have a choice of six tactics (or combinations of them):

    1. Sloppy PVF
    2. Kitchen Timers
    3. The Docking System
    4. Natural Consequences
    5. Charting
    6. The 1-2-3 (different version)

When dealing with some trouble with a child, therefore, you will need to first determine if you have a Stop or a Start problem. If you mix up your tactics (e.g., use counting for homework), you will not get such good results or you may get no results at all.

The 1-2-3 for Obnoxious Behavior

The 1-2-3 is a simple training procedure for getting children ages 2-12—whether they are ADD or not—to curtail obnoxious behavior. You use the 1-2-3, in other words, to control or eliminate things like arguing, screaming, fighting, teasing, disrespect, etc. You don't use it to get the kids to do the good things, like cleaning rooms, homework, and getting up and out in the morning.

The 1-2-3 is simple; so simple, in fact, that many parents and teachers don't believe that it will work when they first hear about it. However, 1-2-3 Magic is being used by thousands and thousands of parents (many of them parents of ADD kids) and teachers across the country. The program is also popular with preschools and day care centers.

Here's a brief introduction to the 1-2-3. Let's say you have a four-year-old who is throwing himself around on the floor, kicking and screaming bloody murder because you refused to give him some potato chips right before dinner. (Typical ADD: bad case of emotional overarousal and low frustration tolerance.) In the past you have not known what to do with these frequent tantrums and nothing has worked.

Here's what you do: you look down at the child, hold up your index finger, and say, "That's 1." That's all you're allowed to say.

Your enraged son doesn't care. He carries on in the same way. After five seconds, you hold up two fingers and say, "That's 2." You get the same lousy reaction. After five more seconds, you hold up three fingers and say, "That's 3, take 5."

What does "That's 3, take 5" mean? It means the child had two warnings to shape up, and he blew it—he didn't shape up. So at "3" he's off for a "rest period" or time out: five minutes in his room and then he can come out. You act as if nothing had happened. No lectures or apologies. No "Now are you going to be a good boy do you realize what you've been doing to your mother all afternoon why do we have to go through this all the time you know I'm so sick and tired of your not listening I could..." Nothing is said. If the child misbehaves again, the counting is started again.

Three counts within a 15-to-20 minute period earns a time out. If the child does one thing wrong, however, and then goes 25 minutes with no problem, and then does something else out of line, you start with "That's 1" again. As the children get older, the 15-to-20 minute "window" is lengthened—meaning the kids must stay out of trouble for longer and longer periods of time.

What if the boy won't go to his room? With the little ones—say 60 pounds or less—you "escort" them, which may mean you follow, drag or even carry them. With older kids, if they don't move at 3, you give them a "time-out alternative." The alternative consequence might be a fine, loss of TV or computer minutes or—one of the best—a fifteen minute earlier bedtime.

How long should the time out be? Short and sweet: approximately one minute for every year of the child's life (a five-year-old gets five minutes, ten-year-old ten minutes, and so on).

That's the deal. Counting, of course, sounds too simple. Most parents have heard of time-out procedures. For some Moms and Dads they have worked and for others they haven't. What most parents and teachers don't realize, however, is that the real key to success has little to do with the time out itself. *The fact of the matter is that the 1-2-3 won't work unless you shut up.* By continuing to talk, you provoke your child and confuse your message. But perhaps most important, by talking you take the responsibility for your child's behavior back on yourself. You transform the "discipline" situation into one where your youngster doesn't really have to respond unless you can give him several good reasons—which he agrees with— why good behavior is in order. This approach isn't discipline any more, it's begging. And expecting an ADD child to respond positively to your misguided wordiness is, of course, pure fantasy.

When parents say the 1-2-3 doesn't work, the failure is almost always because the adult in charge won't be quiet. Here, for example, is one frustrated father's version of the 1-2-3: "That's 1... listen young man, I'm getting sick and tired of all your garbage. Do you really want to go to your room... Look at me when I'm talking to you! OK, THAT'S 2! I DON'T KNOW WHY THE HECK YOU CAN'T DO WHAT WE TELL YOU JUST ONCE EVERY TEN YEARS OR SO. THAT'S IT! BEAT IT! OUT OF MY SIGHT—GET UPSTAIRS RIGHT THIS SECOND BEFORE I GET TO YOU! THAT'S 3, DO YOU HEAR ME!!"

That's not the 1-2-3; it's simply a parental temper tantrum. As a disciplinary tool, parental rage is not very effective, though it is a wonderful way to give a kid a great feeling of perverse power.

To count effectively, you just say, "That's 1." Be silent and leave the child with the responsibility for his own behavior. If he shapes up, fine. If not, "That's 2." If you are doing it right, children will start responding (most of the time) at 1 or 2.

After reading this description your mind will be filled with many more questions about managing obnoxious or "Stop" behavior. Unfortunately, we don't have room to answer all of these here. Consult *1-2-3 Magic* directly for answers to questions like these:

- What if the child won't stay in his room?
- Won't this procedure make the kids hate their rooms?
- What about sibling rivalry?
- What if the child counts you back?
- What do you do in public?
- How do you handle testing and manipulation tactics, such as badgering, tantrums, threats, and martyrdom?
- What do you do when you're riding in the car?
- Will counting hurt my child's self-esteem?
- What if my ADD youngster wrecks his room during his so-called rest period?
- What do you do when you're on the phone?

Tactics for Start Behavior

Getting children to do what you want them to do is another story. For what we call "Start" behavior you can use several different strategies. You can also be more creative. You can use one tactic, or you might use two or three for the same problem. Your tactics to encourage positive behavior are the following:

1. Sloppy PVF. Sloppy Positive Verbal Feedback, otherwise known as praise or positive reinforcement, should be given to the kids on a regular basis. Sloppy PVF should be sincere and not too syrupy. ADD kids don't take well to overdone flattery, since it's often incompatible with their self-

concept. Keep in mind that your positive comments to your children should always outnumber your counting—not an easy task at all with ADD kids.

2. Kitchen Timers. Kitchen timers are great helps for lots of Start behaviors, such as homework, getting up in the morning, eating and going to bed. Kids, especially the younger they are, have a natural tendency to want to beat the clock. Timers can also be used to time the time outs themselves.

3. The Docking System. To use The Docking System, the ADD youngster must first have a source of money, such as an allowance. Then the procedure is simple: if the child doesn't do something she's supposed to, such as a chore, you do it for her! That's right. But you also charge her for the service; a reasonable fee comes out of her allowance. If she doesn't feed the dog, for example, you might take 15 cents out of her $3-per-week allowance for each feeding you have to do. No arguing, explaining, or other "little adult" attempts at verbally pounding sense into her head. Let the money do the talking. (The Docking System also works well with adolescents.)

4. Natural Consequences. Here you let the big, bad world teach the child what works and what doesn't. There are times when your staying out of a problem is the best thing to do. Suppose you have a fourth-grader who is taking piano lessons for the first time. She is not practicing like she should, however, and then—the night before her lesson—she is up worrying that her piano teacher will be mad at her.

What should you do? Nothing, at least at first. Some piano teachers are very good at getting uncooperative kids to tickle the ivories on a regular basis.

Or, suppose you have a seventh-grader. He's supposed to make his own lunch, with food that you provide, and then brown bag it to school. But it seems like every other day he is yelling at you about how hungry he was at lunch with nothing to eat. What should you do? Rclax, and give him some encouragement by saying, "I'm sure you'll do better tomorrow."

5. Charting. Charting involves using a diagram like a calendar which you can put on the refrigerator door or on the back of the child's bedroom door. The days of the week go across the top, and down the side each row

represents a different task the child is working on, such as cleaning his room, getting to bed, doing homework and/or feeding the dog. If the child completes the task to your satisfaction, you indicate their accomplishment on the chart with stickers for the little kids (4 to 8) and grades or numbers for the older children.

The positive reinforcement children get from charting comes, hopefully, from two things: parental praise (Sloppy PVF) and the inherent satisfaction of having done a good job. These two forces often work well to stimulate a child to do a good job. However, they don't always work. What if, for example, it seems that your child is just a natural slob, and a clean room means nothing to him? Or your little girl is ADD and LD, and homework provides very little satisfaction for her in spite of your praise?

Here you must go with "artificial reinforcers"—sometimes referred to as bribery (you're not rewarding the kids for doing something illegal). Some kids need to earn something pleasant in order to help them overcome indifference or aversion to a obnoxious project. Artificial reinforcers can be part of one's allowance, or special meals, or baseball cards or staying up later at night occasionally. The best ideas are often things that can be given out in small pieces and given out frequently. Try to be creative as possible in coming up with reinforcers—they certainly do not always have to be material. One little ADD lad wanted to earn minutes off from school for doing homework!

6. The 1-2-3 (different version). The 1-2-3 was described earlier as a method for controlling Stop (obnoxious) behavior. Counting can also be used for Start behavior, but only on one condition: what you want the child to do cannot take over two minutes. Say your son throws his coat on the floor after school, you ask them to pick it up, and he doesn't do it. Say, "That's 1." If he hangs up the coat, fine. If he doesn't, "That's 2." If he gets timed out, he goes and serves the time. When he comes out, you ask him again to pick the coat up. If there is still no cooperation, another time out follows. Keep this up until he gets the idea.

What if he never gets the idea? Switch to the Docking System. You hang up the coat for him, but you charge for your services. Keep any talking to a minimum, and count the whining, arguing, yelling and other forms of hassling your child gives you for your efforts.

12

Behavior Management: Adolescents

A dd Attention Deficit Disorder to adolescence and you often get "adolescence with a vengeance." Teens tend to be weird, emotional, preoccupied, moody, irritable and resentful of parental intrusions in the first place. When ADD also accompanies the picture, relations between parent and child can be strained to the breaking point.

All parents of teenagers have a fundamental problem: when to let go and when to intervene or take charge. There are times when you must bite your tongue as you nervously watch your child push toward greater independence. But, if you sense there is trouble, there are times when you must get involved whether your teen likes it or not.

With ADD adolescents "letting go" is harder for parents because the past has often been so difficult. How do you let go of a child who never seems to do anything right? ADD teens are often running about three years behind in behavioral and emotional maturity when compared to their peers. On the other hand, parents don't want the kids living with them forever, so Mom and Dad have to consider pulling back at some point. When we discuss the Four Steps that parents can use in dealing with their youngsters in the thirteen-to-eighteen-year-old range, you may find as a parent that you are using strategies for your ADD teen that are more geared for adolescents about three years younger. This attitude is not unreasonable as long as you continue to try to let go more and more, and don't continue treating your fifteen-year-old ADD offspring as if he were seven years old.

As we just did in Chapter 11, here we will describe some general principles and some specific methods for managing the behavior of ADD adolescents. One chapter, however, is too short to allow a parent to learn all he needs to know to manage (and not manage) ADD teens effectively without going insane. For more complete explanations, readers are referred to another of our companion programs (book, audio or video), *Surviving Your Adolescents*. *Surviving Your Adolescents* was also developed largely on the basis of experience with ADD children. Let's first take a look at some general principles concerning the "management" of ADD adolescent behavior.

You Come First

Parents are always putting their children first. This tendency is probably instinctive. Did you know that this way of thinking can also be dangerous? As we mentioned before, parents of ADD children undergo unique stress and often themselves suffer from conditions such as anxiety, mood disorders and ADD itself.

Before trying to handle a problem with an ADD teenager, therefore, you had better make sure you're in good enough shape to do so. Otherwise you're likely to do more harm than good with what is sometimes called emotional dumping or "displacement." If you are old enough to have a teenager, you are old enough to be at the point of midlife yourself. This is a time which brings many problems of its own for adults, such as those involving career, health, aging parents and marriage.

Trying to manage any ADD child when you are strung out with serious personal problems can be a great formula for disaster. Perhaps a long hard look at your job, your health, your mental health or your marriage is in order. Self-help books or groups can also be useful in getting your act together, but if these don't work, getting yourself into some kind of counseling may be necessary.

What sort of adolescent do you have?

Being objective about one's own offspring is very difficult, especially when Attention Deficit Disorder has played a large role over the years in helping to shape your opinion. One of the problems with trying to be objective here is the fact that ADD kids can be so obnoxious so much of the time. *It is very hard to think of someone as competent if they are constantly irritating you.* Yet there seems to be a basic rule of psychology that says that most people—children and adults—show their worst behavior at home. That state of affairs may be the opposite of the way we'd all like it to be, but it's very often the case for both kids and parents.

What this Worst-Behavior-Shows-at-Home rule means to parents of ADD teens is that their children may actually perform the basic tasks of their life a lot better than the parents think. It's just that the parents rarely get a chance to see this competent behavior directly. What Mom and Dad do get to see, however, is irritability, petty sibling rivalry, anger in response to simple requests, sloppy rooms and unfinished homework.

These observations do not inspire confidence, but they may represent the worst side of the coin (they also may not!). Therefore it is helpful for parents to take a long, slow, calm look at how their child is doing regarding not only home, but also social life, school, work (if applicable), and general self-esteem. Though you may not think of your adolescent as anywhere near competent, is he really the disaster area that you usually imagine him to be? Consider his strengths as well as his weaknesses. In general, the better your child is doing, the less you will need to be involved when you feel concerned about something.

How do you get along with your ADD teenager?

Next, take a long hard look at how well you and this child get along. Consider three things. First of all, how well do you talk with each other? How often, for example, do the two of you enjoy just "shooting the breeze?" And how good you are at solving problems together? Second, consider how much time you spend having fun with one another. Shared fun certainly is harder the older the kids get! Finally, how much do you just plain like (not love) each other? Do you find one another's company pleasant most of the time?

If your relationship is fairly good, then as a parent you are in a position to intervene or assist your teen when there is a need. If, however, you think your relationship is pretty bad, you have a problem, because *you may be the last person on earth who should try to "help."* What are your choices? First of all, perhaps you should shut up and let your spouse handle things. (If there is no spouse or if your spouse also has a rotten relationship with the child, you may wind up considering professional counseling.) Second, no matter what you need to avoid the Four Cardinal Sins—which we'll discuss in a moment—like the plague. If you don't or can't avoid these, it may be that you are really more out to get your kid than you are out to help him.

Third, if your relationship is not good, perhaps you could consider trying to improve how you get along with your adolescent. This is no easy task when the relationship has been difficult for many years, and in some situations changing a bad relationship is simply impossible. But if you think you have a chance, here are five "tactics" to consider:

1. Avoiding the Four Cardinal Sins
2. Active, sympathetic listening to what the youngster is saying to you, even if you don't agree or like what you are hearing
3. Talking about yourself (interesting stories or experiences, not lessons)
4. Shared activities that are fun for both of you (the best bet—when nothing else seems possible—is probably seeing a movie and then getting something to eat)
5. Realistic, consistent, genuine praise or other kinds of positive reinforcement

These "tactics" are discussed in more detail in *Surviving Your Adolescents*. They require a good deal of commitment and patience on the parent's part and—perhaps above all—the right attitude. To be successful your attitude must be one of really trying to get along better, rather than being filled with righteous indignation whenever your teen frustrates you—once again—with his typical and absurd ADD behavior.

How serious is the problem?

Did you ever stop to think that your level of aggravation about a problem is not always the measure of the real seriousness of the problem. Your ADD teens, in other words, already have their MBAs! These are the Minor-But-Aggravating things that teens do which are very irritating to you, but which are not indications that the boy or girl is in deep psychological trouble.

MBAs may include problems such as messy rooms, clothes, use of the phone, chores, grammar, using your things and so on. If you have an ADD teen and you are spending a lot of time arguing, lecturing, or complaining about matters such as these, you are missing the boat. You're not likely to change the status quo at this point anyway. Very likely you also have other things to worry about that are more important, such as grades, the child's lack of friends, or your difficult relationship with her.

Realistic expectations are very important. If your child has hit the 13- to 18-year-old bracket, you're not likely to revolutionize her. Your job of parenting is about 60 to 80 percent over. With ADD kids this is frightening. Be patient and don't fall into using ridiculous maneuvers such as the Four Cardinal Sins. Keep your mouth shut unless it's absolutely and positively necessary to say something.

The Four Cardinal Sins

These four mistakes are extremely destructive. They are primitive, impulsive and emotional responses that occur without much thought and they mean sure death to any relationship with a child. These diabolical maneuvers include:

1. *Spontaneous discussions about problems.* It's almost impossible to bring up a difficult subject on the spur of the moment with a child and expect to get anywhere. Yet most of us assume that when we're ready to talk about something—no matter how unpleasant—everyone else should be ready too. Spontaneous discussions will almost always increase irritability and decrease cooperation.

2. *Nagging.* Nagging is good for two things: making kids avoid you and making them hate you. Nagging might be defined as a set of repetitive,

often hostile, verbal reminders from person A, who wants to see something accomplished, to person B, who doesn't share person A's enthusiasm for the project. Behind nagging is the parental delusion that the answer to cooperation is the repetition of the request.

3. *Insight transplants*. Otherwise known as lecturing, this cardinal sin is based upon another bit of parental wishful thinking. The notion is that Mom or Dad will take one of his or her wonderful insights about life and send it through the air waves. The potential wisdom will then enter the teen's ears and proceed to the brain, where it will take root, flower and subsequently produce new and more productive behavior.

While on the receiving end of a lecture, kids often think of just one thing: how can I get out of this situation as soon as possible? Parents sometimes need to open their eyes, look at the youngster's face, and ask themselves how many times they've said the same thing before without much effect. The thought here is not that the ideas in Father's Famous Lecture Series are bad or dumb. Quite the contrary is usually the case— the ideas are very reasonable. The problem is that lectures are not heard, and they also produce much aggravation and little change.

4. *Arguing*. Arguing is one of the habits of ADD teenagers (and teens in general) that can drive parents crazy. There are days when the arguments seem endless and everyone insists on having the last word. Arguments have a nasty way of escalating quickly, resulting in events which make everyone feel bad.

What are the alternatives to the Four Cardinal Sins? On the one hand, a parent can't simply shut up and let his child do whatever he wants. On the other hand, no adolescent was ever argued nagged or lectured into genuine submission.

Think of it like this. First, what is the issue at hand? Is it an MBA? If it is, you shouldn't be talking about it. You say you just walked by your 17-year-old son's room and it was an absolute pigsty and so you went and got him immediately and tried to make him clean it? You just committed at least two of the four sins. Keep quiet about MBAs.

Second, if the issue is important (e.g., grades, smoking, hours), make an appointment to talk about it. What!? An appointment!? Is this a business or a family? It's a stressed-out family and where ADD is involved you must try to treat problems in a very businesslike, step-by-step, unemotional manner. Bringing up an important problem on the spur of the moment with lots of emotion in your voice is suicide.

Four Parent Roles

Now that you know something about what not to do, let's consider what to do when there is a problem. There are four roles—or four alternatives—you can consider using in dealing with your adolescent's problems. These options vary in their level of intrusiveness. From least intrusive to most involved they are:

1. Observer
2. Advisor
3. Negotiator
4. Director

Observer. Believe it or not, there are several ways of merely observing. If you are having a very difficult time with your own life due to health, depression, marital problems, aging parents or all of the above and more, you may be in no shape to deal with a troublesome teen. As mentioned before, you can work on your own personal job, health or marital problems, and, if necessary, keep a watchful eye on what's happening with your child.

You can also do nothing by using the "Grin and Bear It" approach. Before intervening, try more aggressively to "let go." Actually, you really don't need to grin. Unfortunately, there are many times when an adolescent can be doing something that irritates the daylights out of you, but you still should not get too involved in it. Perhaps you don't like the way they talk to one of their friends, or they always study with the radio on. Maybe they're eating junk food after school and you think they should have fruit.

Advisor. An advisor is a person who is hired to give advice, but with a condition. The receiver of the advice has the right to reject it. If you are going to try some friendly consultation with your teen, you are not using parental power. Your child has the right to reject your advice.

Unlike most consultants, however, you probably weren't hired for the job. If you are going to give your son or daughter some words of wisdom, remember that it is your idea to do this and not theirs. Keep in mind that spontaneity can be dangerous. Unwanted advice is a problem by itself, but when your unasked-for wisdom comes out of the blue, an irritable response is almost guaranteed. Try written rather than verbal requests occasionally; the sound of your voice can be very irritating, especially when repeated "consults" turn into nagging. And finally, remember that advice is cheap and often not followed.

Negotiator. "We've got a problem here and sometime I'd like to talk it over with you," might be the beginning of an attempt at negotiation. What you are doing here is recognizing that your ADD teen is older, and consequently your son or daughter should have more say about the things that they do. Negotiating is also a statement that you feel it is important that you get involved, because you think the problem is serious or perhaps because it affects other family members. By Negotiating you are saying that—up to a point—you are willing to bargain or make a deal.

Although Negotiating doesn't have to be anything horribly fancy, it is critical that certain minimal guidelines be followed:

1. Agree to negotiate.
2. Pick a good time and place (a ride in the car is a good idea!).
3. Define the problem.
4. Make a deal or bargain you both can live with.
5. Experiment with the "deal," and change it if necessary.

Director. For too many families there are times when no amount of consulting or talking is going to do any good. Things have gone too far, problems have gotten too serious, and relationships have been strained for too long. When matters get to this point, it is time for Mom and/or Dad to draw the line. The Director role obviously isn't easy; for many parents the idea of trying to tell their adolescents what to do—or of trying to force them to cooperate—brings up images of ferocious retaliation.

When a problem is serious enough (drugs) or interferes directly with your life (loud music), you have a definite right to take charge and become the director of a solution. If the child is uncooperative, the relationship is poor, and all other steps haven't worked, the use of power is legitimate—

provided that this use is not just a camouflaged attempt at waging war. Before acting, take a long, hard look at your motives.

For repeated and significant misbehavior (not MBAs), we often use the Major/Minor System. Here we attach certain consequences to certain misbehaviors; the severity of the consequences is designed to match the severity of the misbehaviors.

A three-category (Major/Medium/Minor) system, for example, might look something like this:

Major: offenses could include: out all night, physical violence, party without permission at home with no parents. Consequences for Major offenses could include: $25 fine, no TV for one month, no phone or car for one month, ten-hour chore or project around the house, or grounding for two weeks (can't leave house except for work or school).

Medium: offenses might be behavioral trouble at school, smoking (13-15 year olds), swearing using the "F" word, friends at home without permission. Consequences for Medium offenses could include: $10 fine, no TV for two weeks, no phone for two weeks, four-hour chore, or one week of grounding.

Minor: offenses might include leaving your tools out, swearing using the "F" word, leaving house unlocked. Consequences: $1-2 fine, no TV for three days, no phone for three days, or a four-day grounding. When the misbehavior occurs, you institute the consequence without yelling, lecturing or arguing.

A guaranteed law of adolescent psychology is this: *repeatedly engaging in one or more of the Four Cardinal Sins will always obliterate the effectiveness of any consequence or punishment.*

Taking charge with an teen can also involve professional counseling, hospitalization, or even kicking an over-18 "child" out of the house.

Here's a quick summary of the Major/Minor process:

1. Advice and Negotiation have failed.
2. The problem is important.
3. If both parents are living at home, sit down with spouse, define the problem precisely, and decide how to take a stand.
4. Give written warning; prepare for testing and manipulation.
5. Reinforce compliance, if it occurs.

6. If there is no compliance, implement consequences.

7. Stick to your guns with no arguing.

How Not to Argue

We hope the suggestions made so far will be helpful, but just in case they seem a bit too general, let's conclude with some down-to-earth specifics about how to avoid perhaps the most common of the Four Cardinal Sins, arguing. One of the hardest things to do with ADD teens is to stop arguing. Adolescents love to argue! But arguing is a useless, provocative, depressing, addictive and irritating behavior that too often becomes an irresistible and inevitable part of family life. How can you possibly stop doing it?

It's obviously easier said than done, but parents who learn the art of not arguing can go a long way toward having a much more peaceful home. If you are going to deal with this problem more effectively with your ADD adolescent, you first need to Realize Several Things, then you need to know Exactly What To Do.

Realize Several Things:

1. Arguing doesn't work. No teenager in the history of mankind has ever been argued into sincerely saying, "Gee, Dad, after your brilliant (though somewhat long) explanation of the problem, I now see your point and will comply immediately."

2. Arguing usually escalates. If you participate in some stupid discussion about something that shouldn't even be talked about, the "discussion" will become verbal war.

3. You control about 50 percent of the problem. Arguing takes two people. It's very hard to argue with just yourself making all the noise. Your shutting up can help a lot.

4. Teens love to bait you. They can be clever and sneaky and provocative. Before you know it, you're involved and gabbing your head off. Imagine your adolescent is a fisherman sitting in a boat, dropping a baited hook down into a lake. Imagine you are a fish living in the lake. What kind of fish? A large-mouthed bass. Take the bait and you're dead.

Exactly What To Do:

1. Stop Talking. If you control 50 percent of most arguments, and arguments are purposeless, you should obviously...SHUT UP! This

advice, interestingly enough, is so simple that it sounds almost stupid. The real difficulty, of course, is that your shutting up doesn't end the trouble right away. Why? Because few ADD teens are going to shut up along with you.

2. You need to know how to handle the teen's next move. It will undoubtedly be one or more of the six types of testing and manipulation—those devious maneuvers kids use to try to get their way. These endearing tactics include Badgering, Intimidation, Threat, Martyrdom, Butter Up and Physical Tactics. Without actually having to say it, your message to the adolescent will basically be: "I'm out of this stupid discussion. The next move is yours. If you leave me alone, fine. If you hassle me, I'm ready." Ready, though, does not mean more stupid talking.

Your shutting up, of course, and your teen then leaving you alone is still not that simple. Here are some of the frequent questions that exasperated parents ask about teenagers' testing and manipulation:

Question 1. What if he (the ADD kid) keeps talking? (Badgering)

Answer: Who's controlling your mouth, him or you? Keep quiet.

Question 2. What if I keep quiet, and he just stands there yelling at me and he won't shut up? (Badgering)

Answer: You have two choices. Go about your business and do your best to pay no attention. Try not to smirk or act superior; you'll only make him worse. If that doesn't work, leave. Go out in the car, go to the bathroom, go for a walk. Anything.

Question 3. What if he follows me all around the house yelling at me? (Intimidation)

Answer: You have two choices. Go about your business and do your best to pay as little attention as possible. If that doesn't work, just sit down—with him right on top of you—and try to look at a magazine. If he grabs the magazine out of your hands, just sit and stare at him. Don't say anything! If you feel like crying, cry. But don't talk.

Question 4. What if he has the last word?

Answer: Are you kidding? Words are cheap. Let him have it.

Question 5. What if he threatens to run away or to break something? (Threat)

Answer: If he threatens to run away, don't say anything. If he does leave (Physical Tactic), don't try to stop him. If he's not back when he's supposed to be, there will be consequences for violating his hours. If he's gone into the night, call the police. If he breaks something not so valuable (e.g., a broom), he will have to pay for it later. Don't start talking to him or arguing with him or threatening him. If he starts breaking valuable things (lamps, windows, stereo CD player, furniture) call the police.

Question 6. What if he says, "I know it's hard for you to deal with me, but I really appreciate your working so hard at setting limits in order to help me become a responsible adult." (Butter Up)

Answer: What?

Question 7. What if he says I don't love him and never did, or if he says that I never talk to him? (Martyrdom)

Answer: Shut up.

Isn't this fun? No, but you don't have a lot of options. Either keep quiet or pour gasoline on the fire.

13

Self Control and Social Skills Training

As we saw earlier, "psychotherapy" with ADD children is difficult, but not always impossible. We often have to look at the counseling process more as an encouragment and monitoring kind of operation. But what if we could *train* ADD youngsters to manage their symptoms better? What if we could train them to control themselves more and get along with other people in more mutually satisfying ways?

How would training be different from counseling or supervision? Training would be more than just talking. It would involve putting children through repeated exercises of different kinds that would help them learn new skills. Training might be like learning to play the piano, and it would mean lots of practice. But perhaps practice and repetition might be what it takes to "get the idea through" to these kids.

For a while in the 1980s there was a good deal of excitement and optimism about self-control training for impulsive ADD youngsters. Some of this self-control training fell under the category of cognitive behavior modification (CBM). The "cognitive" part of CBM referred to the hope that ADD children could be taught to *think* differently (or to think at all before acting). The "behavioral" part of CBM referred to the hope that ADD children could be taught to *act* differently—at least in part because of their new thoughts.

CBM techniques often involved what was called self-instruction training or self-guided talk. This approach took the point of view that the ADD child's difficulties with self-control resulted from a lack of an internal language. A non-ADD child, for example, can talk to herself, thus anticipate the consequences of her actions, and then make a good decision about what to do or not do. "If I hit her, I'll get in trouble." Some CBM techniques, therefore, tried to teach the ADD child how to create and use this internal dialogue. With one method, for example, the trainer started by asking the child to say out loud, "If I talk to the kid next to me in class, I won't finish my work, may get a detention, and may have to stay after school." Then the child whispered the same words, and eventually she just said them to herself in her head. The trainer then tried to encourage the child to actually do this in the classroom: to stop and think instead of acting impulsively.

Unfortunately, the results of training in self-guided talk have been disappointing. The problem: ADD children "forget to remember" to use the strategy. Even though the ADD child may be able to repeat the process back to her trainer, when the time actually comes to use the tactic, the new strategy is the furthest thing from her mind. If you have known many ADD children, you know very well that their forgetfulness is not surprising at all. It is, on the contrary, legendary. How many parents have said time and again things like "I THOUGHT I SAID NOT TO DO THAT!" or "HOW MANY TIMES DO I HAVE TO TELL YOU!"

It is obvious that logic and necessity do not by themselves make treatments work. The nature of ADD is that it makes it very difficult to do or say something to an ADD child in an office or group setting, and then have that intervention change the child's life after she leaves the session.

Interest in self-talk approaches has been followed by interest self-control or self-regulation training. This type of training has included what are called "self-monitoring" and related "self-reinforcement" approaches. In one study children in a classroom situation were instructed to evaluate what they were doing whenever a tone sounded (self-monitoring). They were then rewarded with a token whenever their assessment matched that of an adult observer. After a while children were trained to reinforce themselves in one way or another (e.g., "I'm doing a good job!") when they were doing what they were supposed to be doing (self-reinforcement).

Self-monitoring and self-reinforcement have shown some promise. Some studies suggest that these tactics may be more useful when combined with medication therapy, but these types of training may also produce effects of their own separate from the positive effects of medication. There are also some hints that children's self-reinforcement may produce more appropriate and constructive behavior than simple external reinforcement administered by adults.

Even so, self-regulation strategies still involve significant problems. Their effects may not generalize to group instruction times or to classroom settings *different from the one in which the tactics were first learned.* Some type of adult environmental management still seems to be necessary—adults must help with generalization. And some studies demonstrating success with self-regulation did not train children who met full diagnostic criteria for ADD. We would certainly expect that ADD children would be harder to train in self-control than average kids—or than children with other DSM-IV problems—because self-control is so much at the heart of ADD.

Social Skills Training

One of the most heartbreaking experiences for parents of ADD children is to see their child rejected by other kids. The ability to get along with others is not only an enjoyable part of life, but it also helps determine how successful a person will be in many other areas of life, such as one's career. Consequently, social skills is one of the most important prognostic indicators regarding what an ADD child's life will be like as a grown-up.

When it was first attempted, social skills training employed systematic approaches that provided for the introduction and mastery of individual skills in a supportive environment and, hopefully, the generalization of these skills to other settings. For some time it was believed that the most straightforward treatment was to 1) tell the child what to do in situations identified as problematic, 2) show him or her how to do it, and 3) have the child practice the skill before using it in real life. Parents and teachers could then take advantage of opportunities to strengthen the new behavior. A social skills group might last from about eight to fifteen weeks.

A typical "social skills training group" often went something like this. A brave adult leader (or two) would work with a small group of perhaps four to eight children. The first thing the leader and group would do is to define what social skills are. If you stop to think about it, what exactly are social skills? Social skills are habits that are easy for parents and teachers (who themselves are already able to do them) to take for granted. But these competencies do not come automatically or naturally to ADD kids. Social skills include:

1. Introducing yourself
2. Giving and receiving positive feedback
3. Sharing
4. Compromising
5. Dealing with name calling
6. Sending an ignoring message
7. Joining a conversation
8. Problem solving
9. Saying "No" to stay out of trouble
10. Following directions
11. Constructive complaining
12. Complimenting someone else

In social skills training groups, these different behaviors were discussed and then practiced. Each skill might be dealt with separately. A group discussion, for example, might start by defining what it means to compromise. Definitions are solicited from the children about what good compromising is. Then definitions of poor compromising might be solicited and discussed. Next the kids and leader discussed why compromise is important or helpful in getting along with others. Finally, the youngsters were involved in role-play situations, where they acted out examples of good compromising and bad compromising.

Children were reinforced regularly for their cooperation; during the group sessions there would be frequent breaks. Because the transfer of new skills to the non-group "real world" was a concern, "homework" assignments were given to the child in a social skills group. Sometimes parents and teachers were also informed of the skills being learned by the kids, and suggestions were given to these adults for reinforcing these behaviors when they occurred. Since ADD kids don't usually remember on their own to try to do things differently in different situations, having an adult present who could signal them when it was time to try something new—and reinforce their attempt afterwards—might help a lot. This adult signaling was seen as especially necessary since there was no guarantee that other children would provide reinforcement for an ADD child's new behavior, especially because many ADD children already had bad reputations.

In spite of all the effort, our experience to date has shown that social skills deficits are one of the most difficult aspects of the ADD picture to try to change. Ironically, in the groups themselves ADD kids are very good when it comes to defining skills, describing bad behavior, generating new behavioral alternatives and role playing. As it was with the CBM techniques, however, in their everyday lives ADD children just don't remember to use the new thoughts and skills that have been discussed and suggested to them—even if it's still the same day! As we have just seen with self-control training, logic and necessity do not by themselves make treatments work.

The Future

Even though the jury is still out, many creative and compassionate minds continue to work on the problems of self-control and social skills training. When it comes to these issues, parents and professionals feel they have no choice but to do something. Opinions about self-control training also depend on your points of view, long-term or short-term, for example, and whom you consider to be the primary "trainers" of ADD children. If you look at the problem from different perspectives, there may be more room for optimism.

Combined vs. Inattentive. ADD usually involves interpersonal problems, but the nature of these problems depends upon the particular child as well as the type of ADD—and the type of comorbid problems—the child has. There is some truth to the saying that ADD with hyperactivity kids (Combined) will be rejected and ADD without hyperactivity (Inattentive) children will be overlooked. The social problems of Combined Type children often result from these kids being "in your face"—they are loud, intrusive, demanding and often aggressive. Their obnoxiousness can be aggravated when a disruptive disorder, such as ODD or CD, is added to the picture.

Some experts feel that the problem with Combined Type kids represents a *performance* deficit rather than a *knowledge* deficit. In other words, these youngsters know what they should do, but when the time comes to do it, they don't perform. Ask one of these children, after an unfortunate social encounter, what he should have done, and he may correctly tell you "I shouldn't have interrupted and been so loud." Although he is correct, this knowledge does him little good.

Inattentive ADD children, on the other hand, may have more of a knowledge deficit when it comes to peer relations. These kids hang back and don't get involved because they don't know how to get involved. They are also frequently shy and don't know how to manage their social anxiety.

It would make sense, then, that approaches to social skills problems should be different for Combined and Inattentive children. With Combined Type kids the problem is putting their knowledge into action, and somehow dealing with the interfering problem of impulsivity. With Inattentive children, the problem is learning what *to* do and dealing with the interfering problem of passivity (and often anxiety). In fact, preliminary indications are that Inattentive ADD children may be better social skills training candidates than Combined kids. Why? Because impulsivity is harder to manage and because Combined kids have developed bad reputations that are hard to change. With Inattentives, passivity and anxiety are somewhat easier to overcome, and Inattentive children have no bad reputation hanging over their head—as a matter of fact, they usually have no reputation at all.

Medication. Many parents have heard their child's physician say "You must understand that stimulant medication is *only for school.*" This attitude is unfortunate and it is one that does a great disservice to many ADD kids. Today research has made it perfectly clear that stimulant medications help *most* ADD children in social situations—especially

Combined Type kids. Some people say "That's ridiculous. How can a *pill* teach a *skill*?" This comment misses the point: with Combined kids the problem is not knowledge but performance. The medication helps them do what they know they should. They are more able to stop, look and listen. With medication they become less bossy, less intrusive and less noisy.

What about Inattentive children? The situation regarding medication is a little more complicated. For some children stimulants make them a little more active, which can get them more involved socially. For other Inattentive children, especially those with anxiety, stimulants may help them concentrate in school but may make them a little more anxious, which doesn't help their social interactions. For some of these kids other medications, such as antidepressants, can help reduce their anxiety and— combined with training in what to do—can improve their relationships with other children.

What is the point? Medication can help ADD kids a lot when it comes to getting along with others. When meds do help, it is cruel not to use them given the current, severe limitations on the power of social skills training. These children need all the help they can get after school, on weekends and during the summer. In terms of medication response, however, each child must be carefully evaluated to see what works best for him or her.

Peer Helpers. Some of the more interesting, creative and encouraging tactics for helping ADD children socially have involved using other, same-aged children as helpers of one kind or another. For example, one study paired an ADD child with a non-ADD child (of good social standing) and had the two of them work together each day on academic tasks. Both children were working as equals on the same problems; neither was tutoring the other. This "buddy system" appeared to increase the social status of the ADD child as well as to improve the interactions of that child with other children. Some of the non-ADD child's status or reputation seemed to "rub off" on to the ADD child.

Another study involved non-ADD peer "helpers" with ADD children who fell more into the withdrawn and socially isolated category. The "helper" was taught to invite and encourage the ADD child—during times like recess—to become more involved in playing with other children. Adults helped to monitor and assist the helpers. The result was that the

ADD children's relationships with their helpers improved, as well as their relationships with other children. A surprising result was that the ADD youngster also began doing better in other social settings where the peer helper was not present.

School-based programs. Work is being undertaken to set up school-wide social skills programs where all children are exposed to a basic philosophy of interpersonal relations as well as to specific classroom interventions. All teachers, for example, might be required to buy into and support a school program that does not allow rejection or bullying. That might mean that a teacher herself may need to work on not modeling rejecting behaviors toward a difficult ADD child whom she does not like. Kids quickly pick up on adult attitudes, and youngsters can use them as permission for their own hostile actions.

Problem solving and conflict resolution exercises have also been incorporated into the classroom in some schools. One advantage of this is that ADD children are not singled out as needing special help. All kids are exposed to the activities. A disadvantage may be that other children benefit more from the exercises than ADD kids do, or other kids may not need the practice as much in the first place.

Already there are some suggestions that school-based programs such as these may help produce less aggression in boys, less self-critical behavior in girls, and perhaps less delinquency in general. Keep in mind that these finding are preliminary, and they do not necessarily mean that ADD children themselves are benefitting.

The long-term view: parents as models and trainers. Some individuals have pointed out that the apparent failings of self-control and social skills training efforts with ADD children need to be put in a different perspective. Is it really fair to expect, these people say, major behavioral changes in this difficult bunch of kids in so short a period of time? Are you really going to make a dent in an ADD child's functioning in fifteen weeks or even less?

Perhaps not. On the other hand, we do know that ADD tends to moderate—not go away, but moderate—with age. ADD children tend to become somewhat less hyperactive and impulsive, though they may remain just as inattentive and disorganized. In a sense, then, they do mature, even though this maturing process progresses much more slowly than it does in other children. Can we help to foster and improve—and perhaps speed up just a little—this maturation over the long haul?

We probably can, but the job won't be done by one self-control or social skills training group or one summer camp experience. These activities may very well provide some useful "booster" sessions every now and then, but the real, everyday trainers are going to be parents. For one thing, kids learn a lot through modeling, and they are definitely going to imitate the behavior of their parents. If Mom and Dad exercise reasonable self-control, their children will *tend* to do the same. If parents model good social skills, their kids will tend to do the same.

This is another reason why it is important to treat Mom and Dad as well as the ADD child. Parents themselves often suffer the effects of ADD as well as the effects of disorders such as anxiety and depression. These problems can interfere with their effectively modeling good self-control and effective social interactions.

In addition to being models for their kids, parents must also be trainers. You really don't have much choice. Even if you sent your child to a training group for his whole life, you would still spend way more time with him than he ever would in his group. Time with you offers ample opportunities for training. Training means not only discipline; it also means (in addition to modeling) finding friendly ways to reinforce (and sometimes prompt) your child's efforts at self-regulation and positive social interaction.

Here's an example. Research tells us that ADD kids run into more social problems in unstructured situations. Research also tells us that ADD children, especially Combined Type, often do much better in social interactions with the help of medication. What some parents do is help their ADD child set up a get-together with another child—often someone from their class or neighborhood. But the other youngster doesn't just "come over to play" and the two children don't just do whatever they want. Instead, the ADD child takes his medication about an hour before the potential friend shows up and their time together is structured. Perhaps the two kids watch a video, or go out with a parent for ice cream or to a ballgame. The visit is short, and activities like competitive games are avoided. The parent tries to find the structure or activity that makes the experience pleasant for both children. The parent also acknowledges and reinforces appropriate self-control and positive social behaviors when her child shows them.

Could you set up something like this once a week for your ADD child? It's a fair amount of work, but in one year the boy or girl would have fifty positive social experiences. The other possibility is he might make a friend. Some experts believe—and they have a point—that just having one friend by itself might do more good for an ADD child's skills and self-esteem than a hundred counseling sessions or training groups.

The research clearly tells us that ADD has a strong hereditary component. That means that parents—no matter how hard they try or how good they are at parenting—cannot prevent their child from being ADD in the first place. What parents do have something to say about, however, is how severe the their child's ADD will be and whether or not comborbid conditions will eventually come along for the ride. By their modeling and training efforts over the long term, parents have a lot to say about how satisfying a life their youngster will have.

14

Medication

A ll parents worry about the idea of their children taking medication for Attention Deficit Disorder. A trusted doctor may have told them that medication for their child would be worth trying, but parents have many questions. Can a medication actually change behavior? If a drug does work, how long will it have to be taken? Can a pill help a child get along with peers or improve performance in sports such as baseball? Do the pills have to be taken every day? What about side effects? Are these medications addictive? Will they suppress appetite or stunt growth? Will *my* child look dazed or drugged?

Some parents (and ADD adults) feel the logic of medication treatment is suspect. Does it make sense to give a controlled substance to a child for a behavioral or emotional problem? Isn't this actually encouraging the youngster to use drugs and thus increasing the later risk of substance abuse? And what is the logic behind giving a stimulant medication to a hyperactive child or to a restless ADD adult in the first place? Won't that simply speed him up even more and result in more trouble?

Parental concern about drug treatment is often heightened by two things: 1) myths about medication treatment that still persist and 2) treatment of the subject by TV, newspapers, magazines and radio. Medication *myths* include the notions that the stimulants used for ADD do no good, that they cause terrible and irreversible side effects, that they are addictive, stunt growth and that they can't be used after mid-adolescence.

Media treatment of the use of medication for ADD, unfortunately, also frequently increases parental worries. Presentations that may appear compelling, factual and objective often show little regard for scientific evidence or longstanding practice. Instead, in the interest of heightening entertainment value, parents see, read or hear stories that focus on controversy, on the unusual and on trouble and misfortune. Positive outcomes do not always make for "good" news.

Balanced against parents' worries about medication is the reality of their ADD child. Concerns about drug treatment are abstract thoughts, but their child is flesh and blood. And it is often all too obvious that ADD is dramatically interfering with his day-to-day functioning, with his overall welfare and with his happiness. He is growing up quickly, he is growing up ADD and his life is not right. He has no friends, but he does have a bad reputation for being too bossy, selfish and aggressive. He hates school and it is obvious—despite her protests to the contrary—that his teacher does not like him. Academically he is falling behind his classmates further and further. Homework is a pitched battle every night. The child does not respond well to discipline and has a terrible time going to sleep. Dad and Mom argue more and more frequently about their son. Dad is becoming more distant and Mom more depressed.

So the dilemma many parents face is this: drug treatment is scary. It is an *unknown* quantity—it hasn't been tried by them. Parents may have been exposed to information about medication treatment that has gone from one extreme to the other.

ADD is also scary, but it is a *known* quantity. Parents realize ADD is already interfering with school performance, home life and peer relationships. It is taking the joy out of their child's growing up and wrecking his self-esteem.

Where should parents start? Mom and Dad should begin by getting some accurate, reliable information about medication treatment for Attention Deficit Disorder. Not information from newspapers, magazines, radio or television, because information found there is too often inaccurate. Many adults consider the media to be a public service of some kind, instead of what it really is: a multitude of *for-profit* operations whose dollar sales depend primarily on entertainment value—not accuracy or scientific precision.

What We Know about Medication Treatment

Several points can help provide significant reassurance about medication treatment for ADD. First of all, stimulant medication treatment for ADD has been extensively researched, so we actually know quite a lot about this kind of therapy. Over two hundred controlled studies have been completed.

Second, two of the most commonly used stimulant medications for ADD, Dexedrine and Ritalin, have been on the market for about fifty years. This longevity would not be possible if these drugs did not help, or if they regularly produced disastrous or even harmful results.

Third, the Food and Drug Administration (FDA), the government agency that approves prescription medications in the United States, is probably the most conservative organization of its kind in the world. The FDA is not perfect, by any means, but it is very cautious. The agency requires that careful research be done by drug manufacturers before a new compound is approved.

What has research told us about stimulants? Research has repeatedly shown that stimulant medication is remarkably effective as well as safe. A stimulant medication (Dexedrine or Ritalin) prescribed for ADD is quite helpful about 75 to 80 percent of the time (Adderall looks like it is equally effective). The stimulant will usually help reduce impulsivity and hyperactivity and it will also help improve concentration by increasing attention span. What's more, if, when starting medication treatment, you try two different stimulants in sequence to see which works best (as you should), the effectiveness statistic for stimulant treatment rises to over 90 percent of the ADD population.

What about side effects? Side effects prevent the continued use of a stimulant medication less than five percent of the time. When side effects do occur, they are usually mild and many disappear over a short period of time. Side effects will almost always disappear after the medications are stopped, though discontinuation is not necessary in most cases. Side effects may also disappear if a different medication is tried. (We'll discuss side effects in more detail in a moment.)

Some people respond to this information by saying, "Kids shouldn't be taking medication in the first place and *any* side effect is too much to have to tolerate." What are these people forgetting? The fact that ADD has its own "side effects." What are we going to do about this child's underachievement in school, miserable home life and lack of friends? When the child is a teenager what are we going to do about his inclination to smoke, drink or engage in antisocial activities?

Over the years research, as well as practice, have also taught us other things about medication treatment for ADD. Medication treatment, for example, is a trial-and-error procedure. Before prescribing a particular drug, we only know the probability that it will succeed. Its exact effects, however, can only be determined by actually trying it for a while. Fortunately, the stimulants (Dexedrine, Adderall, Ritalin) are "quick studies"; the effectiveness of one drug can often be determined in several weeks. But which stimulant is the best one for this child? We have to try at least two to find out.

Ritalin is not the only medication used to treat ADD, nor is it clearly the best medication for ADD. Few people seem to realize this. Ritalin is certainly a good medication, but the effectiveness and the side effect profile of its regular form (three-to-four-hour duration) are probably about the same as the effectiveness and side effect profiles of Dexedrine and Adderall. Ritalin, however, may generally be the *worst* slow- or sustained-release stimulant (five-to-eight-hour duration) preparation, since it only comes in a 20 mg tablet (that should not be broken); with some people it kicks in slowly, with some people it fades too quickly, and with many individuals the potency of the 20 mg SR pill is much weaker than two 10 mg regular tablets taken three to four hours apart.

In other words, Ritalin is simply the most well-known and most frequently used medication for Attention Deficit Disorder. For sustained-release (longer) action, Adderall and slow-release Dexedrine will probably work better with most individuals.

Another thing we have learned is that medication should not be the only intervention for Attention Deficit Disorder. This kind of short-sighted approach ignores the frequent needs for counseling, education about ADD, parent training in behavior management, and school accommodations. These other nonbiological strategies—or the lack of them—can make or break treatment. Because the stimulant meds work so well, people often forget how short-acting they are! Even with three or even four doses per day (of regular forms) or two doses per day (of SR forms), what are you going to do with this kid the rest of the time? What about bedtime and what about getting up and out in the morning?

We also know now that ADD very often is accompanied by other psychiatric or psychological conditions, such as anxiety, depression, bipolar disorder, conduct disorder, oppositional defiant disorder, learning disorders and so on. Education, parent training, school interventions, and sometimes individual counseling can also help with these conditions, and so can certain medications other than the stimulants. These other useful medications frequently are antidepressants, but the group also can include mood stabilizers, antihypertensives and antipsychotics.

Does this mean, then, that an ADD child or adult may wind up taking *two* medications? Yes. And often, when a comorbid condition is present, that non-ADD condition should be treated first before using a stimulant for ADD. Why? Two reasons. First, some comorbid conditions are "ADD look-alikes," and when they are successfully treated, what may have looked like ADD disappears. This type of metamorphosis may happen with bipolar disorder, and sometimes with anxiety or depression. In other words, there really was no comorbidity in the first place. Second, some comorbid conditions (e.g., anxiety, bipolar disorders, sleep disturbances) can be aggravated by stimulant meds. In these cases a stimulant may be inappropriate, or it may still need to be used, but only after another medication is in place.

Before beginning an attempt at drug therapy, however, several things should be discussed with the child, family and/or ADD adult. Any attitudes or opinions these individuals have about the use of medication need to be brought out and listened to sympathetically. Then these ideas must be clarified and discussed, and an attempt made to provide accurate information. All parents are concerned—and some are extremely worried—about the prospect of their child taking any pills at all. ADD adolescents are also much more resistant to taking meds than we ever dreamed. Time should be taken to listen to objections and concerns and to provide the needed information. Understanding the treatment rationale and a knowledge of the potential side effects of different medications are also essential before parents or adults can give valid, informed consent.

Medication Choices

Several kinds of medications have been found to be useful with children and adults who have Attention Deficit Disorder, as well as with those who have ADD plus one or more other psychological disorders. The stimulants Dexedrine, Adderall and Ritalin, have the most powerful anti-ADD effects. (Another stimulant, Cylert, is still available but is no longer considered a first-line drug because of recent concerns about liver toxicity.) The biggest drawback to the stimulants is that their effects don't last very long.

A second category of medications used with ADD individuals is the antidepressants. Drugs such as Tofranil, Norpramin, and Pamelor, which are chemically known as "tricyclic" antidepressants, can actually help with the basic ADD symptoms of inattention, impulsivity and hyperactivity. Their anti-ADD effects are not as potent as those of the stimulants, but they last longer. Tricyclics are also useful for some comorbid conditions, such as sleep disturbances, depression and anxiety.

Most SSRI (selective serotonin reuptake inhibitor) antidepressants, on the other hand, such as Paxil, Zoloft, Prozac and Luvox, don't do as much to combat ADD symptoms (although irritability and emotional overarousal are often reduced). SSRIs, however, are helpful for some comorbid conditions such as depression and anxiety.

Two other antidepresants that have shown some promise with ADD are Effexor (venlafaxine), an SSRI, and Wellbutrin (buprorion), a chemically unique antidepressant that has also recently been used successfully for smoking cessation.

After the antidepressants we have some antihypertensive medications which, it just so happens, can also help with the ADD symptoms of restlessness and overexcitability. These antihypertensives, such as Catapres (clonidine) and the longer-acting Tenex (guanfacine), however, don't seem to help with concentration a whole lot. They are good anti-tic meds, though, and can also help with sleep.

The final category of medications used might be called the "other" category. These meds are often used when ADD isn't the only—or the primary—diagnosis. This list includes drugs such as Tegretol and Depakote (an anticonvulsant), lithium (a natural salt), and Risperdal (a major tranquilizer).

The Stimulants

Many people find it nonsensical that stimulant medications would be able to calm down a hyperactive child, but this is in fact what usually happens. The theory here is that the brain and central nervous system of the ADD person—the "governor" of his behavior—is actually understimulated, or, in a sense, lazy. Because this governor is lazy, chaotic behavior results. It is thought that the stimulants in some way energize the governor to do its job correctly, with the result that the ADD individual is able to be more focused and more organized. There is more and more evidence to support this point of view.

Ritalin. By far the most frequently prescribed drug for ADD is Ritalin (generic name: methylphenidate). Ritalin comes in a 5, 10, and 20 milligram regular form, the effects of which can last generally from three to four hours. After taking the medication, positive effects—if they are going to occur—will show up in approximately fifteen to forty-five minutes, provided the person is at an appropriate dose. The maximum recommended daily intake of Ritalin is 60 mg.

Ritalin also comes in a 20 mg slow-release (SR) form, which is supposed to last seven or eight hours. For many children a big advantage of the SR Ritalin is not having to take a second lunchtime dose during the school day. Unfortunately, although Ritalin SR works fine for some children, it tends to be erratic and should be watched carefully, especially in the beginning. Many kids can't take it because it takes too long to kick in, it fades too quickly, or it just doesn't seem to work at all—even though the regular form of the medication may have worked well.

In addition, for small children (under about sixty pounds) 20 mg is usually too much of a dose and the SR cannot reliably be split. In fact, parents must be careful their kids don't chew this medication, because chewing can make too much of the drug available too quickly. This "rush" can cause either temporary drowsiness or increased hyperactivity.

Also worth watching carefully is the generic form of Ritalin, methylphenidate. Although it is much cheaper, for many kids it does not produce results that are as good as those produced by the brand medication.

Dexedrine. Dexedrine (generic name: dextroamphetamine) has a track record, with regard to benefits and side effects, that is just as good as that of its more famous sister, Ritalin. For some reason, though, Dexedrine is not used as often, with the result that many kids suffer. Remember that we can't tell which stimulant is best for a child until we try them.

The regular form of Dexedrine comes only in a 5 mg tablet which lasts about four hours and which kicks in about as fast as Ritalin. The maximum recommended dosage of Dexedrine per day is 40 milligrams. Milligram for milligram, Dexedrine is about twice as strong as Ritalin (e.g., 10 mg of Ritalin equals 5 mg of Dexedrine). This should be taken into account when switching from one of these medications to the other.

Dexedrine also comes in 5, 10, and 15 mg slow-release capsules called "spansules." This form of the drug can last approximately six to nine hours. Dexedrine SR seems to be more reliable than Ritalin SR, and should be considered as a possibility much more frequently than it is. Unfortunately, it is occasionally difficult to find the medication in stock at the friendly neighborhood pharmacy, but this problem can usually be solved when the pharmacy knows in advance what a family will need. With the Dexedrine spansules the flexibility of having three different dose sizes is also an important advantage.

Adderall. Adderall is the new kid on the stimulant block, and actually had a prior use for weight reduction in the 1950s. So far this medication is showing very promising results. Adderall is actually made up of four different amphetamines. The manufacturers of Adderall wanted to produce a medication that lasted longer and that also could be divided into smaller pieces so that dosing could be more individualized. Therefore,

Adderall comes in 5 mg, 10 mg, 20 mg and 30 mg tablets, all of which are double-scored so they can be broken into two or four pieces. This makes fine tuning a dose very convenient—though fine tuning is not done as often as it should be. In terms of potency, Adderall dosages are considered to be roughly equivalent to those of Dexedrine SR spansules.

For some physicians, Adderall is now their first choice among the stimulant medications. Doctors cite two reasons for this selection. First of all, Adderall lasts longer. One study, for example, found that Adderall lasted 30 percent longer than the regular form of Ritalin. Some doctors, though, have found that it can last six hours or longer with some children and adults. Second, Adderall's side effect profile may be "softer" than that of the other two stimulants. Adderall seems to leave the system more slowly, for example, so that the side effect of "rebound" is less of a problem.

We'll learn more about Adderall as more research is done. But at this point this new medication is a very useful addition to our medication toolbox.

Cylert. Another available stimulant medication is Cylert (generic: pemoline). Studies have shown that Cylert takes longer to work than Dexedrine or Ritalin. In spite of the recent concern about liver toxicity, Cylert is still used on occasion if the other stimulants have not worked or if the person who is to take the medication has a history of substance abuse (Cylert has no abuse potential).

Cylert is different from the other stimulants in several respects. First, it comes in strange doses, the smallest pill being 18.75 mg. There is also a 37.5 mg tablet and a 75 mg tablet. Cylert is only a long-acting medication, and when it works its effects can last nine to twelve hours (some say even longer). This can certainly be an advantage if the medication stays around long enough to help with homework! Cylert may kick in a little more slowly than the other stimulants, and the maximum recommended dose per day is 112.5 mg.

Unlike Ritalin and Dexedrine, Cylert must be taken every day to maintain adequate blood levels. It can also take up to three weeks or so for it to begin working, even if the appropriate dose has been reached. We estimate that 37.5 mg of Cylert is about the equivalent of 20 mg of Ritalin (or 10 mg of regular Dexedrine). Since the warning about liver toxicity appeared, however, and since monitoring liver enzymes requires blood testing (which requires needles!), Cylert is no longer considered as a first choice stimulant.

The Stimulant Titration (Adjustment) Process

Too often stimulant medications are not prescribed and adjusted in ways that make sense. Overdosing, underdosing, improper titration and lack of titration are still all too common. Mistakes like these can result not only in poor results but also in uncomfortable side effects and noncompliance.

Before beginning stimulants, several important considerations should be kept in mind:

1. The use of a particular medication in the beginning is only a *trial*, not a sure thing or a lifetime project. Which medication will work best is unknown, and it is very important that a proper diagnosis has been made.

2. Any child or adult about to take psychotropic medications for Attention Deficit should have had a recent *physical exam* that is relevant to the medications being considered. A baseline blood pressure for example, would be important before Dexedrine or Tenex is used, a baseline EKG is usually recommended before using one of the tricyclics, and a liver function should be completed before using Cylert. There should be no other medical conditions that might complicate treatment.

3. Sometimes there are contraindications for certain medications right off the bat. The presence of psychosis, for example, rules out the use of any stimulant in any child. Certain cardiac problems require caution when using stimulants or tricyclic antidepressants. Limited ability of a family to follow through with medication administration can also be a serious drawback. Other patients or a family member may have a history of drug abuse, so the use of Schedule II drugs must be reconsidered or even eliminated as a possibility.

4. Medication is *not a cure*. Medication should not be used by itself, but should be combined with other needed treatments, such as counseling, school interventions and parent training. Many parents who have kids successfully taking stimulant meds know how difficult mornings before school and evenings—with homework and bedtime—can still be!

Which drug should you begin with? With uncomplicated ADD (no comorbid conditions), the answer is a stimulant: Dexedrine, Adderall or Ritalin. After an adequate trial of one drug is completed, a second medication ought to be tried unless the results with the first were positively dramatic (which they often are). Too many people think Ritalin is the only game in town. Dexedrine has been, in a sense, the "forgotten" drug in the treatment of ADD, and now we also have Adderall to consider. Different children respond differently to the different stimulants, as yet we have no way—other than medication trials—to determine which drug is best for which child. Recent studies indicate that if careful trials were to be done with at least two stimulant medications with each ADD child or adult, the positive response rate might increase to 90 percent! Although the multiple-trial procedure is obviously the best way to go, there is still considerable difficulty getting prescribing physicians, who still lean too heavily on Ritalin alone, to cooperate with the process.

Let's take a look at a good way of starting, adjusting and managing medication. How would you determine the right starting dose of Ritalin, for example? Research indicates that a *very general* rule of thumb for Ritalin is that .5 milligrams per kilogram (2.2 pounds) of bodyweight will be an appropriate therapeutic dose—if the medication works. This is only a general guideline, of course, because children vary so much in terms of their medication sensitivity.

You can use this formula to guess what might be the most helpful, or therapeutic, dose. Then after you have made that estimate, you start the child out on a *slightly lower* dose. This tactic gives the child a chance to get used to the meds gradually, protecting those children who might be more sensitive.

One way to calculate the dosage is this: take the child's weight in pounds and divide it by four. That will give you the total daily amount for the morning and lunch doses together (but not including any after school "boosters"). You might expect an 80-pound child, for example, to do well with about 20 mg (80/4) per day, 10 mg in the morning and 10 mg at lunchtime.

You would not start the child on a 10/10 regime right away, however. You would drop down to 5 mg per dose, to be on the safe side. This 5/5 dose would then be tried for three to five days. If there were no beneficial effects and no side effects, the dosage would then be increased to 10/10. If no positive or negative effects are noticed in another three to five days, the dose would be increased again by 5 milligram increments. This adjustment continues until one of three things happens: 1) a good therapeutic effect is achieved, 2) side effects occur which can't be tolerated, or 3) the recommended limit of 60 mg per day is reached. The 60 mg "limit" is a flexible guideline, not a law. Older and larger children sometimes take more.

What if the child is smaller, say 40 pounds? Divide 40 by 4 and you get approximately 10, so you might expect the best dose to be 5 mg in the morning and 5 at lunch. You still do not want to start right at 5 mg with a small child, so the pills should be broken in half, providing doses of 2.5 mg each. Then you go three to five days on that dose, and if no benefits or side effects are seen, you increase the dosage by increments of 2.5 milligrams. For children under sixty pounds, 5 mg jumps in dosage are often too much.

Dexedrine is about twice as strong as Ritalin, milligram-for-milligram, so Dexedrine doses would be about half what you would use according to the formulas above. Adderall doses are comparable to Dexedrine slow-release doses.

Note several things about the medication titration process described here. First of all, for stimulant medications the trial period for one particular dosage is relatively short, three to five days. If a doctor says take this dose and call me in a month, you may wind up wasting three weeks, which isn't funny when the child is terrorizing both school and home. Second, you do not simply come up with a body weight estimate of the dosage and then sit on it forever. You start lower, and then go carefully upward. Sometimes the therapeutic dose exceeds the original rough estimate. Our 80-pounder, for example, might wind up taking 15 or even 20 mg of Ritalin (or perhaps 10 mg of Dexedrine) per dose. Third, frequent monitoring of the medication's effects is essential, especially in the beginning. Monitoring can be accomplished by using symptom checklists, side effect checklists and followup interviews. Legitimate criticism of medication treatment is most often based upon poor follow-up.

What about medication holidays? Medication holidays are days on which the child doesn't take the pills. Some children with ADD do not take the stimulant medications after school, on weekends or during summer vacations. This is becoming more and more unusual, however, because most ADD kids need the medication during those times. For most ADD children, stimulant medication therapy is not "just for school." The effects of meds on behavioral difficulties, social functioning and special situations (vacations, scout meetings, Sunday school, family picnics, etc.) should also be examined. Medication may assist with—but should never be a replacement for—sound discipline and training.

It is amazing, though, how many people still think stimulant medications are no help with a child's social life. Research now clearly shows that stimulants help *most* ADD children to get along better with their peers. While it may be true that no medication will "teach" a child social skills right on the spot, these drugs can help the child calm down, and be less impulsive and pushy. Very often the ADD child simply becomes a whole lot less irritating to others. In a child where this important benefit occurs, it seems grossly unfair to let the youngster go out and play during the summer or after school without the medication.

Some ADD kids, on the other hand, can get along fairly well outside of school not taking the medication. They may take it only now and then for special situations. This "PRN"—or as needed—use can be a lot of help to everyone, and it may not require a lot of extra doses. With the approval of the prescribing physician, of course, using the medication for short periods of time to help manage things like long rides in the car, birthday parties, soccer and the annual family picnic may be a very good idea.

Stimulants: Possible Good Effects

Just about any symptom of ADD can be helped temporarily by stimulant medication. There is no guarantee, however, since medication treatment is a trial-and-error process. Though kids react differently, research shows that the following benefits do occur regularly:

- Improved attention span
- Reduced impulsivity

- Less hyperactivity and restlessness
- Improved grades
- Less aggressiveness
- Less noisiness
- More cooperation with requests
- Less disruptive behavior in the classroom
- Better performance in some sports (soccer, baseball)

Although the child's IQ itself does not increase due to the medication, the child's school grades will usually improve. Oddly enough, though, a number of studies have showed that even with prolonged (over several years) medication therapy, scores on standardized achievement tests do not, on the average, improve for ADD kids.

Stimulants: Possible Side Effects

More than 95 percent of the ADD children who take stimulant medications do not experience side effects which prevent them from continuing drug therapy (provided the medication also works). In addition, negative reactions that do occur usually occur in the beginning of treatment, and they almost always disappear with the discontinuation of the drug or a switch to another stimulant.

The list of unwanted side effects associated with stimulants includes the following:

- Appetite suppression: very common but most often tolerable; significant weight loss is not usually a problem
- Insomnia: rare when meds are titrated properly
- Headache: can occur in the beginning of therapy, usually goes away
- Stomachache: same as above
- Sadness/irritability: rarer, but may necessitate discontinuation; watch carefully for this in adolescents, where it may cause noncompliance
- Drowsiness: usually a sign—believe it or not—that *too much* medication is being taken

- Increased hyperactivity: fairly rare
- Tics: oddly enough, stimulants may aggravate or reduce tics, depending upon the child

Some parents report a kind of "backlash" or "rebound" problem with kids taking Ritalin or Dexedrine. Backlash often occurs after school right about the time the boy or girl is returning home. What seems to happen is that as the medication is leaving the child's system, the youngster may become extremely irritable, sometimes teary, harder to manage and often much worse than his or her regular ADD self. This difficult period often lasts less than an hour, but some parents have reported that in some kids it seems to go on all evening. In those cases it's hard to tell if this is due to a continuing, internal chemical adjustment or if the bad start to the evening itself did irrecoverable damage.

Rebound occurs with perhaps 20 percent or so of those children who take stimulants. There are several ways to try to manage it. Some parents just try to stay out of the youngster's way during the dangerous half hour after school. This is not the time, Mom and Dad have learned, to ask him about homework or to demand that he clean his room! More often, however, adding a smaller booster dose (about half the size of the last school dose) can help carry the child safely into the evening (and help with homework). When a booster dose is used, backlash doesn't usually occur at dinnertime. With other children reducing the last dose in the school day may make some difference with rebound, but one must be careful that concentration and behavioral benefits are not compromised at school.

As usual, solving the problem of rebound is a trial and error procedure. As mentioned before, some doctors feel Adderall has less likelihood of producing rebound, since it both enters and leaves the system more gradually than Ritalin and Dexedrine.

Discontinuing Stimulant Medication Therapy

ADD children who benefit from stimulants will need to continue taking these medications for a number of years—most likely through high school and college. This idea follows logically from the fact that ADD is not something that will be outgrown, as well as from the fact that meds do not cure the disorder. Unfortunately, some children will discontinue drug therapy prematurely because their parents saw a misguided news show on TV, or because grandma read a disturbing article in a magazine and began giving Mom substantial grief about her child's "taking drugs." The amount of personal, human tragedy caused by such unfortunate decisions is impossible to calculate.

A very small number of ADD children will be able to discontinue meds—for the right reasons—while they are still in school. How this happens we are not sure, since ADD is normally not outgrown or cured by treatment. Perhaps these children are extremely intelligent, have only marginal cases of ADD, or were diagnosed very early. Perhaps, while on the medication, they also learned a bunch of new habits and compensatory skills that were powerfully reinforced.

Many professionals recommend trying a child off stimulant medication every year or so to see if she can be successful on her own. If you consider taking this step, several rules should apply in order to make the holiday most beneficial as well as least aggravating:

First, the periods off stimulant medication should be very short: no more than a few days to a week. Sometimes all you need is one or two days to tell you emphatically that things are not working! Don't punish the child and everyone else by keeping him off the medication.

Second, explain to the child what you are doing, and that there is a very good possibility that he will need to continue using the medication. Sometimes we tell children, "You'll get one vote, your teachers get one vote, and your parents get one vote." It's obvious, therefore, that the child might get outvoted. With adolescents, of course, this is a trickier process.

Third, sometimes "accidental medication holidays" have already told parents and teachers that the child is not ready to go off medication. An accidental medication holiday occurs when the child goes to school after forgetting to take the medication in the morning. Many parents under these circumstances are *guaranteed* of a call from the school, because the child's behavior and attention are suddenly so much worse.

Fourth, never in September! *Never do a medication holiday in the beginning of the school year if the child was doing well with the medication at the end of the previous year*. This idiotic idea has ruined school years for countless children, teachers and parents. Let the child start out the new year on the best foot, then consider trying him off meds in November or February (not December because of holiday excitement).

Summary: First Choice Stimulants

Adderall (mixed salts of a single-entity amphetamine)
Dexedrine (generic name: dextroamphctaminc)
Ritalin (generic name: methylphenidate)

Adderall
DOSES AVAILABLE
    5, 10, 20, 30 mg (each tablet is double-scored)
DURATION OF ACTION
    5 to 7 hours

Dexedrine
DOSES AVAILABLE
    5 mg-regular
    5, 10, 15 mg-slow-release
DURATION OF ACTION
    regular: 3 to 5 hours
    slow-release: 5 to 9 hours

Ritalin
DOSES AVAILABLE
    5, 10, 20 mg (regular)
    20 mg (slow-release)
DURATION OF ACTION
    regular: 3 to 4 hours
    slow-release: 5 to 7 hours

Adderall, Dexedrine, Ritalin
EXPECTED BENEFITS
    Improved attention
    Calmer
    Reduced impulsivity
    More cooperative

POSSIBLE SIDE EFFECTS (Stimulants)
Reduced appetite
Headache and stomachache
Irritability/Sadness
"Rebound" (probably less with Adderall)
Insomnia

The Antidepressants

Another kind of medication used with Attention Deficit Disorder is the antidepressant. As we saw before, there are two major kinds of antidepressants: tricyclics and SSRIs. Tricyclics can help with ADD and comorbid conditions, but they are sometimes less used because of side effects. SSRIs usually help only with comorbid disorders—not with the symptoms of ADD. SSRIs are known for having fewer side effects than tricyclics—except, perhaps with teens. Both kinds of antidepressants have a longer duration of action (one or two doses can cover a whole day) that sometimes makes them more attractive than the shorter-acting stimulants.

The tricyclic antidepressants, such as Tofranil (generic: imipramine), Norpramin (generic: desipramine), or Pamelor (nortryptiline) may be given consideration in several different situations. The first situation is where the stimulants have not been successful or have produced side effects that could not be tolerated. (Be careful here, though, because too often stimulant trials merely follow the "Ritalin-or-nothing" program—totally ignoring the existence of Adderall and Dexedrine.) A difficult ADD child who does not respond to any stimulant presents a vexing problem to himself and others, and many times the antidepressants can help quite a bit.

There is another situation in which antidepressants might be the first medications to be tried: when a child is also experiencing a good deal of anxiety or depression. Antidepressants, of course, were originally intended to deal with depression, but they can also have a significant effect on anxiety. An SSRI antidepressant is likely to be tried first with an anxious or depressed child, especially if the presence of ADD is not clear. Tricyclics, on the other hand, are often more helpful with sleep.

In a third instance, a tricyclic antidepressant may help when a stimulant is already being used, but the benefits from the stimulant simply last too short a period of time. Some children, for example, do well on a stimulant medication during the day, but these kids are still holy terrors at night in spite of the best parental efforts at firm management. To cover these evening periods—and perhaps even the difficult mornings—medications like imipramine and desipramine can be helpful.

Many of the tricyclic antidepressants come in 10, 25, 50 and 100 mg sizes, as well as larger pills. Adults taking these medications for depression can usually achieve consistent therapeutic blood levels after three weeks or so by taking the medication only once a day. Some children can do this, but because of their higher metabolism kids may require dosing of two or three times a day. In order to maintain blood levels these drugs should be taken every day, seven days a week. Even though they are not addictive in any way, sudden discontinuation can cause temporary, flu-like symptoms (e.g., headache, nausea) and anxiety.

There seem to be differing opinions as to how long it takes the tricyclic antidepressants to kick in after beginning therapy. It is often predicted that it will take ten to fourteen days before results are seen, but this prediction may be largely based on data gathered from the treatment of adult depressed patients. With children results are often seen sooner, but "results" can mean different things. Within a few days many children will sleep better with a tricyclic antidepressant. Anti-anxiety, antidepressant and anti-ADD effects, however, may take a little longer to appear.

Therapeutic doses with the tricyclics have been found in the ranges between one to five milligrams/kilogram per day (Pamelor, though, is about twice as strong as Norpramin and Tofranil). A 75-pound youngster, for example, taking 100 mg of Tofranil each day would be at approximately the 3 mg/kg level. Initially tricyclics were dispensed rather liberally, with higher doses not uncommon. Then it seemed that most physicians were reluctant to exceed the 3 mg/kg point, due to concerns about possible cardiac side effects. The general feeling today is that higher than 3 mg/kg doses are often necessary to achieve a therapeutic blood level, but that any treatment with tricyclics should be accompanied by appropriate cardiac monitoring, such as baseline and follow-up EKGs and blood testing. Sometimes benefits from tricyclics appear to stop after a period of time, but clinical experience shows that gradually increasing the dose can result in improvement that lasts.

Tricyclic antidepressants can produce behavioral effects similar to those produced by the stimulants. With the antidepressants, though, these effects may last longer. Studies have reported the positive effects to include reductions in hyperactivity, impulsivity and sometimes aggression. Parents often report that children taking antidepressants are more compliant and their moods are more stable. Some of these medications have also helped with things like bed-wetting, night terrors and sleepwalking.

Concentration improvements that do occur with the tricyclics are not as dramatic as those resulting from stimulants. For this reason, some children will take a stimulant *and* an antidepressant concurrently. The stimulant provides concentration benefits during the school day, while the antidepressant may help with behavior *all day*.

Side effects with tricyclic antidepressants can include the "anticholinergic effects," such as dry mouth, constipation and blurred vision. Nausea and drowsiness are also possible. Many people react poorly to these side effects, and as a result compliance with tricyclics is often a problem. There has also been a good deal of concern about possible cardiovascular side effects of the tricyclics. Minor increases in blood pressure, pulse and cardiac conduction times are not uncommon, but these effects are usually not associated with physical discomfort. Though there is still disagreement about the utility of the EKG in this situation, a baseline EKG is usually recommended before starting therapy with tricyclic antidepressants, and the EKG is often repeated with dose increases.

Summary: Tricyclic Antidepressants

Tofranil (imipramine)
Norpramin (desipramine)
Pamelor (nortriptyline)

Tricyclic Antidepressants
DOSES AVAILABLE
10, 25, 50, 100 mg
DOSES PER DAY
1 to 3 times

Tricyclic Antidepressants
EXPECTED BENEFITS
  More cooperative
  Less impulsive
  Calmer
  Better concentration
  Mood improvement
  Reduced anxiety
Tricyclic Antidepressants
POSSIBLE SIDE EFFECTS
  Dry mouth
  Drowsiness
  Blurred vision
  Dizziness
  Constipation
  Cardiac irregularities

Wellbutrin

Wellbutrin (bupropion) is a newer antidepressant that does not chemically fall into either the tricyclic or SSRI class. Wellbutrin has been shown to be useful with both ADD children and ADD adults. Since it is an antidepressant, this medication can also be helpful with depression and possibly with anxiety disorders. Dosing for adults is usually divided during the day and may go up to 300 mg or more.

There may be a certain "kind" of ADD individual who responds especially well to Wellbutrin, but as yet we cannot predict exactly who these people will be. An interesting phenomenon can occur with this medication. Bupropion, in its slow-release or long-acting form, is the same drug that is known as Zyban—the drug that has been recently marketed to help people stop smoking. A number of individuals, not diagnosed as ADD, have taken Zyban for smoking and have noticed improvements in both their concentration and their mood. These changes, of course, suggest the possibility that either ADD and/or mood disorder may have existed in these persons and was being "accidentally" treated by bupropion. This phenomenon is more interesting since we do know that both ADD as well as mood disorders frequently lead to smoking, which for some people may provide both concentration and mood regulation effects.

Antihypertensives: Catapres and Tenex

A third category of medications that may help with some ADD symptoms includes some antihypertensive drugs. Catapres (generic: clonidine) and Tenex (generic: guanfacine) are actually medications used primarily for people with high blood pressure. While this may sound odd—using an antihypertensive for Attention Deficit—it is probably no more conceptually strange than using a stimulant or an antidepressant.

What type of ADD children might be considered candidates for antihypertensives? According to some writers, the optimal responders are highly aroused ADD children who are very overactive, extremely energetic and who have very low frustration tolerance. Children who experience explosive outbursts as well as ADD kids who also are conduct disordered may benefit. Parents and teachers described ADD children on antihypertensives as more cooperative, more willing to complete homework, more willing to carry on conversations, and as having better frustration tolerance.

Antihypertensives are also sometimes considered when the stimulants either don't work or don't work well enough. In the latter case, the antihypertensives have been combined with stimulant medication therapy. Keep in mind that the stimulants are better when it comes to helping with attention and distractibility, though at this point there are suggestions that Tenex may produce some concentration benefits. The two medications appear quite similar, but clonidine has been more researched than Tenex.

Two other considerable benefits that antihypertensives can provide include reducing tics and assisting with sleep. Clonidine and Tenex can safely be used when tics accompany stimulant use, and can also help when stimulants make it more difficult for a child to sleep or—as is the case with many ADD kids—when the child simply has trouble falling asleep in the first place.

As with medication treatment in general, follow-up and careful monitoring are critical, especially when an antihypertensive is used along with a stimulant. Some people feel that the generic (clonidine) is some-times not as effective as the brand medication (Catapres). The maximal effects of clonidine, if they occur, may not be evident for one to two months. Now that's a slow kick-in period! Often there are initial side effects of sleepiness and lightheadedness, but these subside after a few weeks and the patient remains calm and alert. A gradual maturation may unfold as the child is able to calmly apply his strengths to the problems of living. Some parents say they're not sure if it's the medication or if the child has simply "grown up some and matured the way he's supposed to."

Doses of clonidine sound extremely low, but remember that you cannot equate milligrams across different medications. An average 10-year-old may start on as low as .05 mg (1/2 tablet) of clonidine once a day for three days, gradually building up to 0.2 to 0.3 mg per day. Clonidine also comes in skin patches, which can be worn on the back. The skin patches can survive showers and sweating, but often produce skin rashes.

Tenex has the advantage of lasting longer than clonidine, so that two doses per day may be required instead of four. That can make life a lot easier. Daily doses range from .5 mg per day to about 3 mg per day.

Antihypertensives should not generally be used with children who may be depressed or have a history of depression, children who are psychotic or have thought disorders, and kids who might qualify as Inattentive Types. Blood pressure is obviously a concern and should be monitored carefully.

Clonidine and Tenex are promising medications. Their ability to reduce hyperactivity and impulsivity, and to increase frustration tolerance around-the-clock is attractive, especially since the stimulants do not last all day and often cannot be given at night.

Summary: Antihypertensive Medications

Catapres (clonidine)
Tenex (guanfacine)

Catapres
DOSES AVAILABLE
Tablets:
0.1 mg (one-tenth mg)
DOSES PER DAY
3 to 4 times

Catapres Patch (Transdermal Therapeutic System):
TTS-1 0.1mg/day/1 week
TTS-2 0.2mg/day/1 week
TTS-3 0.3mg/day/1 week

Tenex
DOSES AVAILABLE
1 mg and 2 mg
(Tenex) DOSES PER DAY
2 (teenagers)
4 (younger children)

Antihypertensive Medications
EXPECTED BENEFITS
 Less impulsivity
 Reduced hyperactivity
 Better frustration tolerance
 Less irritability
 Increased cooperativeness
 Improved sleep
 Tic reduction

Antihypertensive Medications
POSSIBLE SIDE EFFECTS (all generally lower with Tenex)
 Fatigue/drowsiness

Dry mouth

Lower blood pressure

Sedation

Dizziness

Depression

Sleep disturbance

Medications for Comorbid Conditions

Oppositional Defiant Disorder

Children with ODD present extreme behavior management difficulties, and medications are usually less helpful. Stimulants can help with hyperactivity, impulsivity and sometimes emotional overarousal. Stimulants may also help these children focus in a way that improves compliance.

Stimulant treatment for ODD children has its limitations, however. The early mornings and evenings, when these meds are not operating, may still present problems. Side effects must also be monitored carefully. An ODD child may experience rebound after school or get more irritable and depressed when on the drug. ODD is bad enough by itself. Sometimes trying another stimulant may help, or adding a booster after school for rebound.

Many ODD kids experience an underlying mood disorder, so that antidepressants can sometimes be useful. The changes in some children who are treated with a tricyclic or SSRI can be quite dramatic. They may become less irritable, more cooperative and even more affectionate!

Conduct Disorder

As is the case with ODD, there is no one medication that is a surefire help for conduct disorder in children. We certainly wish there were. When underlying mood disorders are part of the picture, antidepressants can help. Sometimes bipolar disorder is involved in delinquent behavior. In these cases the bipolar condition should be treated first (see below).

Stimulants can help CD kids who are also ADD, but the risks of drug abuse or drug diversion must be kept in mind with this population. Cylert again becomes one option in these situations. Some clinicians have also had luck with Risperdal (risperidone) or Zyprexa (olanzapine) with aggressive children or "CD-to-be" kids. Though these "antipsychotic" medications do little for most ADD symptoms, in some situations they seem to reduce irritability and impulsive, antisocial acting out as well as explosive and/or aggressive bursts of temper. (Catapres may help as well with these kinds of youngsters.) One must keep an eye out, however, for the possibility that the sedating effects of an antipsychotic may actually make concentration worse. One may then be confronted with the question, "Which is the worse of the two evils: antisocial aggression or poorer attention?"

Anxiety

SSRI antidepressants, such as Prozac, Zoloft, Paxil and Luvox may be the treatment of choice with most anxiety disorders. These medications are safe, have fewer side effects, and can often provide round-the-clock coverage. Luvox has been shown to be effective with symptoms of Obsessive Compulsive Disorder.

Tricyclics have also been used for anxiety. Tofranil, for example, was often used for what used to be called School Phobia. In the past tricyclics have also been used in the treatment of panic disorders.

Buspar (buspirone) has been used successfully for anxiety in children. One of its attractions is that it is not a benzodiazepine, but a drawback is the fact that its effects may not appear for several weeks.

When a condition such as Generalized Anxiety Disorder (formerly Overanxious Disorder of Childhood) is thought to possibly coexist with ADD, the GAD is usually treated first. The reason for this is because poor concentration and restlessness can be caused sometimes by anxiety alone, and what looked like ADD may disappear with the successful treatment of the anxiety. Another reason for treating anxiety first is the fact that stimulants may produce a side effect of *increased* anxiety, especially in older kids.

Depression

The SSRI antidepressants are the ones usually thought of first for depression. Although they are more expensive than the tricyclics, they generally have fewer side effects, and help with depression about 75 percent of the time. Side effects of SSRIs can include agitation, changes in weight, nausea and increased anxiety in children and teens.

If a child's "depression" appears to be only school-related and ADD is also involved, stimulant treatment is begun first. Many of these children are gloomy only on Sunday nights and on school days and evenings. Their mood picks up on Friday night as well as before and during vacations. When a stimulant helps significantly with school, the mood of these kids shows a corresponding improvement.

When ADD appears to be involved, but the child's depression is more pervasive and consistent, the depression should be treated first. As is the case with anxiety, poor concentration and restlessness can be caused sometimes by depression alone, and the ADD "symptoms" may remit with the resolution of the depression.

Other children will still show ADD symptoms, such as difficulty focusing in school, even after their depression is gone. In such cases stimulants may be added to the antidepressant treatment.

Bipolar Disorders

Some experts feel that over 90 percent of bipolar youngsters also meet criteria for ADD, i.e., they are inattentive, restless and impulsive. When these children are younger, stimulants may actually be safely used to combat these symptoms. As bipolar children get older, however, they begin to show greater variations in mood—from hypomanic to dysphoric. Bipolar disorder worsens with age, and as it does the risk of a stimulant— or an antidepressant —medication triggering a manic episode increases.

To avoid this risk, stimulants or antidepressants should not be used first with bipolar kids, especially older children. Instead, "mood stabilizers" should be used in the beginning. Mood stabilizers include lithium as well as anticonvulsant medications: Tegretol (carbamazepine), Depakote (valproic acid) and Nerontin (gabapentin). Because of the long-term effects of lithium on the liver, kidneys and thyroid (as well as more immediate side effects), many physicians prefer to use the anticonvulsants.

If treatment is successful in stabilizing mood and if ADD "symptoms" also go away, there is no need for stimulant medication. Many children, however, are both ADD and bipolar. In these cases stimulants should be added to the mood stabilizers.

Tics

The treatment of ADD and comorbid tic disorders has been an area of recent interest. For many years it was thought that stimulants could not be used in patients who also had a tic disorder, or that stimulants had to be discontinued when tics occurred with stimulant treatment. Now these notions have been challenged.

Studies have shown, for example, that not all people with a tic disorder have their tics worsened by stimulant treatment. On the contrary, 70 to 80 percent of tic patients show no change in their symptoms while taking stimulant drugs. Sometimes the stimulants even seem to reduce the severity of the tics.

Research also seems to show that although tic disorders and ADD often go together, they run separate courses. For many individuals their tics are going to run their course—often getting worse and then better with age—no matter what is done about the ADD. In addition, ADD-tic comorbidity—unlike other comorbidities—does not worsen the prognosis for an individual.

What has also been realized more recently is that when tics do occur, they are *usually* mild to moderate, and not a significant interference with a person's life. Barking or swearing loudly in a room full of people, for example, is not a common behavior of tic sufferers. How much tics interfere, of course, depends not only on the tic itself, but on the perception of the person with the tic and his or her family and friends.

Therefore, the following alternatives for medication treatment are considered when both ADD and tics (or the possibility of tics) are present:

1. Stimulants may still be tried with an ADD individual who has tics or who has a family history of tics.
2. If tics occur with treatment, they may be tolerated (if mild to moderate) or a non-stimulant medication (e.g., Tenex, clonidine, Haldol) may be added to the treatment.

3. If tics occur with treatment, a stimulant medication may be replaced by a tricyclic antidepressant. Tricyclics, as we have seen, often help with ADD symptoms and may also be "tic neutral," i.e., they have no effect on the tics.

Sleep Disorders

About 30 percent of our ADD children will have sleep problems, usually difficulties that involve getting to sleep. According to clinical psychologist Dr. Tom Brown of Yale University, the first approach to the problem should be nonmedical. Sleep "hygiene," he says should be restructured. There should be a regular bedtime, and a regular and calming routine for preparing for bed. Floor fans, or other noise or music machines, for example, are sometimes helpful.

If going to sleep remains a problem, Dr. Brown suggests trying the antihistamine Benadryl first. The Benadryl should be taken one to one-and-one-half hours before bed. If Benadryl doesn't work or can't be taken regularly, the next alternative he suggests is clonidine. Surprisingly, there are also some ADD kids who go to sleep better when they take a small dose of a short-acting stimulant a half hour or so before bed.

Learning Disabilities

There is no research, unfortunately, indicating that there are any effective medications for learning disabilities. It may be true, however, that 30 percent or more of LD children may also be ADD. How many of these LD kids have been given a trial of medication?

Avoiding Medication Mistakes

As we have seen, the use of medication can be one of the most dramatically helpful parts of the multimodal treatment package. In order to maximize effectiveness, certain errors must be avoided. The most common are the following:

1. Inadequate prior medical histories or physical exams
2. Not trying any medication at all

3. Inadequate follow-up, both during the critical initial titration phase as well as long-term

4. Ambivalence about using drugs. Mixed feelings due to poor information, for example, can cause mistakes such as underdosing with a potentially helpful medication, or the discontinuation of any attempt at drug therapy after only one drug has been tried.

5. Underdosing or overdosing due to strict adherence to bodyweight formulas

6. Overlooking family problems or comorbid diagnoses

7. Summertime medication holidays that ruin a child's social and family life

8. Medication holidays right when a child returns to school in September

9. Stopping medication abruptly without talking to one's doctor

10. Believing that medication cannot be used when the diagnosis is ADD, Inattentive Type. Most Inattentive children benefit greatly from stimulants.

11. Discontinuing medication simply because a child has hit midadolescence; people can still benefit from medication at age 18, 30 or 50.

12. Using only one medication when more than one would be most helpful

Medication can be one of the most potent parts of the treatment package for Attention Deficit Disorder. Always remember, though, that medications should be used in conjunction with education about ADD, counseling when necessary, parent training, school or work adjustments, and appropriate social interventions.

15

Working with the School

Patricia A. Graczyk, Ph.D.

Because symptoms of ADD are often most evident in the school environment, parents of children with ADD need to interact with school personnel on a more frequent and intense basis than other parents. It is important, therefore, that parents become informed of the legal, procedural and intervention options that may be available through their child's school. The purpose of this chapter is to provide a broad overview of such topics and inform parents of ways they may work together with school staff to insure that their children are provided with positive school experiences throughout their academic careers, including college.

In recent years, many positive events have occurred that have increased the likelihood that children with ADD will be successful in school and that their parents will be able to function as active partners with school staff in making decisions relative to their academic program. These include the following:

1. The U.S. Department of Education issued a memorandum to all state and local educational agencies which stated that students with ADD may be eligible for support services in school under Public Law 101-476, the Individuals with Disabilities Education Act of 1990 (IDEA), or

Section 504 of the Vocational Rehabilitation Act of 1973 (commonly referred to as Section 504).

2. Several well-written resource manuals for teachers are now available that include a compilation of school interventions for children with ADD (e.g., CHADD's Educators Manual).

3. More teachers are aware of ADD and the needs of children with ADD who are placed in their classrooms.

4. Educators have a greater awareness that effective home-school partnerships are necessary to ensure that students are successful in school.

5. A wealth of information regarding ADD is now available via the Internet.

IDEA and Section 504

In 1975 Congress passed Public Law 94-142 (PL 94- 142), the "Education for all Handicapped Children Act." This important law (and its downward extension, Public Law 99-457) guaranteed that children with disabilities were entitled to a free and appropriate public education. This law also established procedural guidelines to protect the rights of children with disabilities. When 94-142 was reauthorized in 1990, it was renamed the Individuals with Disabilties Education Act (IDEA).

Both PL 94-142 and IDEA delineate the handicapping conditions they cover. Students with ADD who are found eligible for services or programs under IDEA are frequently served under the categories of learning disabilities, seriously emotionally disturbed or "other health impaired." In the IDEA Amendments of 1997, the definition of "other health impaired" was expanded to specifically include "attention deficit disorder" and "attention deficit hyperactivity disorder" as two conditions that may render children eligible for special education support, if the condition adversely affects their alertness to the educational environment and their educational performance.

If students with ADD do not qualify for support through IDEA, they may still be eligible through Section 504. A student with ADD would be eligible for school adaptations and interventions under Section 504 if it is determined that ADD substantially interfered with a "major life activity," such as learning.

Both IDEA and Section 504 require a school district to conduct an evaluation to determine if a student has a handicapping condition that warrants educational interventions. In the IDEA '97 revisions, "parent input" has been added to the list of sources from which the public schools should seek information in order to determine a child's eligibility for special education support. Both IDEA and Section 504 require that interventions be implemented in the "least restrictive environment." This assures that the student's educational program differs from the standard educational program only to the extent necessary to meet his/her educational needs in a satisfactory fashion.

If a child is eligible for educational support through IDEA, an Individual Education Program (IEP) is written and delineates the specific difficulties the student is experiencing in school and the steps to be taken to address those difficulties. According to IDEA '97, parents must be given a copy of their child's IEP at no cost and without having to request it. If a child is eligible for support through Section 504, an Accommodation Plan that contains similar information will be developed. The parents' role in educational planning for their children with a handicapping condition is stipulated by law. Many references are available that explain both students' rights and those of their parents. These can be accessed through such sources as public schools, public libraries, organizations such as CHADD, or via the Internet.

Guidelines for Effective Home-School Partnerships

There are several obstacles parents may face in dealing with school personnel. Parents may, for example, underestimate or overestimate what school professionals can do. Conversely, school staff may underestimate or overestimate what parents can do. The most common obstacle voiced by many parents is that they feel intimidated by school personnel. This feeling may in part be fueled by the parents' belief that school personnel are the "experts" and that they, as parents, have little to offer in discussing and planning their child's educational program. Unfortunately, some educators may also hold the same belief, and they may convey this attitude either openly or through the manner in which they treat parents.

What, then, can parents do to ensure that their child is provided an appropriate education? First, they need to remember that they are their child's first teachers. In working with school personnel, parents should present themselves as active, contributing and essential participants in the educational decisions made for their children. Parents and school staff should work to establish and maintain a working relationship based on mutual trust and respect. Both parents and school personnel should view each other as equal partners in solving the problems a child with ADD may face. Parents should also continue to educate themselves on the needs of children with ADD (yours, in particular!) so they may take a greater role in the decision-making process.

This decision-making can be viewed as a "problem-solving" process in which the parents of a child with ADD will participate with school personnel, given that ADD symptoms are typically most evident in school. Therefore, it is important for parents to be familiar with the steps involved in the problem-solving sequence. The following information is offered as a general framework parents can utilize in their collaborative efforts to work with school personnel in order to address the difficulties their child may face in school.

In order to demonstrate how this process may proceed we will take a fairly common problem children with ADD have in school: not completing assignments.

Step 1: Problem identification. You may be thinking to yourself that this is an easy step because we already know what the problem is, i.e., the student is not completing assignments. However, in this step, we need to take the problem as stated and define it more specifically. In what class(es) is Jimmy not completing his work? Are all his assignments partially done or just some of them? What kinds of assignments is he more likely to leave incomplete? How often does this happen? What purpose does this behavior serve? All of these are examples of questions that may be asked to help clarify the problem as much as possible. Once there is a clear understanding of the extent and specific aspects of the problem, you then proceed to step 2.

Step 2. Look at the factors that may be contributing to the problem. Is Jimmy not completing his work because...he doesn't understand how to do it?...he's not using allotted time wisely?...the assignment is lengthy and he is unable to attend for more than 10 minutes at a time?...there are too many distractions in his work area?...he uses that time to socialize instead?

At this step you would also attempt to look at the extent to which the identified factors may be working together to cause and maintain the problematic behavior.

Step 3. Brainstorm alternative strategies. By brainstorming, participants in the problem-solving process attempt to generate as many solutions as possible to the problem. All possible solutions are accepted without criticism (and are often written down). Once all the possible solutions are generated, you proceed to the next step.

Step 4. Discuss alternative strategies and choose the ones that look most effective. At this step, you consider the advantages and disadvantages of each brainstormed "solution" in a systematic fashion until you agree on the interventions that appear most appropriate to the problem. At times school personnel will have the primary responsibility for implementing chosen strategies, but at other times it may be the parents. For example, if Jimmy is not completing his work because he doesn't have a quiet place at home to study, his parents will be the ones who are responsible for finding that quiet spot for him and encouraging him to use it.

It is most important that individuals who are charged to implement interventions are, in fact, in agreement with them. After all, they are the ones who will be expected to do the work! Often the person doing the implementing is the classroom teacher. IDEA '97 requires that at least one regular classroom teacher be a member of the IEP team. Try to be sensitive to the extra demands that children with ADD present to their classroom teachers. Similarly, don't agree to carry out things at home that you as a parent don't agree with or cannot do.

Step 5. Specify who will be responsible for what. In Step 4 it should be made perfectly clear who will implement each of the necessary interventions. Other tasks, however, may also need to be carried out in order to implement the intervention. These other tasks should be delineated and specifically assigned to someone to insure that the chosen intervention doesn't "fall between the cracks." The ways in which the effectiveness of the intervention will be evaluated should also be discussed at this time. The formality and comprehensiveness of the evaluation process should be determined by the type of problem and its severity.

Step 6. Initiate the intervention.

Step 7. Evaluate the effectiveness of the intervention. This appraisal can be done on an informal or formal basis. Minor changes in the intervention can occur informally in order to "work out the kinks" as the intervention is being implemented. More formal evaluations may include progress review conferences by members of the problem-solving team. At these meetings participants should review what has been done, how successful it was, and the next steps to be taken.

When Your Child is Being Evaluated for ADD

By the time a child is diagnosed with ADD, parents may have already been actively involved with their child's teacher and other school personnel. Since ADD symptoms are typically most apparent within a school environment, it may even be the case that school personnel were the first to mention to parents the possibility that their child has ADD.

Some parents prefer to conceal the fact that their child is being evaluated for ADD from school personnel. Such parents believe it is a family matter and not one for which the school should be informed. This point of view can actually impede the accurate diagnosis of ADD, because an accurate assessment of a child's school performance is a major component of the assessment process. Typically the clinician doing the evaluation will request a verbal or written report from the child's classroom teacher(s). As part of the evaluation, teachers are often asked to complete behavior rating scales specifically designed to provide information regarding the school difficulties most often encountered by children with ADD. Most teachers are quite willing to provide such information.

Once a Diagnosis is Made

Once a diagnosis of ADD is made, it is helpful to inform the school. If a trial of medication is recommended, information from the classroom teacher is usually crucial in determining the appropriate medication and its optimal dosage.

It is a good idea for parents to provide the school with a report from their child's doctor that stipulates a diagnosis of ADD has been made. In the report doctors sometimes choose to include recommendations they believe would facilitate the child's school progress. It's best to give this report to the school principal (or, for older students, the child's guidance counselor) with a request that it be shared with appropriate school personnel, especially classroom teachers.

Depending on the severity of the student's needs, he may be eligible for a variety of educational interventions. According to the Professional Group for ADD and Related Disorders, 50 percent of children with ADD can have their educational needs met successfully through modifications in the regular classroom. Of the children with ADD who do require special education, 85 percent are successfully maintained in the regular classroom for a significant proportion of their school day. Approximately 30 to 50 percent of children diagnosed as having ADD also experience other difficulties such as learning disabilities, poor eye-hand coordination and low self-esteem.

Support personnel such as school psychologists, counselors, resource teachers and social workers may also be available to provide supportive services to a student with ADD. These professionals often have had extensive experience with ADD children, and they can serve as powerful resources to students, parents and teachers in meeting a child's educational needs. In addition to classroom modifications or academic assistance provided by teachers, support personnel may also be able to provide assistance in the following ways:

1. Providing parents with information regarding home management techniques, local parent groups or community activities available for children with ADD

2. Helping the classroom teacher to implement an effective classroom management program or to provide instruction more in line with a child's needs

3. Working directly with children to improve their social skills and peer relationships

4. Providing counseling for children experiencing low self-esteem

Transitions from One School Year to the Next

Both parents and school personnel want to see students start a new school year "on the right foot," and there are steps parents can take to facilitate successful adjustment. Don't wait until the beginning of a new school year to get going!

Toward the end of the current school year parents can request a progress review and planning meeting with their child's current classroom teacher(s), the principal or guidance counselor, and other relevant staff members. At this meeting the child's progress should be reviewed— including what tactics worked and what didn't—and both parents and staff should project what the child will need in order to be successful in the following year. The plan may include:

- a particular teacher (if there is more than one class per
     grade) or homeroom teacher
- a behavior management program
- preferential seating
- a peer buddy system
- a daily assignment sheet
- a meeting with the receiving teacher(s) just before the
     start of the next school year of very early in the year
- additional services outside the classroom (e.g., academic
     support or counseling)

Once a child's new teacher (or homeroom teacher) has been named, parents should make an appointment early in the year to initiate a working relationship. Parents can provide teachers with information regarding their child's unique needs as well as general guidelines for classroom strategies that work for students with ADD. Parents should assure their child's new teacher that they are willing to work with her in meeting the needs of their child. Parents should also acknowledge the challenge that a child with ADD can present to a classroom teacher.

Whenever meetings are scheduled to discuss their child's educational needs, parents should make every effort to be present and actively participate in the discussion. It's also helpful to request that summary reports of such meetings be written and distributed to all participants. Such summaries provide a record of the issues discussed and decisions made. They also help insure that any recommended follow-up is implemented.

As mentioned earlier, more educators are sensitive to the needs of the child with ADD than was true even a few years ago. Although major gains have been made in home-school collaboration, there may still be times when parents and school personnel do not agree about the ways to provide a child with a satisfactory educational experience. When parents have depleted all cooperative avenues, they may need to utilize the services of a parent advocate or exercise their due-process options. All states have parent advocacy groups. The public library should be able to provide parents with information about such advocacy groups and due-process options.

The Big Transition: Off to College

Many students with ADD can be successful in college. However, prior planning will greatly facilitate their success. Although the average high school student may spend one or even two years researching colleges and universities, college planning for students with ADD should actually begin four years sooner, i.e., by planning for their success during their high school years. Why so soon? For two main reasons: (1) It is through earlier school successes that a student gains the self-confidence needed to even consider attending college; and (2) college placement decisions are based on performance. Thus, the better a student with ADD does in high school, the greater the likelihood he/she will attend and be successful in college.

All colleges and universities receive federal funds. Therefore, all public universities and many private colleges are required to offer accommodations for individuals with disabilities. However, the amount and comprehensiveness of this support can vary greatly from one institution to another. As an entry requirement, most institutions require standardized admissions tests such as the ACTs or SATs. However, students with ADD may be eligible for accommodations such as breaks or extra time when taking one of these tests. Directions on how to apply for such accommodations are typically included in the application packet. Usually high school guidance counselors or special education staff also know how to apply for accommodations.

Most universities and colleges require documentation of a prospective student's handicapping condition and a current psychoeducational evaluation that includes measures of intellectual and academic achievement in reading, math and written language. If the student's high school has completed a case study evaluation in the past year, this report may include the needed information and a copy of it can be sent to the college. If not, parents may request that an updated psychoeducational evaluation be done by the high school or by a qualified private clinician.

In addition to test results, colleges often request a listing of recommended accommodations. College students with ADD can experience difficulties with the following: organizational skills, note-taking, paying attention to class lectures, completing work on time, structuring themselves to complete lengthy assignments such as term papers, interacting with faculty and other students, and following rules. A student with both ADD and another handicapping condition, such as a specific learning disability, may experience additional needs in college.

The following is a list of some (but not all) accommodations colleges and faculty may provide students with ADD:

- reduced course loads
- early registration
- waiver of certain requirements such as foreign language
- support groups
- taped textbooks
- permission to use a tape recorder in class
- preferential seating
- advanced organizers or study guides
- frequent and specific feedback and instruction
- modified assignments
- modified test-taking procedures (e. g., extra time, alternative
        format, quiet area,opportunities to request further
        clarification of instructions)

Although accomodations may at first be recommended in a psychological report, the list may be modified—and/or others added—as the school year progresses.

In addition, students with ADD can help themselves! Depending on their unique needs, they can be encouraged to:

- advocate for themselves
- learn who and how to ask for help
- employ coping strategies and relaxation strategies when needed
- sit near the professor during class
- use a tape recorder or note taker
- use a planner or assignment book
- use a quiet place to study (e.g., the quiet room in the library, dorm room)
- ask questions when they do not understand an assignment or test question
- utilize support services (e.g., support groups, counselors, writing clinics) offered at their college

With each passing year of their school careers, young people with ADD will face new teachers and new challenges. Their parents will be the one consistent factor providing continuity throughout their school years. Parents need to be active and confident in their partnership with the school, whether it be an elementary school, middle school, high school or even college. Parents have the knowledge, experience and concern for their children that are unique and important in helping individuals with ADD be successful in school.

Emphasize strengths!

In closing, there is still one very important point to make that is relevant not only to children's school careers but also to all other facets of their life: always keep in mind a youngster's strengths. Children with ADD are typically some of the most energetic, enthusiastic, alert, creative and perceptive students we have! Although the focus of this chapter has been on ways to accommodate the problems these kids may face in school as a result of ADD, it is important not to lose sight of the many talents these children have—and to help them discover new ones!

16

Classroom Management

ADD statistics suggest that there will be approximately one ADD child in each classroom of 20 to 25 children. In some years, of course, a teacher might get lucky and have no ADD kids. At other times, the law of averages may betray her, and she may have more than her share. A cardinal rule for teachers is this: never become known as the ADD expert in your school! A concentration of ADD children in the same class can turn the school year into a nightmare.

Even when there is only one ADD child in a class, that child is very likely to take up a disproportionate amount of the teacher's time and effort, especially if that child represents the Combined Type of ADD. The suggestions in this chapter are designed to keep the time and effort required to manage ADD as manageable as possible, while still providing the necessary direction and support for the ADD youngster. Assertive and reasonable management of an ADD child also makes the school days, weeks and months more enjoyable and productive for *all the other kids in the class*.

Managing Your Own Thoughts and Feelings

Believe it or not, an ADD child will take you to task—whether you're a parent or a teacher—regarding an important segment of your own philosophy of life. In particular, you will find yourself—and your spontaneous thoughts and feelings—exposed and clearly defined along a continuum that goes from angry/judgmental at one end to understanding/ helpful at the other.

Imagine you're driving down the street on your way to work. Another driver comes out of nowhere, cuts you off and speeds away. After getting over our fright, most of us think something like "What a jerk!" and feel angry. It's what happens next that makes the difference. Some people continue with the angry thoughts, focus on them and even feed on them. "He has no right to do that to me, that S.O.B. There's no reason for that kind of behavior!" The angry thoughts build and some individuals will even speed up themselves—chasing the offender to either teach him a lesson (revenge) or at least give him a piece of their mind.

After recovering from the inital blast of fear and anger, people with a more understanding or charitable bent think, "Maybe he's heading to the emergency room with some kind of medical crisis" or "Maybe she's late for work and afraid of losing her job." As this kind of person entertains possible reasons or motivations for the obnoxious behavior, the feeling of anger diminishes inside and revenge is not considered as an option.

This is not a sermon. The fact of the matter, though, is that your thoughts, feelings and actions are often connected. Thinking, "That S.O.B. He can't do that to me. There's no reason for that kind of behavior!" makes one angry and want to strike out and defend oneself. Thinking "He's heading to the emergency room with some kind of medical crisis" lessens anger and makes a person feel there's no need for self-defense.

While alone in your car, of course, you have the luxury of thinking whatever you want. You also don't have a reliable way of guessing what the "offender's" motivation was. If you don't eventually precipitate another "road rage" incident, it makes little difference, perhaps, what you think or do (other than your own state of agitation). You're by yourself, and whatever the actual motivation of the person who cut you off might have been soon becomes irrelevant.

Things are different, however, when you're in a classroom presenting a lesson to 25 children and this time it's an ADD child who cuts you off (again) with an impulsive and inappropriate remark. After the initial irritation—and this behavior is irritating!—what mode are you going to get into: angry/judgmental or understanding/helpful?

ADD children force their caretakers into this dilemma many times every day. On the one hand, irritation over obnoxious behavior does not produce an incentive to be of help; rather, anger naturally inspires negative judgments and motivation toward revenge or counterattack. On the other hand, though, a teacher has the welfare of 24 other kids, the ADD child and herself to worry about. Getting into a "war" with the ADD child—even though it may be tempting—will do no one any good.

How does an adult make the switch—over and over again—from an angry/judgmental stance to an understanding/helpful one when attempting to handle an ADD child? In many ways, each of us has to come up with our own answers, but responding to that question is what this chapter is about. Don't ever kid yourself: managing an ADD child is hard emotional work. The very first step is to understand and to think clearly about ADD.

Thinking ADD

When you think about it, no one—whether a teacher or a parent—should really expect normal behavior from a handicapped child. You don't, after all, expect a girl in a wheelchair to run like the wind. ADD, however, is different from physical handicaps in two important ways. First, with ADD the handicap is "hidden." The child looks normal, so you tend to think, "Why on earth can't he behave like the other children?" Second, your heart goes out to the little girl in the wheelchair. You feel bad for her and you are sympathetic. Your heart does not naturally go out to the ADD child who is irritating you with impulsive, inattentive and hyperactive behavior.

"Why on earth can't he behave like the other children?" This statement is usually an expression of extreme frustration, but it should not be treated as a rhetorical question. It should be treated as a real question.

The answer to the *legitimate* question, "Why can't he behave like other children?" is: the child can't behave normally because he has Attention Deficit Disorder which he can't turn off at will. While a teacher's goal is to work on normalizing the child's behavior as much as possible, you must start with what you get. That means *this kid the way he is*.

One good way to accomplish this kind of reality check is for the teacher to make a list of ADD symptoms and then to rate the child on each one. After a few weeks have gone by in the beginning of the year and she has gotten to know the youngster, a teacher can do a rating of the extent to which the child shows each ADD symptom or trait. The DSM-IV lists (Inattentive and Hyperactive/Impulsive) or our eight characteristics (Chapter 2) can be used.

For example, here's the list Mrs. Simpson made to describe nine-year-old Jeff (10 means "a lot," 5 means about average, and 1 means "very little" compared to the child's age group):

Inattentiveness: 9
Impulsivity: 7
Difficulty delaying gratification: 6
Emotional overarousal: 7
Hyperactivity: 6
Noncompliance: 8
Social problems: 9
Disorganization: 8

This is the child Mrs. Simpson will get every morning, five days a week. Not a nice child, not a cooperative child, not really a normal child. The rating exercise helps define the difficult job this teacher has, but any job is at least a little more tolerable when one accepts it at face value. No wishful thinking is allowed in this business.

An even better idea is to do the symptom rating, have the parents do the same rating, and then discuss the results with the parents. This exercise helps the teacher and parents be more realistic about what to expect from this boy or girl. It also helps them sympathize more with one another. This ADD child, in other words, is capable of torturing both teacher and parents—through no fault of anyone—in similar ways both at school and at home.

Thinking ADD also helps to accomplish several other things. First of all, it gives the teacher a down to earth idea of what an ADD child's behavioral repertoire really is. Second, it clarifies for the teacher that the problem is ADD, not a lousy parent, a kid who's out to get her, or major faults in her competence as an instructor. Third, thinking ADD reduces (not abolishes!) anger because it makes expectations more realistic. Anger is always aggravated the greater the discrepancy between what you expect and what you get.

Managing Your Feelings Toward the ADD Child

Learning to manage your own feelings toward an ADD child, obviously, is no mean feat. In some ways this skill flows directly from thinking ADD. Here's the problem in a nutshell: how do you consistently teach, care for and offer help to a child who is obnoxious and uncooperative more often than not? No teacher likes to admit that she doesn't like a child. Yet the fact of the matter is that there are plenty of ADD kids who are not liked by their teachers, their therapists and/or their parents.

Psychotherapists call a problem like this "countertransference." Countertransference refers to feelings that a therapist may have toward his or her client that sometimes interfere with the therapy itself. Hostility is a common countertransference problem in many helping and caretaking relationships.

What's a teacher to do? There are no simple or easy answers, but here are a few suggestions:

1. Admit the irritation to yourself (not to the child). Don't feel guilty about this anger and don't try to cover it up with syrupy words or behavior.

2. On the other hand, don't start a war. Don't repeatedly direct spiteful—subtle or otherwise—attacks toward the child. For example, "John, did you take your medication today?" said in front of the entire class is a thinly veiled attack. So is this: "All of you who feel John is acting like a first-grader, raise your hand." Revenge is a perfectly common and normal human motivation, but it can get you into a cycle of attack and counterattack. Who suffers? Among others, your entire class.

3. Adjust your expectations. If you are really mad, it's very likely that your expectations are out of whack with reality. You are out of touch with what's really possible at this moment. Psychotherapists have to make this

kind of attitude adjustment *constantly* in working with their clients. What can you reasonably expect from *this* kid? Not from most kids, just from this one. Do the symptom ratings.

4. Learn about ADD. When it comes to human beings, increased knowledge about a person, his motivation and his behavior almost always leads to less anger. Increased knowledge *means* being more understanding. Two key points for school personnel are these: 1) Can you understand what it means to have a neurologically-based problem with self-control? and 2) Can you take to heart the fact that ADD is a hereditary problem that is not caused by bad parenting?

5. Try to be useful/helpful to the ADD child. Accept the fact that these kids need direct, frequent interventions from you. These interventions, of course, include positive reinforcement, directions and limit setting. Remember the paradoxical-but-true old adage: if you want to get to like a difficult person, try doing him a favor. The more enterprising and energetic a teacher is in trying to solve the problems presented by an ADD child, the more she is likely to like that child—and the higher her (the teacher's) self-esteem will be.

6. Teaching an ADD child is hard enough without what we call mental "add-ons." Try to avoid these common, seductive-but-mistaken notions:

> a. This kid is out to get me, drive me crazy and insult me.
> b. This kid's behavior shows I'm not a good teacher.
> c. This kid's behavior proves his parents are nuts.
> d. This kid's behavior is deliberate and malicious.
> e. This kid's a brat or a jerk—or both.

These judgmental thoughts are not only unrealistic, but they also increase anger and the impulse toward revenge. More understanding—but also more realistic—replacements go as follows:

> a. This kid's inattentive, impulsive and hyperactive behavior
>   is frequently very irritating.
> b. This kid's behavior taxes my abilities as a teacher.
> c. ADD is not caused by bad parenting; chances are 100

percent this child aggravates his parents in the same ways he aggravates me.

d. This kid's behavior, unfortunately, is unintentional, careless and poorly thought out.

e. I'm in the habit of thinking that obnoxious behavior proves that the perpetrator of that behavior is a complete idiot.

General Intervention Principles

Now that we've discussed the critical and extremely difficult issue of understanding—or attitude adjustment—it's time to discuss intervention strategies with ADD kids. There are hundreds of tactics, and some of the best have been developed over the years by teachers who work with ADD students. Different strategies work best with different teachers and different kids. It is important to keep in mind, however, that any strategy can be undermined by an underlying base of ignorance and hostility.

Russell Barkley has proposed a number of general principles that apply to the management of difficult ADD behavior. Several of these will be discussed here, and they apply to parenting as well as teaching. Using these principles usually means more thought and more work, but, as mentioned above, ADD kids don't give you a lot of choice. You will react to these children—one way or another!

One of the reasons for describing these general principles before making more specific suggestions is this: many teachers are very creative at coming up with their own *specific* ideas if they already have some *general* ideas about how a task needs to be accomplished. The task here is managing inattentive, impulsive and hyperactive behavior.

Here are some basic principles:

Immediate feedback and/or consequences. ADD kids learn best from feedback that comes quickly. Praise for positive behavior as well as reprimands or consequences for problem behavior should be given as soon as possible. This means just a few seconds after, when possible, not hours or minutes after.

Frequent feedback. To keep them on task, ADD children need to receive friendly reminders and other kinds of helpful messages more frequently from adults. ADD involves a problem with sustaining motivation, especially when feedback or reinforcement is sparce and the child sees the task as boring.

Stronger consequences. Reinforcers for ADD children must be more powerful than those used with other kids. Reinforcers must have more "pull." In addition to words, for example, rewards might include tokens, points on a chart, colorful cards or the right to engage in special activities.

Incentives before punishments. The irritating behavior of ADD children naturally inspires reprimands and punishments from adults. Positive reinforcement, rewards and praise, unfortunately, will not flow as naturally. Positive consequences, however, should be used *first* and should also be used *more often* than punishments or reprimands.

Actions speak louder than words. As we saw earlier, in our brief discussion of the *1-2-3 Magic* program, nagging, lecturing and pleading don't work well, especially in the long run. Consequences should be used instead. To Barkley's advice on this point we might add that these unhelpful tactics also make the adult using them more emotional. The more you talk, the more excited you get; the more excited you get, the more you talk. An overly emotional adult trying to handle an emotionally overaroused ADD child is not a formula for success.

Consistency. ADD children do much better when there is predictability and structure in their everyday lives. These kids have a hard time handling change. If the rules—or the ways the rules are administered—are subject to adult whim or emotion, the result will be confusion and then chaos.

Advance planning for problems. If you're thinking ADD and have an idea what kinds of problem traits and problem situations a child is going to present, it is a good idea to plan management strategies in advance. Perhaps standardized achievement testing is coming up, or the child always has trouble with transition times during the school day. Thinking ADD means replacing "I hope today he behaves himself for a change" with "What can I do to help him manage better this time?"

Remind child of the plan. Just because you are aware of the plan or the rules doesn't mean the ADD child is aware of them. And, as you know by now, one of the hallmarks of ADD is a major case of forgetfulness! Don't think, "By this age she should be able to remember..." Do think, "ADD kids are running about 30 percent behind their peers in emotional and behavioral maturity, therefore..." Remind yourself to remind the child—concisely, of course—what the plan is and what the rules are.

Now let's take a look at some specific suggestions for the classroom management of ADD children. You'll notice that these suggestions often incorporate some of the general principles just mentioned; they also represent only a few of the many intervention strategies that exist.

Behavior Management

As Ann Welch, a Virginia special education teacher and educational consultant, points out, two basic rules apply to the classroom. First, children are in school to work/learn; there is a job to do. Second, kids' behavior should not interfere with the work/learning of others. Inattentive ADD kids usually have trouble with the first rule; Combined Type ADD children usually have trouble with both.

The instructor's first task here is to divide children's potential problem activities into three categories:

1. Behavior that can be ignored (violates neither rule)
2. Nondisruptive but inattentive behavior (violates only the first rule)
3. Disruptive misbehavior (violates the second rule and often the first as well)

1. Behavior that can be ignored. ADD children, both Combined and Inattentive, will often do things that—at first glance—look like trouble, but which really aren't. Some of these "activities" are expressions of hyperactivity and restlessness, while others look like inattention but really aren't.

Manifestations of hyperactivity and restlessness include fidgeting with hands and squirming around in the chair. You can't ask an ADD child to sit still—that's a lost cause! But many ADD children can—with a teacher's help—learn to express their restlessness within certain limits without violating either of the two rules mentioned above. Some children, for example, come up with some very creative body postures while they work! They may work just fine while kneeling on the chair or they may do better reading on the floor. Some ADD children are natural fidgeters; their hands always have to be doing something. For these kids, what Ann Welch calls "legal fiddlers" can be helpful. These are objects, such as a rabbit's foot or pipe cleaner, that can be constantly fiddled with without making any noise. Gross-motor restlessness (arms and legs) can sometimes be reduced by one of the prevention tactics known as Legitimate Movement (see below).

Also in the category of "ignorable" behavior are postures and actions that make the ADD child look as though she's not paying attention, when in reality she is. Many ADD kids, for example, don't make good eye contact with a teacher when the teacher is talking. These kids may be looking out the window, or staring at an object on the wall. Some are paying attention and some are not. By gently asking them a question or asking them to repeat directions, a teacher can eventually learn which kind this particular ADD child is, or the teacher can learn when this child is likely to be spacing out and when she is not. Apparent inattentiveness can then be ignored; real inattentiveness can be dealt with using a secret signal (see below).

2. Nondisruptive but inattentive behavior. When a child is off-task but bothering no one else, a simple signal may be given by the teacher to the child. Many teachers prefer a "secret signal"—one that is, hopefully, known only to the teacher and the child. This maneuver is an attempt to avoid embarrassing the youngster and also to engage him in a kind of mutual problem-solving game. When the ADD child is off daydreaming, for example, the teacher gets in a position to be seen and produces the signal—tugging on her ear, scratching her forehead, tapping her elbow with her finger, or whatever she and the child earlier agreed upon. A simple hand on the shoulder or finger on the child's desk can also work quite well.

3. Disruptive behavior. For the behavior that interferes with the work of other students, the "1-2-3" method can be used (see Chapter 17). Verbal warnings or "counts" are given immediately after the behavior in question. After the third count, a consequence will take place. The consequence can include:

1. A brief time out in a predetermined area of the room

2. Time away: time spent in another classroom with another teacher who has agreed to cooperate
3. A response cost consequence: the student loses tokens or points which are being accumulated to "purchase" or earn a special privilege or reward

Goofing around or other violations of time out may result in immediate withdrawal of an imminent privilege, such as recess or lunch, involvement of someone like a principal, and/or a notification of parents. When using any kind of counting or warning system, of course, the teacher should avoid excess talking and should remain as calm as possible.

After they are well into the school year, some teachers reduce the number of warnings that may be given prior to the final consequence. Instead of two warnings, children may only receive one. Eventually kids may be consequenced for the first instance of a misbehavior when the teacher feels that the problem behavior is fairly serious or disruptive and enough time has gone by for the children to be very familiar with the rule involved.

Problem Prevention

Several tactics can go a long way toward preventing problems before they occur. These include the following:

Legitimate movement. Allowing the child brief periods of time to move around is often a real blessing for everyone. These times can include going to the bathroom (though not 19 times a day!), sharpening a pencil, stretching, doing classroom chores and taking special trips for the teacher down to the principal's office. Sometimes movement can be used as a reward for good behavior, but this strategy should be used carefully because many ADD kids need to move regularly—not just at special times.

Other examples of allowing for legitimate movement include the child being able to move from one desk to another to do his work. Standing work stations or the use of a podium allows some kids to get a break from sitting while they continue their work. Bean bag chairs on the floor and rocking chairs have also helped, as have exercise breaks for the whole class that involving moderate—not frantic—movement.

Teacher-led instructional activities that require movement on the part of all students also allow the ADD child an opportunity to be active. Holding up "Yes" or "No" response cards to answer the teacher's questions or the use of dry-erase boards can be useful.

Desk placement. An ADD child usually does best when his desk is up in front of the room, fairly close to the teacher. This arrangement more closely approximates the kind of one-on-one situation in which ADD kids perform better, and it also makes it easier for the teacher to structure work for the child, monitor progress and provide appropriate reinforcement. If the child is facing toward the front of the room, seating in the front also minimizes distractions; visual and associated auditory stimuli coming from the other children are behind the ADD student.

Be careful with cooperative education or team learning. Many ADD kids don't do well when they are asked to work in small groups. Desks that are close together, for example, may mean increased distractions as well as three other youngsters within kicking distance. Some teachers, however, say that some of their ADD kids handle team learning well, so this is another time when gentle experimentation is needed to find out how *this* ADD child does in *this* group. Rarely does it work to have more than one ADD child in the same work group.

Maximize the child's strengths. It is useful for a teacher to try to discover what this particular ADD child is good at, whether it's math or reading, or simply loving to do errands. Giving a child ample opportunity to express her strong suits, and then verbally recognizing and reinforcing her efforts increases the youngster's willingness to cooperate with other tasks as well.

Structure is essential. Structure means that the classroom is managed in such a way that at any one time each child knows what he is supposed to be doing. ADD children present a problem in this regard because they don't "self-structure" very well. While many children can return from recess or lunch and remember to get to work on their next assignment, an ADD child will return from recess or lunch and get involved with whatever comes first or whatever is most interesting. The activity "chosen" might be looking out the window, teasing another student, or checking out the contents of the wastebasket.

Helping the ADD child to structure his time is aided by routine. Doing things at the same time and in the same place—as much as is reasonably possible—will help the ADD child focus. Verbal instructions of what the agenda is before an activity are also useful. Friendly reminders during the activity also may be necessary; these reminders may take the form of praising the ADD child—or a child sitting near him—for staying involved with the appropriate task.

The importance of structure to the ADD youngster, of course, has another side to it. On days when change or disruption of the usual routine is inevitable, a teacher can prepare for that fact by realizing that the strategies discussed in this chapter will need to be intensified. Such disruptive changes include field trips, visitors to the classroom, days before holidays and standardized testing. Days when a substitute teacher is needed, of course, provide a double whammy: a different teacher is a big change to start with, and the regular teacher is unavailable to help. Different schools have different methods for dealing with these days, but lack of preparation of substitute teachers, unfortunately, remains a problem.

Encouraging the Best Work

Here are some suggestions for getting the maximum academic effort out of your ADD kids:

Clear the work area. Help the child to clear his desktop of all materials that are not part of the task at hand (with the exception of "legal fiddlers").

Divide work into small, manageable units. Some children, for example, do better when they start with a work sheet that is folded in half so they can't see the whole thing. Long-term writing assignments often give older ADD children (or at least their mothers) fits. Separate due dates for outline, notes, rough draft and final copy can be very helpful.

Giving directions. When giving the instructions for an assignment, try to establish eye contact with the ADD child before beginning. Use the child's name, if necessary, to keep him with you as you speak and try to keep the directions as short as possible. Using multiple modes, such as visual and auditory, in presenting instructions or new material probably makes things a bit easier for all children.

Attention checks. Sometimes it is helpful to see if the Attention Deficit child has really understood the task that the teacher just described. Some of these kids have become adept at looking you right in the eye while they are paying absolutely no attention to what you are saying! If it is feasible, ask the child in a non-accusing manner what is supposed to be done.

Doing the work. Frequent checks to insure the work is being done are often helpful. It is certainly true that there are 24 other kids that also need to be checked on, but our ADD charges are the ones most likely to wander off task. Many ADD kids start out with a bang and then fizzle out quickly. If the child is off task, secret signals can be used to bring him back. ADD kids do best with frequent verbal or physical reinforcement. So do other children, of course, but Attention Deficit students fall apart much faster when reinforcement is not available.

When the work is done. ADD kids often lose it! This unfortunate problem occurs more with homework, of course, but it can also affect work done at school as well. Helping the child to immediately store his work in an orderly, consistent manner is essential. Color-coded notebooks can help. Assignment sheets or notebooks for unfinished work or homework should be filled out and checked by the teacher. Even though they are in the seventh grade, many ADD children are simply unable to do this.

Dealing with Parents

Maintaining a positive and consistent relationship with an ADD child's parents is essential—and often very difficult. School-home communication becomes more and more important the more trouble the child is having. It is axiomatic that it is very hard—or next to impossible—to discuss serious, emotionally loaded issues with strangers. Therefore, teacher and parents (plural!) should meet before the year starts.

Teachers need to remind themselves that these parents did not cause their child's difficult ADD behavior by the way they raised him. In addition, mothers of ADD kids are the ones to whom teachers talk more frequently, and many of these mothers will come across as angry, blaming, anxious, depressed, disorganized and extremely intense. The internal reaction of many teachers to this presentation is something akin to "Heck, lady, if I had a mother like you, I'd be hyperactive myself!" It is important to keep in mind that this temperamental parental behavior may, in fact, reflect the exact opposite reality: Mom's upset may be a manifestation of the long-term effects of this child's behavior on her.

For their part, parents need to remember that the teacher has 24 other kids in the class to worry about; the teacher's day does not revolve around their child. Mom and Dad must also give the teacher the right or freedom to have the same negative emotional reactions to their child that they do at home. Parents cannot expect semi-infinite patience from a teacher simply because she was trained to be a teacher. And when a teacher does voice her frustrations, parents should try to realize that criticism of their child is not the same as criticism of them. Whether or not the teacher admits her frustration, she has a right to be aggravated.

When teacher and parents meet, experimental and flexible thinking is needed. There are quite a few recommendations in this chapter, for example, for managing the ADD child in the classroom. There are hundreds more. It is obviously impossible for any teacher to apply all— or even a significant percentage—of these ideas to any one ADD child. It is also true that not all techniques will work equally well with all ADD children or with all teachers.

Teachers and parents, therefore, should take a provisional and pragmatic attitude toward the problem, trying to find the strategies that do the most good and that are most realistic in terms of the teacher's time, energy and experience. The "experiment" can be accomplished in the following way:

1. The teacher sits down with the parents and asks them what strategies have worked best with their child in the past.

2. The teacher looks at the list in this chapter (or in other books) and also searches her own experience, identifying tactics that she thinks would be useful.

3. Parents and teacher agree on certain techniques. These will be the ones tried out initially during the year. If they work, fine. If they don't, there's no sense in beating a dead horse—something else should be tried.

ADD kids are notoriously "teacher-sensitive." The person in charge of the classroom can have a wonderful—or devastating—effect on what kind of year they have.

Medication Basics

Many teachers say that they are not physicians, do not prescribe the medication, and feel uncomfortable getting involved in this aspect of ADD treatment. Though these thoughts are certainly understandable, they need to be modified to some extent. A teacher's knowledge about medication and involvement in the medication adjustment process can help immensely with the overall treatment plan.

Why? For one thing, many ADD kids are lousy historians; they have great difficulty accurately describing their past experiences, including their positive or negative responses to medications. For another thing, because of the short duration of action of the stimulant medications (often three to five hours) and the fact that—unfortunately—many doctors still prescribe medication only for school, sometimes behavioral changes due to medication are there to be seen only during the school day.

What this means is that much of the time the only reliable observer of positive and negative drug effects—who is around while the drugs are active—is the teacher. And for treatment to succeed, a teacher's classroom observations of an ADD child on medication must be communicated to parents and doctor one way or another. Teachers, consequently, need to know some basics about the different medications and how they work. It is very important for them to have a general idea of what positive effects might be expected from stimulants, for example, and also what some of the possible side effects might be (see Chapter 13). It is also helpful if a teacher is aware of the fact that you don't have to wait a month (with most stimulants) to determine if a drug is working; three to five days usually does the trick. Thus if the teacher knows the child has been taking a particular dose of a certain drug for two weeks and nothing has happened, it's time to say something.

Teachers certainly don't prescribe meds themselves, but they can pass on critical information to parents and/or directly to the prescribing doctors. In doing so, they can help the ADD child immeasurably. They also help make their classroom a much more positive learning environment for everyone.

Part IV

Adults with Attention Deficit Disorder

17

A Lifelong Proposition

For a long time people believed that Attention Deficit Disorder would be outgrown by the time the individual who had it was an adolescent. This idea probably came from the general observation that most hyperactive children seemed to calm down some as they got older; their gross-motor restlessness decreased. Since the most obvious symptom of the disorder—moving around a lot—lessened, people tended to assume that the rest of the problem had gone away too.

Unfortunately, this is not the case. Most ADD children carry their ADD symptoms into adulthood and also suffer added problems that arise from "growing up ADD." Among the more prominent of these "extras" are lowered self-esteem, a pessimistic view of life, problems establishing an independent lifestyle, and major interpersonal difficulties. Growing up ADD also contributes to comorbidity; ADD adults usually will qualify for more than one diagnosis.

For the therapists trying to treat them, Attention Deficit adults can be among the most enjoyable and rewarding of clients as well as among the most frustrating. ADD adults can, of course, present the same paradox to their friends and family! Since they are no longer being dragged into treatment by their parents, ADD adults also have a choice about whether to pursue counseling and medication or "do it on my own."

ADD Characteristics in Adults

The Inattentive and Hyperactive/Impulsive lists of DSM-IV are used in diagnosing ADD adults as they are with ADD children. The problem with this procedure is that for many ADD individuals, their symptoms "mellow" (but don't go away) with age. This mellowing process, however, affects the two DSM-IV lists differently. Hyperactive and impulsive characteristics are likely to diminish more in severity with the passage of time; patterns that involve inattentiveness, disorganization and trouble with follow-through will decrease less.

Two results may follow. First of all, many adults who are still truly troubled by Attention Deficit Disorder may not qualify for the diagnosis. Some people, for example, may not qualify for six of the nine symptoms on either list, even though in their everyday lives they are still significantly impaired by ADD. The other possibility is that people who were formerly true Combined Types will begin to appear—according to DSM-IV—as though they were Predominantly Inattentive Types; they will meet at least six of the nine inattentive criteria but will not fit more than six Hyperactive/Impulsive traits.

Some experts have suggested, therefore, that the DSM criteria should be modified for adult diagnosis. Perhaps only four or five items per list, they suggest, should need to be endorsed before one or the other ADD diagnosis is made. This idea is receiving serious consideration at the present time.

The eight ADD traits which we described before in ADD children also appear in modified form in adults. With adults, however, broad modifications occur in these symptom patterns because life itself has been transformed: school, for example, has been replaced by a job, and the role of being a child has been replaced by being a husband, wife or parent.

1. *Inattention* (Distractibility). Adults with ADD will still find themselves having trouble concentrating on a number of things. They may have trouble staying on task when they are at work, with the result that they do not finish as much as they—and their supervisors—would like them to.

Distractibility can also affect the ADD adult around the house, where he can go enthusiastically from project to project without ever finishing any one task. Many ADD homemakers find that they can't seem to stay on top of household chores; the day is one endless series of frustrations.

Inattentiveness also frustrates Attention Deficit adults in social situations, where they can have considerable difficulty focusing on conversations. Some ADD men and women find big parties or family get-togethers frustrating because so many conversations are going on at the same time, and their mind keeps getting drawn away from the conversation they are supposed to be paying attention to. The result is frequently embarrassment when it becomes apparent to other people that the ADD individual has lost the train of thought. ADD adults may also appear to other people as if they are bored, because they are restless, do not always maintain eye contact, and sometimes interrupt or abruptly change the subject.

2. *Impulsivity*. Impulsivity is often more restrained in ADD adults than it is in ADD children. This difference may be due to the fact that by the time they are adults, ADD individuals may have been burned so much by past impulsive actions that they are more or less "forced" to exercise more self-control. (Their learning curve may be slow, but it's still there!) By this time in their lives, many ADD adults are downright nervous about social situations for fear of what they might do or say. This discomfort may be especially strong in social situations where the ADD man or woman doesn't know other people well. In fact, some ADD adults will be quiet and appear shy when confronted with strangers! When together with familiar people or family, however, Attention Deficit adults often show a marked tendency to interrupt, blurt things out, talk very loudly or even yell. Impulsivity can also appear when an ADD adult is behind the wheel of a car, although ADD drivers may not be that much worse than your average road maniac.

3. *Difficulty delaying gratification*. Impulsivity and difficulty with delay are related problems. Impulsivity refers to action taken without thought and without waiting. Difficulty with delay is the sense of impatience and severe frustration stimulated in a person with ADD when he is *forced* to wait and think. During conversations ADD adults may have an awful

time waiting to express their opinion about something; they become squirmy and lose eye contact. They also may have trouble finding the patience for academic, "schoolish" tasks such as balancing a check book, filling out and filing a tax return, paying bills or even reading a magazine. Like ADD schoolchildren, adults with ADD want to get these boring tasks over with as quickly as possible. This frustration and difficulty with perseverance often result in messy, unchecked or undone work, resulting in problems that later come back to haunt the individual.

Some ADD adults also have serious problems managing money because they spend it so quickly. Since credit cards today offer the promise of never having to wait for anything, credit limits may be quickly pushed to the max. Unfortunately, spending money is sometimes seen—by ADD and non-ADD people alike—as an antidote to boredom and other dysphoric moods. ADD adults often find that when they are inactive they are very easily bored. This boredom can all too quickly evolve into a sense of emptiness and melancholy that is hard for them to describe, but which they will do almost anything to avoid. Unfortunately, even though the dollars are not really available, going shopping (at the mall or on the Internet) can become a frequent—but ultimately self-destructive—exercise in financial self-medication.

4. *Emotional overarousal.* This is one of the ADD characteristics that is, for some reason, conspicuously absent from the DSM-IV list. In our ADD children, you recall, emotional overarousal manifested itself in the "hyper-silly" routine in groups and in ferocious fits of temper. With ADD adults hyper-silly behavior in groups is much less common. Perhaps these adults have learned that this type of display doesn't go over too well with other people, or perhaps these individuals just don't feel like goofing around as much as they used to.

Temper is another story, however. ADD adults often continue to have tempers that are about as bad as those they had as children and their outbursts can be quite intimidating to other people. Though their emotional eruptions may be more restrained in public, ADD adults may come across on the job as irritable or moody. At home, unfortunately, temper can be unleashed on spouses and children. Spouses often find that they have a very hard time asserting themselves with their ADD husband or wife, because so many of their conversations seem to produce angry responses. Displays of temper can also be aggravated by alcohol or drug abuse. Spouses begin to feel like they are always walking on eggs, and that the mood of their ADD mate is quite unpredictable.

In addition, an ADD parent may continue to show a problem with low frustration tolerance when it comes to dealing with his or her kids. Even average children are very frustrating on a regular basis. Since ADD tends to be hereditary, ADD adults tend to produce ADD children. Thus we wind up with an adult with low frustration tolerance who has children who are extraordinarily frustrating. Unfortunately, this combination can result in abusive episodes. On the other hand, some ADD parents have said that their being Attention Deficit themselves sometimes helps them understand their ADD kids better, because they know what the youngsters are going through and can better imagine what their children feel like inside.

People who are not Attention Deficit probably have no idea what kind of strain the symptom of emotional overarousal puts—day in and day out—on the self-control of an ADD adult. These adults certainly do not ask that everything feel like a big deal, but it does. Non-ADD adults know what it is like to be more irritable at the end of a long day or perhaps after a few drinks, but this is an unusual experience for them. For ADD adults it is a regular, daily occurrence. It's almost as if the same event stimulates in an ADD individual four times the amount of adrenalin that it does in someone else. It certainly is difficult to like or to understand an irritable person with a bad temper, but the old saying, "Walk a mile in my shoes," does comes to mind here.

Whatever underlies the problem of emotional overarousal and difficulty with emotional control may also underlie the comorbidity of adult ADD with anxiety disorders and depressive disorders. Everyone feels anxious and depressed from time to time, but when the frequency, intensity and duration of these feelings become excessive, anxiety or depression may be diagnosed. That is exactly what happens in many adults with Attention Deficit Disorder.

5. *Hyperactivity*. As they get older, most individuals with ADD will tend to move around less. Gross-motor hyperactivity may be replaced by a general kind of fidgetiness or restlessness, and some ADD adults are still

described by those familiar with them as not being able to sit still for very long. Other ADD men and some ADD women will continue to be hyperactive, but the "hyperactivity" will take a verbal form. Their speech may be rapid, nonstop and have an anxious or driven quality to it. ADD individuals may also have great difficulty stopping long enough to listen to what someone else is saying without feeling compelled to interrupt in order to make what they feel is an important point.

6. *Noncompliance.* As most people get older, they generally have less of a problem following rules and staying out of trouble. This tendency applies to ADD adults as well. Part of this positive change is simply due to the fact that ADD adults are in fewer situations where other people are trying to tell them what to do. As parents they may now be trying to tell their ADD kids what to do! Still, some studies indicate that as many as 25 percent of ADD adults may have a serious problem with antisocial behavior. Other retrospective studies of incarcerated adults suggest that large percentages of these people look as though they grew up with unrecognized Attention Deficit Disorder.

Many ADD adults function well enough in the workplace because they are their own bosses. Others, however, may have quite a bit of difficulty with supervision, which tends to stir up some of the old "anti-parent" antagonisms that were experienced when they were kids (remember that some research has shown that nine out of ten interactions between ADD kids and their parents are negative). Rules and supervisors, therefore, may stimulate a kind of automatic opposition; managers and bosses may be easily perceived as stupid and irrational.

Because of their frequent inability to get their act together around the house, as well as their emotional lability, the spouses of ADD adults may sometimes feel like they have another child to deal with rather than an equal partner. Trying to parent your own ADD spouse, however, is fraught with danger, because attempts at advice or correction are often met with temper outbursts. Many non-ADD spouses, therefore, simply keep their mouths shut, but inside they feel considerable resentment toward their "partner."

7. *Social problems.* How one gets along with the rest of the human race is extremely important to anyone, and adults with ADD are no

exception. Unfortunately, many feel isolated and rather lonely—though this feeling may wax and wane. For ADD individuals it is often hard to maintain long lasting relationships, and by the time they are adults some have simply quit trying. Inside they may blame everyone else for their problems, but they may also, from time to time, have the feeling that they are the primary source of their own troubles.

At home, the temper and bossiness of an ADD man or woman can pose persistent difficulties to his or her spouse and kids. On the job coworkers may find the ADD adult hard to be with due to his talkativeness, restlessness, tendency to complain and general irritability. On the other hand, sometimes ADD adults are enjoyed for their lively personalities and their ability to get a discussion—or a party—going, and this skill can help their social life considerably.

8. *Disorganization.* Many ADD adults have trouble juggling the different aspects of their lives. They can have trouble with dates, times and appointments, and—as it is with ADD kids—their memory can be amazingly erratic. The homes of men and women with ADD are sometimes monuments to the tendency to start and not finish things. The bathroom upstairs has been torn up for the last six months, there are still paint cans on the floor of the kids' half-painted bedroom, and the car again had to be parked outside all winter because the garage cleaning project never got done.

On the job, adults with ADD have difficulty staying with a task, especially if they see it as boring and especially if it is entirely up to them to keep at it. (Supervision can be a necessary but aggravating evil!) An ADD adult may also feel like he is a born procrastinator. Because he is easily bored, he tends to avoid tasks—like paper and pencil jobs—that he feels are uninteresting or obnoxious. He also tends to find the easiest or most interesting thing to do right at the time. The problem with this way of operating, though, is that the job chosen may not be the one that most needs to be done at that moment.

Procrastination has gotten many ADD adults into significant trouble. Over time the undone tasks build up. The ADD employee begins to feel more and more embarrassed about the jobs left undone, but he still can't bring himself to face the unpleasantness. Then he is confronted by an angry supervisor who finally discovers the gap in the work, and the ADD adult can provide no reasonable explanation for what happened.

Many ADD men and women, of course, handle life reasonably well. Most will be married, have jobs, and be self-supporting. Some adults with ADD who are bright, have good social skills, and who can use their extra energy to good advantage, will be outstanding achievers. Attention Deficit Disorder will continue to add some rough edges to their existence, but these men and women will feel justifiably proud of their achievements.

Note: For more information about ADD in adults, see the video *Adults with Attention Deficit Disorder*, by Thomas W. Phelan, Ph.D.

18

Diagnosis with Adults

If three to five percent of school children are Attention Deficit, and 80 percent of these kids don't outgrow the condition, then about two to four percent of our adult population is likely to have ADD. That's a lot of people! Many mental health professionals who work with ADD wonder where all the Attention Deficit adults are.

How do ADD adults get into treatment? Obviously most of them don't. Undoubtedly, many ADD adults avoid treatment because they are sick of it. Now that the decision is up to them, they don't especially care to see another mental health professional or another physician, partly because they may feel that as kids they were dragged to every doctor in town. Our current data certainly indicate that ADD treatment compliance decreases with age.

On the other hand, there are many ADD individuals who stick with treatment through their adolescent, young adult and adult years. They have realized that this perseverance makes a big difference in their lives, and that it also makes those around them a lot happier. As one ADD adult put it, "I'd rather be happy than go around pretending I'm perfect and shooting myself in the foot all the time."

What about ADD men and women who were never diagnosed as children or teens? It is very common for adults to seek treatment for themselves after their ADD child has been successfully diagnosed and treated. In the course of their son or daughter's evaluation and therapy, these parents learned that ADD is usually hereditary and that it is not outgrown. When discussing the developmental histories of their children, many adults can't help but reflect on their own childhoods, which are often remarkably similar to those of their kids. Involvement in parent support groups may also help to reinforce the idea that residual—or adult—ADD exists. During such meetings parents may meet other parents whose situations are similar to their own, and Mom and/or Dad may start wondering, "What about me?"

Motivation for treatment can also come from other sources. A frustrated wife, for example, may know she has an ADD kid but also feel convinced that she has an ADD husband. Many women try to "encourage" their husbands to do something about the possible problem. Some are successful. Other times, however, the "ADD suspect" is defensive and denies having anything wrong with him. Unfortunate arguments can result which reduce—rather than increase—motivation for treatment. It certainly is no help if one feels that seeking an evaluation for Attention Deficit is like eating crow.

Some adults have done a bit of their own "diagnosing" by trying out their child's stimulant medication on their own. This is not a recommended procedure, since it can backfire for a number of reasons. The medication may be appropriate, for example, but the dosage is not. Other adults have such a good response that they bite the bullet and go into treatment, realizing they can't borrow meds from their kids for the rest of their lives.

After doing a fair amount of soul searching, many adults will come in the office stating that they are convinced they are ADD adults. Though some of these people are correct (keep in mind there may be other diagnoses as well), the competent therapist will carefully check the available information and conduct an evaluation that is in many ways similar to what would be done with a child. In some cases, people "shop" for a diagnosis. Some people who are not Attention Deficit, for example, may consider the diagnosis of ADD to be more benign than other diagnoses they may have been given before, such as bipolar disorder, chemical dependency or schizophrenia.

Though it doesn't solve the problem entirely, one of the most helpful considerations for the evaluator in this regard is chronicity. *To qualify as an ADD adult you must have been an ADD child* (whether diagnosed or not). ADD does not just start up suddenly when you hit 35; there must be evidence of chronic, ADD-based impairment. The diagnostician, therefore, must carefully look at presenting complaints, take a complete history (no mean feat with some disorganized, over-40 adults!), and use structured interviews, questionnaires and standardized rating scales to help pinpoint the real nature of the person's difficulties.

The diagnosis of adult ADD requires several steps which are similar to those included in the evaluation of a child, but there are important differences. The steps with adults include: 1) self-reports of the adults themselves, 2) structured interviews, rating scales and questionnaires, 3) observations of office behavior, 4) interviews with spouses, parents or others who know the adult being evaluated, and 5) the collection of other information.

1. Adult Self-Reports

Therapists who work with ADD in adults are very familiar with the impatient phone call that says, "I'm an ADD adult and I'm ready to do something about it." The message is, "Let's get going—I'm frustrated and in pain! Why waste any more time now that we know what the problem is?" Sometimes it takes quite a bit of effort to persuade a possible ADD adult to submit to the entire process of evaluation, which takes three or four sessions plus a bit of "homework."

Just like their younger counterparts, ADD adults are not always good historians. Though they may be able to describe the things that currently cause *them* emotional pain, they may minimize problems in which their angry, intrusive or hyperactive behavior causes trouble for *others*. Just plain poor memory can also make sifting through past years a formidable task for both client and evaluator. Disorganized thinking and a tendency to jump from topic to topic also put pressure on a mental health professional to structure the interview so that the necessary information is retrieved.

In addition to the interviewer's skill and sticktuitiveness, two other evaluation strategies (which we'll discuss in a moment) are very useful. If they are available, other people, such as spouses, friends and parents, can help a lot in providing more objective information about past and present. Also, structured interview formats, questionnaires and rating scales can assure that the all relevant subjects are covered and the necessary data is gathered.

What problems do ADD adults describe when they come in? As we mentioned, some start by giving you their diagnosis. Other adults describe presenting complaints that involve mood (depression and/or anxiety), job concerns, and marital dissatisfaction. Both men and women can report the pervasive feelings of melancholy and dissatisfaction with life that accompany depression, or the agitation and discomfort of anxiety. Women are often more honest in describing the low self-esteem that often accompanies mood problems, while ADD males may vacillate between blaming everyone else for their troubles and being able to discuss their own shortcomings.

Men mention job concerns more often than women. Their concerns include difficulty concentrating, procrastination, trouble getting started, poor organizational skills and difficulty getting along with others. Add all these up and the adult often feels that he isn't progressing as quickly as he would like at his place of work. These problems have been brought up by supervisors in periodic performance appraisals, often leaving a residue of intense anger as well as nagging self-doubt.

Marital problems are brought up more often by women. One reason for this is that, in general, females look for more out of a relationship than males do, so women are usually the most frustrated with the state of the union and thus more likely to seek help. Since women often are affected by the Inattentive Type of ADD, they may report that their husband criticizes them for the disorganization of the household. These women also feel that in discussions (and arguments) with their spouses they cannot hold their own; they get mixed up, flustered easily and have trouble expressing themselves. This confusion is infuriating because it adds to the conviction of their spouse that he was correct in the first place.

In marriages where one spouse turns out to be an adult version of the

Combined Type of ADD, the non-ADD spouses—whether male or female—will also have a great deal of difficulty asserting themselves with a person who doesn't listen well, interrupts frequently and has a ferocious temper.

With some ADD adults presenting complaints are less specific and presented in a confusing manner. These complaints can include not being in a very good mood much of the time and vague hints regarding low self-esteem. One theme that often jumps out is how aggravating other people are, and the list of culprits may seem endless, ranging from kids and wife to "friends," coworkers and government. Other less well-defined complaints may have to do with not feeling well organized, difficulty persevering with a wide range of tasks, and a sense of memory loss or confusion.

2. Structured Interviews, Questionnaires and Rating Scales

The good news about structured interviews, questionnaires and rating scales is that they can help organize the evaluation process so that it is more reliable and valid. Structured interviews help the evaluator assist the person being evaluated to stay on task. Questionnaires and rating scales, which can be mailed out before the first office visit, give the possible ADD adult time to think and reflect. The bad news, however, is that a paper-and-pencil task that requires reflection is not the kind of job that someone with ADD relishes!

Several instruments are helpful for taking a closer look at presenting complaints and comorbidity. The Structured Clinical Interview for DSM-IV (SCID) can take the interviewer and client through the DSM-IV diagnoses in a way similar to what the DISC does with parents of kids. The SCL-90 (Symptom Checklist 90—Revised) and The Personal Problems Checklist for Adults are broad band scales that look at a wider range of symptoms, such as anxiety, depression, hostility and obsessive-compulsive traits. Some evaluators still employ the Minnesota Multiphasic Personality Inventory and the Millon Clinical Multiaxial Inventory. Though these scales have no proven ADD-specific patterns, they can provide useful information about an individual's approach toward life as well as indications about comorbidity.

The daunting task of completing an accurate history can be aided by using the Wender AQCC Scale (Adult Questionnaire-Childhood Characteristics) or Goldstein and Goldstein's Childhood History Form. In Attention-Deficit/Hyperactivity Disorder: a Clinical Workbook, Barkley and Murphy also provide Developmental History, Health History, Employment History and Social History forms that can be duplicated at no charge. Some professionals ask that these forms be completed not only by the person being evaluated, but also by a spouse, friend or parent.

ADD specific (narrow-band) intruments include the DSM-IV ADHD Symptom Rating Scale. This scale allows each of the possible eighteen ADD symptoms (nine Inattentive, nine Hyperactive/Impulsive) to be rated for severity on a 4-point scale, rather than the all-or-nothing format which is usually employed with the DSM-IV criteria. Clients as well as spouses can fill out the form to describe an individual's current functioning; clients and parent(s) can fill out the form to describe the individuals functioning as a child. The Attention Deficit Disorder Evaluation Scale (ADDES) also has adult versions that include evaluations of social life and employment.

Other narrow-band instruments can help the evaluator take and look at specific non-ADD areas. These scales include Locke-Wallace Marital Adjustment Scale, the Hamilton Anxiety and Depression Scales, and the Michigan Alcohol Screening Test.

3. Office Behavior

While 80 percent of ADD children will sit still in a doctor's office and not show their ADD stuff, the same is not true of ADD adults. For children the office visit may be new and somewhat intimidating, but for adults, in general, it is not. The office behavior of ADD adults will frequently reveal a number of characteristics that are related to, or the result of, Attention Deficit Disorder.

Rapid speech is very common, and a steady flow of ideas may almost overwhelm the interviewer. The ideas, however, are not often very well organized—shifting from one to another. The listener may struggle to try to figure out what the point of a particular story is. An ADD adult may seem quite anxious, restless and driven, sometimes presenting an almost "haunted" look, as if he can't escape some dark cloud that follows him everywhere. Eye contact is often broken, and the individual will sometimes appear as if he were lost in thought—pausing for a few seconds and staring off into the room.

One of the most common occurrences in interviews with ADD adults is their tendency to interrupt the interviewer. This trait takes some getting used to! The symptoms of difficulty delaying gratification and impulsivity seem to operate here. The person suddenly gets a good idea and simply can't wait to share it, so—no matter what the interviewer was saying—he just bursts in with his thought. Many ADD adults are aware of this tendency and tease themselves about it from time to time, though that insight doesn't necessarily cut down its frequency.

The overall mood of the Attention Deficit adult may alternate between sadness, excitement and irritation. So many things seem to bother these men and women; the emotional aftermath of this aggravation is sadness, brief depressive episodes and a feeling that life is generally very frustrating. Though ADD adults often blame their troubles on the behavior of other people, after they become comfortable with the interviewer they can begin to get in touch with and express their doubts about themselves.

4. Find Mom! Interviews with Spouses, Parents and Others

It is very important for the therapist or evaluator to talk with other people who know the possible ADD adult. ADD adults—just like ADD kids— are not always good historians, and they don't remember a lot of things that are important. In addition, adults with ADD are not always objective, and they may show a distinct tendency to minimize certain aspects of their problems. While they might be quite candid, for example, when discussing their concentration difficulties, they may omit a lot when it comes to how they express their hostility at home with the family.

Often a spouse will be included in the evaluation. Another reason for involving the spouse, of course, is that this person will be not only helpful but necessary as treatment progresses. The spouse should be seen separately, at least part of the time, so she can talk freely. Many times the stress she feels is painfully obvious, and she will welcome an opportunity to ventilate her own frustrations. She may describe her ADD mate as a moody individual—with the predominant moods being anger and depression. She may also feel it is very difficult to talk to her husband and get anywhere, since he appears to take everything as a criticism. Other problems spouses describe include intolerance of the children, arbitrary and inconsistent discipline, excessive use of alcohol, chaotic spending and money management, and a host of unfinished projects around the house. Some spouses describe a feeling of guilt because they avoid their ADD husband or wife and feel relieved when their partner is not around.

5. Other Information

With suspected ADD adults, much of the same information is helpful that is useful in diagnosing ADD kids. The only problem is that the information is not as available. School records, for example, including report cards, achievement tests and reports describing special education interventions are extremely enlightening if they can be located. Once they are retrieved, these pieces of information are also quite interesting to the person being evaluated, and this data can help stimulate other important—and often painful—memories.

If records of psychological testing can be found, these reports can be very helpful. Most clients are very curious about test data ("What's my IQ?") and appreciate having it explained to them. If psychological testing was never done, it is sometimes a good idea to consider something like an adult IQ test and some achievement tests that have adult norms. Keep in mind here that if medication is to be considered later as a possible treatment alternative, the choice of a medication and its titration should probably be done before the testing is done, so as to get the most accurate results.

Performance appraisals from work, in the form of evaluation scales and/or written narratives, can often provide a more accurate picture of an individual's strengths and weaknesses on the job. Perhaps equally important is the adult's attitude toward and feelings about these appraisals. What feedback from his past supervisors does he agree with and what does he see differently? How well has he liked his immediate superiors? Some adults who come in for an evaluation are willing to have a mental health professional contact their current boss or supervisor, but many, of course, do not wish to reveal to anyone at work that they are going to see a "shrink."

A health history is an important part of the ADD evaluation. Sometimes a physical exam is needed as well. Gathering this information is probably even more important with adults, because adults have had a greater period of time in which to incur physical problems, may have a greater range of possible problems, and may also have had some difficulties with drug or alcohol misuse. Certain physical conditions may also produce symptoms that mimic ADD. These conditions include diabetes, cardiac difficulties, thyroid dysfunction and chronic pain. As mentioned earlier, the chronic nature of ADD and its early onset often help distinguish it from other physical as well as emotional problems.

Diagnosis Shock

For the adults who are diagnosed as having Attention Deficit Disorder the discovery that they have a particular problem is something that has a number of positive as well as negative sides to it. Many ADD adults are in something of a state of shock for a while as the "news" sinks in. "You mean it has a name!?" There is, in a sense, something inside me—a diagnosable disorder—that has been causing all this trouble. And this *thing* is not the same as my inner self or the "real me."

On the positive side, therefore, the diagnosis brings with it the idea that all the problems may not have been my fault. It wasn't "just me" that was doing it. And all the people who criticized me in the past didn't know the whole story. The ADD adult may also begin to feel that he is not alone. Other people, in fact, lots of other people, also suffer from the same problem, and comparing notes with other ADD adults can often be a beneficial experience.

Also on the positive side is the feeling that perhaps something can be done about the problem. I don't have to be this way all the time. One of the most dramatic examples of this realization for many people is their first experience with medication. Some ADD men and women have experimented with their children's stimulant medications; others have waited for their own prescriptions. For those who respond well to medication, the experience often feels like some kind of religious awakening. On medication ADD adults can look at things and actually see them, paying attention to details that were previously unrecognized. With the help of drug treatment these men and women may suddenly be able to sit still during a conversation and really listen to what someone else is saying, without feeling the restless urgency to either speak or leave. Daily activities can be organized better and work becomes more productive.

Many ADD adults will take antidepressant medication, either in addition to or instead of stimulants. Though the effects of these drugs can take a week or two to kick in, a positive response to antidepressants can also be an enlightening experience. Some people say that they never knew how depressed they were until they started feeling better; that lousy feeling had just been taken for granted all these years.

The diagnosis of ADD, however, may also have a dark side. It can bring a sense of many wasted years. "If only I would have known, I could have been saved a lot of trouble." The diagnosis can also generate considerable anger toward those who didn't do anything constructive about the problem in past years—especially parents. Even though this anger makes little sense—way back when there's no way anyone's parents could have known much about this kind of problem—the resentment can still be strong, especially when the ADD trait of emotional overarousal adds its emphasis to the feeling.

Following the diagnosis, as a person learns more and more about Attention Deficit Disorder, other negatives can arise. Dramatic initial responses to medications, for example, can generate hopes for a permanent cure or permanently altered state of being. Over a period of time, however, the realization hits that ADD doesn't go away; it is not curable. In addition, the effects of stimulant medications only last for a short period of time, and most people can't take them in the evening due to the possibility of insomnia. Some adults also find—as do some children—that the ADD symptom of disorganization makes it hard for them to stick to a regular medication regime.

There can be other negatives. Medications involve expense, and the expense can be considerable. For many people— a great many people!— the idea of taking pills for the rest of their lives is also not very appealing.

Why can't I just bite the bullet and do it myself? Perhaps it's the old American tradition of "rugged individualism" that makes the idea of chemical assistance for mood or behavior unsavory.

By and large, though, a valid diagnosis of Attention Deficit Disorder offers the possibility for new ways of looking at life, much greater success and more satisfying relationships with other people.

19

Adult Treatment

Treatment of Attention Deficit in adults is in some ways similar to treatment for children; education about ADD, medication and counseling can all be helpful. But there are important differences when it comes to treating ADD in adults. Adults come in of their own volition, whereas the children do not. Adults also can make more choices about treatment depending upon the kind of work, social involvement and recreation they pursue.

Treatment of ADD in adults is a relatively new phenomenon and there is a lot more that needs to be learned about it. In dealing with Attention Deficit adults, many therapists do their best by making educated guesses based upon what is known about counseling and psychotherapy in general, and also based upon what is known about medication treatment of children. But ADD adults are more complex and have more comorbid conditions to watch out for. And the fact that they—rather than their parents—now make the decision about pursuing treatment can definitely be a mixed blessing! The good news, though, is that more and more ADD adults are being treated and more research is being done.

Education About ADD

Adults must be educated about ADD just as parents and children are, but ADD adults are usually more interested in learning about the disorder and how it affects them. Today a good deal of educational material—in the form of books, audios, videos, newsletters and support groups—is available. Many adults with ADD prefer to learn by means of videos or discussions with other people, and they find it very interesting to become acquainted with the basic symptoms of ADD and then to use this knowledge in shedding light on their own past and present behavior.

Education about ADD is actually the beginning of counseling. The very fact that there is a hereditary condition known as Attention Deficit Disorder and that it produces identifiable effects in one's life can be the basis of a restructuring of a person's view of herself. As Kate Kelley and Peggy Ramundo have said, an ADD adult may begin to realize that she is not "stupid, lazy or crazy." As everyone who has ever gone through the process knows, however, old, self-critical messages die a very slow death. The job of reeducation needs to be constant—and probably lifelong.

Seeing oneself differently also means that self-esteem can change and that a new kind of self—and life—may be possible. If I'm not the perverse dope that I always thought I was, what am I really? What unrealized potential do I have? These thoughts are exciting and, as Kevin Murphy points out, they can be the basis for legitimate hope that life can actually improve. Maybe I can get along with other people better. Perhaps I can do my job differently. Maybe I can even go back to school and consider the possibility of a different kind of work.

Medication

The medications available for adults are similar to those used with children, with the exception of the antihypertensives (Tenex and Catapres), which are not prescribed as much. In the stimulant category, Adderall, Ritalin and Dexedrine—and less often, Cylert—are commonly used. These medications provide the most potent anti-ADD effects, though some studies indicate they may not be effective with as large a percentage of adults as they are with children. With the exception of Cylert, the biggest problem with the stimulants remains their short duration of action. When multiple doses are needed each day, the odds increase tremendously that ADD forgetfulness and disorganization will interfere with treatment.

Bodyweight formulas applicable to children in estimating therapeutic dosages of stimulants, however, are not relevant with adults because of lowered metabolism. Usually much less of a stimulant drug is needed. A 170-pound adult, for example, may do well with only 10 or 15 mg of Ritalin per dose, or 15 mg of Dexedrine slow-release or Adderall per day.

The tricyclic antidepressants (TCAs), such as Tofranil (imipramine) and Norpramin (desipramine), offer several advantages for adults. A single dose may last all day, there is very little potential for abuse, and these medications can also help with comorbid conditions, such as anxiety, depression and sleep problems. Though these drugs are usually not as potent in their anti-ADD effects as stimulants, they still can help with concentration, impulsivity and hyperactivity and they can also be taken concurrently with stimulants. This strategy—taking two medications—can help minimize "rebound" problems as well as the up-and-down "rollercoaster" effect that is sometimes a byproduct of using a stimulant alone.

Though they are frequently helpful with ADD in adults, the TCAs as a group are often overlooked. This may be due in part to the general focus these days on newer antidepressants (SSRIs), such as Prozac, Paxil and Zoloft, even though these newer medications do little for ADD itself. Tricyclic antidepressants are also hard for some people to tolerate due to their side effects, such as dry mouth, constipation and blurred vision. Nonetheless, TCAs should not be forgotten because they do work well with many adults. They are also decidedly cheaper!

Some people have suggested that the MAOI antidepressants can also be useful with ADD adults, but others worry that the necessary dietary restrictions required with these medications and the impulsivity and disorganization of ADD individuals will make for a dangerous combination.

On the other hand, a unique antidepressant, Wellbutrin (buproprion), has been found useful with a significant percentage of adults with ADD. Wellbutrin acts in some ways like a stimulant, increasing the availability of dopamine in the central nervous system. Since it is an antidepressant, it can also be helpful with comorbid anxiety and depression.

In its sustained-release form, buproprion is currently marketed as Zyban, a drug that is helpful in smoking cessation. The connection between ADD and smoking is an intriguing one. We know that ADD adults are more often smokers than non-ADD individuals. Does nicotine provide a stimulant effect similar to that of Dexedrine, Adderall or Ritalin? We do know that more than one ADD adult, while being treated with Zyban for smoking, has found that he could suddenly concentrate a lot better. Others adults have found that they could not only concentrate better, but were also in better spirits. In other words, for some people the use of buproprion for smoking cessation resulted in the "accidental diagnosis" of ADD—and sometimes mood disorder as well.

With one exception, the SSRIs are not generally effective for ADD in adults or children. These drugs do not alter inattention, impulsivity or hyperactivity. However, many physicians still prescribe them for ADD, possibly because spouses of ADD adults—and sometimes the adults themselves—occasionally report that the ADD individual is "so much easier to live with," "less irritable" or "more mellow." Perhaps these changes are due to the SSRIs' having an effect on the mood disorders that often accompany ADD. The SSRIs may also alter symptoms such as emotional overarousal and irritability, which are not included in the DSM-IV lists for Attention Deficit Disorder.

One SSRI that may have some anti-ADD efficacy is Effexor (venlafaxine). Several studies have indicated its possible usefulness with ADD. Effexor is also frequently prescribed along with a stimulant for adults with ADD.

Many adults find that the best medication regime for them involves using a stimulant and an antidepressant in combination. The stimulants help best with the core ADD symptoms, but they are short-acting. The antidepressants (other than the TCAs) do not help usually with core symptoms of ADD, but they do help with what you might call temperament—and their effects can last all day long. With a stimulant and an antidepressant, therefore, an ADD adult may achieve a concentration benefit during the day, when it is most needed (at work), and may also maintain a kind of temperamental "mellowing" effect during the evening while at home with family or out with friends.

When it comes to medication treatment, one important rule applies to both children and adults: the principle of individual differences. Medication must be carefully adjusted, and the process frequently involves trial-and-error learning. What is best for one individual, in terms of both medication type as well as dose, may be quite different from what works for someone else.

Counseling

As we saw before, education about ADD is the necessary beginning of individual counseling. Education about ADD provides both bad news and good news. On the bad side, a therapist may need to assist an ADD individual in expressing his dismay and resentment for having ADD symptoms. "I'm sorry you're stuck with ADD, but here's what we can do about it." That's part of the good news; something can be done about it.

ADD symptoms may explain present and past behavior, but they are an excuse for nothing. Part of the therapist's job is to help an adult with ADD take responsibility for being the way he is and deal with it. Accepting the fact of emotional overarousal in one's personality, for example, is not to be taken as license to abuse one's spouse or children.

Individual counseling can also help ADD adults come to a more realistic sense of self-esteem, an aspect of their existence which has usually taken quite a pounding over the years. Many ADD adults have an excellent sense of humor; amusing anecdotes about forgetfulness and disorganization are now plentiful. Individuals with ADD may find it healthy to take themselves with a few grains of salt, while at the same time working hard to improve their overall effectiveness.

Marital counseling is often helpful with ADD adults and their spouses. Husbands' and wives' tales about years of frustration should be listened to (although not beaten to death) and something done to try to prevent the future from being as difficult as the past was. Since the non-ADD spouse has often been the chronic underdog in the relationship, a therapist can help a couple come up with a more democratic way of dealing with each other. The entire focus of counseling should not just be on Attention Deficit Disorder, however, since the ADD individual will also have legitimate gripes about his or her partner that need to be addressed.

Part of the focus in counseling should also be on helping the couple to have fun again—something that "ADDers" are usually very good at!

Periodic family counseling can assist children and parents in dealing with the usual problems that come with daily living, as well as those that are related to ADD. It is quite common, of course, for ADD parents to have ADD kids, and this unfortunate combination can make things very difficult around the house. An ADD adult and spouse will find it helpful to learn some specific parenting strategies, such as counting, charting, or positive reinforcement, rather than just shooting from the hip when problems come up with the little ones.

Individual counseling can also be the forum where someone with Attention Deficit Disorder learns to develop his or her organizational skills. Keeping a daily planner, for example, where everything—work, social and recreational—is written down can be extremely useful. The next step is developing tactics in order not to misplace the planner! Also useful can be the development of memory-jogging gimmicks for taking medication, learning to use computers to aid in planning and completing daily tasks, and having someone teach the mechanics of balancing the checkbook and filing out income tax returns.

For adults, social skills training often takes place in the context of individual counseling. Therapists working with ADD find it a refreshing change to work with an adult who wants to change his or her ways of relating to other people, rather than with an ADD child who is still blaming all of his social ills on everyone else. Compared to children, ADD adults also have more motivation to generalize their learning from the therapist's office to the real world, and many are delighted with the benefits of their efforts.

Medication can play a big role in effecting this social change. Listening skills, for example, are often enhanced tremendously by stimulant medications prescribed in conjunction with counseling. Antidepressants can have a kind of calming effect that reduces the restlessness and fidgetiness that children, spouses and co-workers find so irritating.

More and more groups for ADD adults are available these days. These groups include support group meetings that may take place monthly, as well as more intensive experiences in weekly groups. Being in a small room with seven other ADD adults for an hour and a half can be a trying experience, but it can help people get a perspective on the disorder and realize they are not alone.

Although it does not quite fall into the category of individual counseling, a newer strategy for helping ADD adults is known as coaching. The coach helps encourage, support, organize and direct the individual with ADD, but the contacts are usually much more frequent than those involved in counseling. Instead of talking once a week or less, the coach and client communicate a number of times per week via phone, voice mail or e-mail. Sometimes the contacts are daily, but they are of shorter duration than counseling sessions—perhaps ten or fifteen minutes. This frequency of contact is an attempt to respond to the basic ADD problem of sustaining motivation over time.

Coaching is intended to be present oriented, practical and task- or goal-directed. The coach hopes to provide some friendly accountability for the ADD adult to help him stay on task, accomplish his goals and get more out of life. Coaches who work with ADD, of course, need to be very familiar with Attention Deficit Disorder. The coaching movement has been building up steam recently, and in a few years we hope to have some solid research attesting to its usefulness.

On the Job

For most ADD adults the curse of school is replaced by the world of work. Unfortunately, like the previous academic setting, the work world may turn out to be no picnic either. Tasks that are repetitive, annoying coworkers and bothersome superiors can make the days seem endless.

With the help of a sympathetic counselor, an ADD adult can begin to sort out "how much of the problem is the job and how much is me." In the big, bad world there certainly are plenty of boring jobs, irritating associates and incompetent supervisors! In counseling, an adult with ADD can take a long look at several questions: Is this the job for me? Do I have any choice? Is this the job for me if it could be altered in some ways? Should I look for something else to do? Should I even—gulp—consider going back to school?

According to psychologist Kathleen Nadeau, director of Chesapeake

Psychological Services of Maryland, the worst jobs for ADD adults share several characteristics. These jobs are sedentary, long on paperwork and short on opportunities to move around or interact with others. They involve long-term tasks, lots of detail and a distracting work environment. Poor jobs for ADD individuals are uninteresting, require long hours working alone, and are especially difficult if these characteristics are combined with a boss who is unsympathetic and demanding.

With the inclusion of ADD as a disability under the Americans with Disabilities Act, employees with ADD may be eligible for accomodations to help them function more effectively. The basic principle is similar to that involved when kids with ADD are assisted by a 504 Accomodation Plan in a school system.

Even though the idea of job accomodations makes some sense, however, there are some very real problems with its application. First of all, an employee must demonstrate conclusively to his employer that he is ADD and that being ADD interferes seriously with job performance. This means more than just a cursory letter from a doctor and it also means that a person must admit to problematic job performance. Second, some ADD individuals who did declare their disability to their employers have felt that, as a consequence, they were no longer considered for promotion and may also have been pulled off more desirable jobs. Their declaration, in other words, hurt them more in the long run. Certainly, telling your employer "there is something wrong with me" is a risky business. These days, too, there is no doubt that there is backlash against the notion of ADD—especially when some people see it being used in a way that they consider to be an excuse.

Dr. Nadeau suggests two possible ways of handling the issue of ADD accomodations on the job. One is to not declare the ADD unless it is a last resort—either to save a job or to try to buy time if one is close to being fired. The second idea—and perhaps a better and surely less desperate maneuver—is to work out "accomodations" with one's employer without calling them accomodations and without talking at all about ADD. If the relationship between employer and employee is good, there are a number of job modifications that might be helpful:

1. A private office or less distracting place to work
2. Working at home
3. Tape-recording meetings
4. More frequent—rather than less frequent—performance appraisals!
5. Getting instructions in writing
6. E-mail supervision
7. Flex time
8. Extra clerical support

While working with a counselor, ADD adults can also take a look at how the work they do might be affected by the use of medication. Most ADD children will benefit considerably from stimulants because they have to be in school all day, where they have to sit still and concentrate on material they see as boring. There is more diversity in the lives of ADD adults, however, so the uses of stimulant medication are more varied.

An ADD adult who reviews insurance forms all day, for example, may need to take medication regularly, just as a child in school would. An ADD adult who drives a delivery truck for a living, on the other hand, may not need medication at all for that job. Another ADD person who does outside sales may not need the meds while driving around the city making calls, but she may need the stimulant medication when Friday afternoon rolls around and it's time to fill out her expense reports. She might also use the medication periodically for recreational reading.

During the process of reevaluating their job situations, many ADD adults reconsider the possibility of going back to school. Initially, the thought of school may inspire anxiety—or downright terror. After experiencing the concentrational benefits that medication often provides, however, many of these men and women decide to take the plunge. Organizational skills, note taking, reading strategies and test-taking tactics must be worked on. That old nemesis, the Homework Monster, must also be attacked aggressively. The good news, however, is that for many ADD adults going back to school—and succeeding—is an absolute thrill.

The Big Question

We have seen that treatment for adult ADD exists. Education about ADD, medication, counseling and taking another look at one's job can make life much more satisfying than it ever was before. Self-esteem can rise as a person becomes proud of her accomplishments and develops more satisfying relationships with family, spouse, children and friends.

Treatment is not perfect, though; it involves a lot of work. Treatment for ADD takes time and money and effort. Sometimes it's boring; sometimes it may seem like it's doing no good. Tackling life's big and little jobs that have been chronically avoided, or managing emotions that are persistently exaggerated, requires a lot of elbow grease—day after day.

So what's the Big Question about treatment for adult ADD? It's this: *Will treatment for ADD be pursued or will it simply become one more item on a long list of unfinished projects?*